30130211675789

D0636717

TOTON ENGINEMAN

THE AUTOBIOGRAPHY OF A RAILWAYMAN

JOHN HENRY WOOLLEY

EDITED BY NIGEL HARRIS

DEDICATION
This book is dedicated to all railwaymen, past and present, of every grade and to their families. It is also for my dear wife who supported me throughout my railway life. She never once complained about the unsociable hours demanded by my career. It must have been a very lonely life for her.
And last but not least, it is for the enthusiasts who would love to know: What was it like?

CONTENTS

Published by Steam World Publishing,
First Floor, 2 King Street, Peterborough, PE1 1LT
Telephone: 01733 555123
Email: steamworld@choicemag.co.uk

First published: December 2013.
Designed by Nigel Harrist

Printed by Hung Hing Offset Printing.

British Library Cataloguing in Publication Data.
A catalogue record for this book is available from the British Library.

ISBN 978-0-9927398-0-5

© **The mark 'Steam World Magazine' is a registered trade mark.**

**Previous page: For its entire 96 years as a steam depot, Toton was a
heavy freight shed whose job was moving millions of tons of coal from
the Nottinghamshire coalfields to London, on the Midland Main Line.
The articulated Beyer-Garratt 2-6-0+0-6-2s became emblematic of Toton
Motive Power Depot from the 1930s to the late 1950s, when they all
succumbed to the cutters torch. Not a single example of the 33 built
survive. On June 26 1957, No. 47969 digs in whilst running bunker-first
at Wellingborough. *Ken Fairey/Colour Rail.***

FOREWORD
BY SARAH MIDDLETON-WOOLLEY

My dad began work at the very bottom at Toton Motive Power Depot – as an engine cleaner he started with no more than an oily rag. But his aim was to be an express driver – and he achieved that ambition. In an age when practical experience was everything, he worked hard over many years to climb the promotional ladder. He had never really enjoyed school, which had been a difficult and unhappy time for him, and he left as a consequence without any academic qualifications. It was the railway – and the steam locomotive footplate in particular - that gave him the opportunity to prove himself. He seized that opportunity with vigour and determination from his very first day. On that first morning he was in charge of an oily rag: on his last afternoon he was in charge of freight operations over a huge area from Toton, including Worksop, Leicester, Peterborough, March and Parkeston Quay. My mum, sister and I could not be prouder of what he achieved and this book stands in tribute to his successful career.

After grafting first as a cleaner in the dirty and primitive conditions of Toton engine shed, and then serving as a fireman he finally became a main line driver in 1967. He worked hard at Toton MPD and in the 1970s, after steam ended, he also attended night school, where this time he was determined to further his education and to gain the qualifications needed for management.

To be promoted on the railways, you had to prove yourself worthy by working hard, week in, week out, and learning every last aspect of a very complex job. It wasn't as simple as signing-up on a management course and applying for promotion - you really had to earn each upward move. You were judged entirely on your merits.

Dad was passionate about the railway and passionate about his job, to which he devoted his working life. He was a very determined man and this helped him achieve his goals. I am keenly aware that my words here are very personal – but the railway *was* personal in those days. My dad's life on the railway represented a lifetime of devotion to 'the job' and for him the railway really was like a second family. He spent so much of his life there - but I knew him best as my dad.

As a child I remember he was frequently away. He worked long hours and often had to stay elsewhere overnight. Even when he was at home, the constant reminders from mum to "…be quiet, your dad is in bed, he's on nights this week," loom large in my memory. So I would walk down the entry beside our house on my roller skates, rather than roll on them, so that the noise of the wheels wouldn't disturb him. Maybe that's why my skate wheels ended up square.

Essentially we shared dad with his work - and this is a story familiar to wives, sons and daughters of long-serving industrial shift workers everywhere. Dad worked very hard for us all, and when he did have time at home, there would often be someone's car in pieces on the street at the front of our house, with the engine out and parts carefully placed across the pavement! There would be tools everywhere and my mum would be cursing him for ruining yet another decent shirt because he hadn't changed into an old one.

Our family holidays in the early days were camping breaks in Cornwall. Dad would spend a few days preparing the car - a Hillman Hunter - for our holiday in the hope that it wouldn't break down. In those days we always had old, second hand cars.

The tent would have been set-up in the back garden in the weeks running up to our holiday to check it for leaks when it rained. Patches would be carefully applied. It still leaked. The car would be loaded, fitted with a roof rack and everything would be packed inside

Right, top: John Woolley (right) as a young fireman spent his leisure time playing guitar in Long Eaton pop band, 'The Deltic Rhythm Group.'

Right, centre: A few years later, aged about 19 - and about to enjoy a beer. In later years, John's home-brew lubricated many a Christmas party for family and railway friends at his Long Eaton home.

Right: John Woolley had railways in his blood and after more than a decade on steam locomotive footplates as a fireman from 1954, he built a new career in the diesel age. When he started in 1954, Toton had just been modernised by British Railways and was at its zenith, handling up to 2m wagons a year. When he retired in 1994, the glory days had long gone in the once-massive yards, but the MPD continued to thrive and he'd be delighted with its important role with leading freight operator DB Schenker today. *All: Courtesy Caryl Woolley*

and on top, my mum making sure that nothing had been forgotten.

Mum, my older sister Helen and I travelled to Cornwall on the train, using the cheap 'privilege tickets' dad's job entitled us to. He would leave the night before in the car with all the gear, driving alone overnight to Cornwall. He would arrive at the camp site in time to put up the tent and then collect us from St. Erth railway station, with our holiday 'home' all ready to move into.

At the camp site in Hayle, mum would unpack all the camping gear and our belongings. This was a perfect opportunity for dad to take Helen and I down to the beach to leave mum in peace. He was an entertaining joker who never tired of rock pools and digging sand.

These holidays were always on a tight budget, but they were great fun and they left me with such lovely, treasured memories that I still take holidays at that same Cornish camp site every summer, with my own family. Nowadays it's in a chalet, not a leaky old tent! If my young son Fletcher ends up with only half the wonderful memories that mum and dad gave me, then I couldn't be happier and he'll be the wealthier for it.

A little later in my childhood, during the 1980s, and after dad had been promoted a few times, we could afford to holiday abroad - to Italy. The first few times involved long, tiring 37-hour journeys by rail from Long Eaton to Naples – but thank goodness for those very cheap 'privilege tickets' which made it possible. We would still feel the movement of the train for a few days after arriving at our destination.

As the years passed, holidays became more frequent and we travelled by air - but it is still those early budget holidays in Cornwall that I remember with the fondest of memories. I say all this because I think it's important to set the context for dad's working life as an engineman and say something about the man we knew at home. He was a family man and a loyal friend. My dad was very sociable and generous and he loved to entertain family and friends. He worked hard but when he wasn't at work, he liked to have fun

and he liked to laugh - a lot. He was busy and gregarious with many varied interests and an unquenchable curiosity for life. On Christmas Eve, every year, my parents threw a party for family, friends and neighbours at our house. These parties were a highlight of my Christmas. Mum would spend all day preparing food and my sister and I made paper chains.

At the time, dad was very keen on making wine, barley wine and home-brewed beer. The kitchen was often turned into a production line. At one of our Christmas parties, there were endless supplies of wine, barrels of home-brewed beer and stacks of 'Party Seven' cans of beer (remember them?) piled high. People gradually filled the house and as the night progressed the music got louder and louder - Fleetwood Mac, Dire Straits, The Eagles and Jethro Tull. The house was full of fun and laughter until the early hours.

Christmases were great family occasions, but dad was always a railwayman and there was always a shift to be worked at Toton – even when he was at home on Christmas day, he was often 'on call.' Even so, my Christmas memories are very fond ones; not of the presents from Santa, but of noisy parties and family fun, led by dad.

He had many interests. In his younger days he had enjoyed motorbikes. He also liked cycling and my parents had a tandem for a while - until it was stolen. He loved music too (which he passed on to me) and even played guitar in a rock 'n' roll band - the Deltic Rhythm Group - in the 1950s. Nowadays, I sing in my own band too. He would have liked that.

He loved photography and building and flying model aircraft and he used to go metal detecting too. I went with him sometimes. We spent most of the time digging holes only to discover a bottle top, a ring-pull or a horse shoe, but it was always fun. For many years, he used to catch rabbits with ferrets, which he bred at home.

He was fortunate to see my sister and I marry and he was with us long enough to enjoy being a Granddad to Helen's two children, Matthew and Chloé. Sadly, he died before my own son Fletcher was born in 2006 – and this is another powerful reason that I'm so pleased this book has been published at last. I want Fletcher to know something of his grandfather's working career, of his passion for the railway, his love of steam and his success at work – and what better way than through an autobiography of his own words? Dad would also be thrilled to see this book finally in print. He retired from the railway in 1994, aged 55, after 40 years' service. He spent his time thereafter doing odd jobs for local businesses, one of them a local brewery. He also discovered a new interest in trout fishing. He then took the time to write this book of his working memoirs.

He was as busy as he had ever been – no 'soft' retirement for him! He worked as hard on this manuscript after his retirement as he worked on the railway for the 40 years before.Then, in the summer of 1997, dad began to feel unwell. By autumn he was very poorly indeed and was admitted to hospital for tests. The following day he was diagnosed with Acute Lymphoblastic Leukaemia. Our world was torn apart by this heartbreaking news. It was shattering.

My dad was so brave. Whilst our family wrestled with the terrible truth that he was not going to recover, Dad courageously carried on with life as best he could. He refused to give in and fitted his interests and socialising around the seemingly endless, tiring trips to the hospital for 'chemo' and radiotherapy. He did go into remission for a couple of months. More chemotherapy was then necessary to try and bring the disease under control, but the treatment didn't work and sadly, my dad died on September 28 1998. He was just 59 years old.

Family and friends were all devastated. Such a huge character and personality was suddenly missing from our lives: it left a huge void. My mum, Helen and I have a strong family bond, however and together we are united, and certainly both Helen and I have inherited our dad's spirit for life. He lived life to the full and never wasted time. We all miss him enormously. We always will.

This book is a personal treasure to us of course – but we also believe that his writing is an important record of social and historical significance and we are delighted others can now share and enjoy it too. It paints a vivid picture of life on the railway he loved so much during the last days of steam and the early years of more modern diesel locomotive operation, which his career so neatly bridged. His character and personality are very much missed in our family but they are forever present in his words, which have been presented here so beautifully and with such care. The *Steam World* team has worked hard to bring my dad's words to life through some magnificent accompanying photographs and we are all delighted with the finished product.

I so wish he could have been here to see how wonderfully well Helen's two children have made their way in the world. I wish he could have been here to see me become a mum and to be a Granddad to my son, Fletcher. I wish he could have seen his book finally published. Most of all, I just wish he was here.

This book is both his legacy and his tribute. My mum, Helen and I really hope you enjoy it. He would have been thrilled to see it - and he would have wanted everyone to raise a glass! So, please do.

Sarah Middleton-Woolley,
Long Eaton,
Derbyshire

August 31 2013

EDITOR'S INTRODUCTION
BY NIGEL HARRIS

There's an old saying that there's no such thing as coincidence – that such things are actually fate's way of nudging you in the right direction. Whichever is true, it's the reason this book was published after more nearly 15 years on the shelf.

As a volunteer steam locomotive driver on the Great Central Railway, in 2012 I was also the rhythm guitarist for 'Top Link' – otherwise known as the 'Loughborough Shed Band' - who often performed at GCR galas and other special events. One evening, we were getting ready to rehearse our repertoire of songs from Buddy Holly and the Searchers to the Eagles, Joni Mitchell and even Robbie Williams. As I tuned my Telecaster, I overheard a conversation between Sarah, our then-new singer and bass player Mick Carr.

"My dad was a driver at Toton shed," said Sarah. "He wrote his railway life story after he retired but it was never published…"

Mick said he'd like to read it sometime and Sarah agreed.

"Yes, me too, if I could," I added, always with my radar pinging for potential material for *Steam World*. A few weeks later Sarah handed me a ring binder containing John Woolley's neatly typed manuscript and I spent the next three evenings reading it. It was superb. I knew within the first few pages that it ought to be published.

Because John's very personal and compelling words aren't just his own story. He speaks for hundreds of thousands of enginemen who made the iron road their life and who served with dedication, commitment and skill. This involved considerable self-sacrifice which their families had to share - and so this book is much more than simply an engineman's tale. It's a story about how significant chunks of England were shaped by hard working men like John Woolley.

Long Eaton and Toton are just a couple of places which, but for the railway, would be known only locally. The same can be said of Horwich, Shildon, Annesley, Tebay, Ashford, Eastleigh, Whitemoor…..the long list of otherwise nondescript English places with a huge railway history is a long and proud one.

And the most important part of that railway history isn't the massive motive power depots, massive workshops, stations or marshalling yards. The crucial ingredient is the people who worked at those places and whose communities grew around the steel web of rails that dominated, sustained and characterised those areas.

Each of those communities had extended railway families whose real families depended on the railway, which provided not only employment, but which also shaped local culture, framed community thinking and gave a common context to literally thousands of lives.

All this left its mark in Toton and Long Eaton, where although the once immense yards are now mere shadows of their former selves, the railway is still the framework around which the local community continues to develop. Unlike Shildon and Horwich, railway activity is still substantial – and with the announcement in 2013 that the massive railway lands are earmarked for the High Speed 2 station to serve the East Midlands, Toton's railway credentials are listed to be upgraded to 300 kilometres per hour.

Sadly, I never knew John Woolley, but I like to think he would have been pleased about HS2. It's obvious from what you'll read that he was a forward-thinking and adaptable railwayman. When steam went he seized the opportunity to forge a second career in management and he excelled at that just as he'd excelled with a firing shovel in the cabs of those massive Toton Beyer-Garratts on the Midland main line. He would certainly have approved of the economic rejuventation that HS2 will bring to Toton and Long Eaton whilst at the same time worrying about those whose homes would be displaced by the new 300kph (186mph) railway.

I hope he would approve of what we've done with his autobiography. It's been a privilege - a real honour - to be entrusted with the task of shaping it from raw manuscript to finished book. I was determined from the start that the only voice you should hear in these pages is John's. I'm indebted, therefore, to his wonderful family for the long hours of hard work that they have spent making sure that John comes through loud and clear on every page.

John's widow Caryl, and his daughters Helen and Sarah (see pictures, below) all painstakingly read my sub-edited version of John's words and their hard work and honesty in helping fine-tune the text and the way it is punctuated has ensured authenticity. I've done my best to find photographs and graphics which reflect, enhance and give life to John's words. Where possible I've used pictures of the locations and even the specific locomotives mentioned. I'm sure John Woolley would have been proud beyond words at his family's determination not only to see this book in print but also that they have been so closely involved in its production.

In the year or so it's taken to put this book together, I'm privileged the Woolley family have become friends. I've come to understand and see at first hand just how much seeing this book published means to them. It's come to mean a lot to me, too. From the moment we decided to publish it as a *Steam World* book, rather than as a serialized set of articles in our monthly magazine, it's become an important part of my life too.

It's ironic that as a driver on today's GCR, I have realised that John and I have a great deal in common and I was fascinated to see that as a Midland man he even spent time working at Leicester Central MPD, so the overlap in our lives is even more poignant. I very much regret that I can't phone him and say "John, I'm booked out driving tomorrow – do you want to come along for the day…?"

His family were always very keen to see this book published and they have all played important parts in seeing it published - but Sarah's contribution has been fundamental in getting this book into print and I bet her dad would have been as proud as punch.

If you enjoy reading this book only half as much as I've enjoyed putting it together - then you'll be well pleased with it.

Nigel Harris,
Tallington,
Lincolnshire.

August 31 2013.

Above, Caryl, Helen, Sarah and John Woolley on holiday in Italy in 1982. *Courtesy Caryl Coolley.*

Above: Caryl, Helen and Sarah, October 2013. The bridge in the background carried Toton's high level goods lines. *Nigel Harris.*

Chapter 1

CLEANING, LABOURING AND FIRST FIRING JOBS

Above: On May 13 1956, Garratt No. 47973 rests alongside No. 1 shed at Toton MPD, where, in October 1954, 15-year old John Woolley started work as an engine cleaner. Of the 33 articulated 2-6-0+0-6-2 Beyer Garratts built, 20 still worked at Toton in 1954 and the author fired them on the main line. By 1957 they had all gone - and none survived. All went for scrap. *C.J.B. Sanderson/J.W. Armstrong Trust.*

Long Eaton is a town between Nottingham and Derby, famous for its lace factories and its railways. I was born there at the beginning of the Second World War. Toton Sidings (a modest title which belies the once-massive scale of the place) lies between Long Eaton and Sandiacre. It was said to be the largest sidings and steam depot in Europe.

My mother was a seamstress and my father an upholsterer. I was educated at the local boys school and from an early age I was fascinated by railways. My school friends and I would rush from school to a local vantage point each day to watch the Up 'Thames Clyde Express' pass through Long Eaton at about 5 o'clock, before going home for tea.

I remember as if it was yesterday the thrill of seeing the express roar out of Trent Station headed by one of the polished green Stanier three-cylinder 'Jubilee' 4-6-0s, named after far away places and famous people....*Bahamas, Fiji, Shovell* ...and the rest.

I remember the smell of the hot oil, the steam, the feel of the boiler heat, the sharp bark of the exhaust and the friendly wave of the driver in his shiny-topped cap and faded blue overalls.

It was during one of these exciting moments that I decided to pursue the dream of just about every school boy of the day: I was going to become a locomotive driver when I left school - and it wouldn't be just a dream, I was quite sure of that!

This book is a factual account, viewed from retirement after a four-decade career, of how life was 'on the rails'. Aside from all the technicalities, I hope that at times you'll find it humorous as well. Wherever possible I have included specific dates and locomotive numbers. It is obvious however, that after 40 years service, my

memories are too numerous to describe in detail and my diaries are somewhat incomplete. But even if I had kept a record of every working day and "every beat of the locomotive", it would be impossible for me to write them all here.

In retirement, never a day goes by without thoughts of my youth, when every working day was an adventure. I feel proud to consider that my working life was spent amongst one of the most professional and dedicated work forces the country has ever known. They were, and still are, 'the salt of the Earth'.

I hope you enjoy reading this snapshot of my years with British Railways motive power as much as I have enjoyed recording them.

I was just 15 when I left school in July 1954. At the time, my father would not hear of me working on the railways. He said: "You won't stick the shifts lad. The hours are terrible and the job is filthy. There's a job at the local factory that would be better for you. No lad, you are not working on the railways - and that's that!"

I worked at the factory for two months. I hated it. How could my parents subject me to this life of pure misery? I put in my notice, but not before filling in an application form for employment in the footplate line of promotion at nearby Toton Motive Power Depot. I

Top: Young John Woolley was inspired to join the railway by boyhood trainspotting experiences at Trent station (closed from January 1 1968). LMS 'Jubilee' 4-6-0 No. 45712 *Victory* rolls over the north junction and into the station on April 16 1959 with the 6pm Derby-St Pancras. *Colour Rail.*

Above; left: Midland Railway Class 2F 0-6-0 No. 58173 - then a Toton engine - rattles over the diamonds at Trent Junction in May 1953 at the head of a short down freight. Trent was built to enable easier transfers for passengers between the various converging routes. *R.J. Essery Collection.*

Above, right: Impressive lower quadrant semaphore signals at Trent North Junction. Derby to the left, straight on for Nottingham. *Colour Rail.*

was accepted subject to passing the medical and eyesight test.

I was wondering what I should say to my parents and how best to break the news. I shouldn't have worried – in the event, the job was done for me. In my absence, the Toton messenger (caller-up) had delivered - by hand - my free travel pass accompanied by an introductory letter to the Medical Officer at Derby. My mother took the letter on my behalf. It had all been read by the time I got home. Suffice to say, there wasn't a great deal of conversation over tea that night!

The day arrived when I had to attend the Railway Medical Centre at Derby. I was spot-on time for my appointment. In the waiting room there were three other boys. One of these was a lad called Les. I had gone to school with him and it was great to see a friendly face.

My time came and I was shown to the surgery. The doctor was a portly man in a white coat and he rather gave me the impression that his job was a chore. It probably was – just another recruit. For me, though, it was very important. He showed very little interest in me at all. In his off-handed, matter of fact way, he examined me, starting with sounding my chest, taking my blood pressure and asking me questions about my general health. He eventually told me that I was as "fit as a fiddle."

The next part of the examination was for general eyesight and colour vision. I had been told, by a neighbour who was also an engineman, that this was the most important hurdle. I half knew

what to expect. I was shown into a room and sat down. The room was darkened. At the far end I could see a pinprick of white light. The doctor explained that as he changed the tiny light, I would be expected to identify four colours: white, yellow, green and red. He warned me that the shades would vary, just like colours would change if they were viewed through a fog or mist.

It was tricky. The white light took on a yellowish tinge but it was still white. The yellow took on a reddish tinge but it was still yellow. I managed to get them all correct.

The next part of the colour test involved a book containing pages of different coloured dots. The dots were arranged in such a fashion that a number appeared if your colour vision was normal, but another (or none) appeared if your colour vision was defective. It was a crucial test because it determined whether or not you could distinguish signals. The book was called an 'Ishihara book' and was so named after the Japanese doctor who had invented it. This book had been the downfall of many a hopeful young lad. Fortunately, I was not one of them and was told that I would be accepted for employment in Toton's Motive Power Department. That lifted a massive weight of worry from my shoulders. I hated to think what would have happened at home should I have failed!

Les also passed the medical and as we travelled home together we chatted happily about our prospects as enginemen. We were elated. I said a temporary farewell to Les and started for home to tell my

parents. As expected, my father went completely 'off the rails'! "You won't stick it five minutes," he told me, in no uncertain terms, "and even if you do, there is no future in a job like that!"

I had to bite my tongue before replying that there was no future in knocking tacks in all day either. My future lay on the railways which had always fascinated and excited me. I couldn't wait.

My first day at Toton Motive Power Depot

Two days later I received a letter advising me to report to Toton Steam Depot at 8.30am on Monday October 25 1954. It was a lovely morning as I walked across the Meadow approach to the steam shed at Toton.

The MPD's Chief Clerk welcomed Les, three other boys and myself by saying to the foreman: "I bet none of them can spell Leicester."

Top: The southern end of the busy down yard at Toton (looking north) with the Erewash Valley main lines to the right of the control tower and the MPD in the left distance. Everything you see here is gone. Incredibly, in 1954, Toton was handling one millon wagons a year.

Above: The northern end of the same up yard from the up hump, with the 'cenotaph' concrete coaling plant of the MPD rising beyond the main lines. Long Eaton is in the distance. *Both: R.J. Essery Collection.*

That was an indication of the capability of young recruits expected by the railways of the mid-1950s 'baby boom' generation. What intelligent man would want to work amidst coal dust, oil, grime and smoke when the country was calling out for labour in other far more attractive occupations in the early post war years? It was possible to

Above: An aerial view of Toton MPD, clearly showing how the oldest building - No. 1 shed - was offset to the later Nos. 2/3 sheds. Note the through 'Garratt' road, squeezed down the left wall of the roofless central No. 2 (and No. 3) shed. This was the only road on which the 87ft articulated engines could be put under cover for repairs. This severely shortened the turntable roads. *Keith Reedman Collection*

Left: 1950s Toton MPD Running Foreman Bill Scattergood (in trilby and suit) with a handful of Toton enginemen, including (centre, back) Driver Harry 'Buck' Walker. *Courtesy Judith Squires.*

get a job almost anywhere. This had been my father's argument, of course.

Perhaps this individual failed to appreciate that for some of us at least, our intention was to make the railways a career, not just a job. To be fair to the chap though, the railways had a tremendous turn-over of young recruits who rapidly departed for those other jobs when they learned that railway work in general – and locomotives in particular - was not a bed of roses.

The Running Foreman, Mr. Scattergood, called for the Chargeman Cleaner, whose name was Sam. He was a white haired old man

who walked with a limp. We were to be told later (and many times thereafter if we would listen) that he limped because of an injury received in India's Khyber Pass! Although very regimental and disciplined in his manner, we were soon to learn that he would be our father figure and would guide us kindly (but firmly) through those early days.

Sam took us to the clothing store for a uniform which included the coveted shiny-topped footplateman's 'greasetop' cap. The Storekeeper was not unlike Sam. His name was Clarence. Both were ex-footplate but had fallen by the wayside because of ill health and were confined to shed duties. Sam then summoned a few senior cleaners and told them to "show us the ropes".

Les and myself were introduced to Terry. He would be our mentor for the day. Terry had started on the railways one year earlier and was about to go to Firing School. When he told me this, he instantly became my hero.

For the first time I was able to look around the very large locomotive sheds. There were three turntables and stabling sheds. No. 1 Shed was off set to Nos. 2 and 3 and was the oldest of the three structures. It housed the oil, cotton waste (for cleaning), the clothing store, the sand drying plant (dry sand was carried on locomotives and was needed to improve adhesion between wheels and slippery rails for starting or braking a heavy train). It also housed the Chargehand Cleaner's office.

The turntable was the shortest of the three and was not suitable for the biggest locomotives. A Stanier Class 8F 2-8-0 heavy freight locomotive would barely fit on the table with only about one inch

On his first day at work at Toton, new engine cleaner John Woolley was given a lifeless, filthy Stanier '8F' 2-8-0 to clean. This is No. 48439 at Toton, in May 1966, five months before the shed closed to steam. *Initial Photographics*.

to spare at either end. It never failed to amaze me in the early days how a driver could stop his locomotive 'just right' within such tight tolerances. On the south side of the turntable there was a straight road leading to the fitter's drop pit. This was a hydraulic device for lowering sets of wheels from under locomotives and was used for the removal of wheel sets for the maintenance of axle boxes and wheel bearings.

No. 2 Shed was a little larger than No 1. It was in line with No. 3 shed so that it was possible to cross 2 Shed turntable and enter No. 3, which was the largest shed of all. Also, there was a long road which avoided the turntables but was under the cover of Nos. 2 and 3 Sheds. This was called 'the Garratt Road'. It was the only line where an articulated Beyer-Garratt 2-6-0+0-6-2 could be placed under cover, for maintenance. Here, it was possible to house three of these 155-ton locomotives in a row. They were over 87ft long.

The drivers' messroom and locker rooms were in No. 2 Shed. No. 3 housed heavy machinery for maintenance and was mostly used as a repair shop. It was a massive complex and I felt proud that I had become part of it.

I well remember my impressions that first day. The first was how

incredibly dirty everything was. You only had to touch anything or anywhere and your hands would be covered in grime!

The second was the smell. It was sulphurous, oily and had the dank aroma of age and damp. My third observation was the construction of the brick built shed walls. They were at least 4ft thick. It was obvious that when the Victorians had built the complex they expected it to last a thousand years. It was clear that the MR had never envisaged any competition from any other form of transport.

Back to that first day. Terry said: "OK John, we've had a quick look around, we'd better get back to the job and I'll show you what we have to do." We returned to No. 1 Shed. In one corner adjacent to the Tool & Oil Stores stood a cold and lifeless Stanier Class 8F 2-8-0. This was the locomotive which we had been booked to clean.

Terry explained that a team of three cleaners was assigned to each locomotive and the task was divided into three parts. One cleaned the boiler, cab and smokebox. Another cleaned the tender spring and axleboxes. The third cleaned the locomotive motion (piston rods, connecting and coupling rods, cranks, wheels, valve gear and frames). The latter was the most demanding and dirtiest job of the

Left: Toton MPD in 1965 - the year before it closed to steam - from the top of the coaling plant. The shed yard still looks comparatively clean and tidy.

Facing page, lower left: Stanier '5MT' 4-6-0 No. 45230 awaits the call, alongside No. 1 shed.

Facing page, lower right: An extremely work-stained and weary looking BR Riddles Class 9F 2-10-0 takes water from a Midland swan-necked shed column in the shed yard in 1964.

Below left: 1924-built LMS Class 4F No. 44463 on shed at Toton alongside the concrete mechanical coaling plant.

Below: Eastern interloper! LNER Thompson Class B1 4-6-0 No. 61313 stands at the end of No. 3 shed. The piles of bricks were used for creating combustion arches in locomotive fireboxes.
All: Lee 'Eggy' Edmonds.

three and was usually assigned to the junior hand – in other words, me.

I was armed with a massive ball of cotton waste, a metal scraper and a bucket of mineral oil. The first job was to scrape off the copious layer of oily slime from all the moving parts. This would be followed by softening what remained with the cotton waste dipped into the oil. Finally, this oil was wiped away with clean cotton waste. The end result would be a shiny set of motions coated in a thin protective film of oil.

They did look very nice indeed when finished - the trouble was however, that I didn't! I was covered from head to toe in black grime and grease. Lunch time came and we washed up in the cleaners' corner, which consisted of about ten stone and white glazed sinks in the corner of No. 1 Shed. All glazing had long since been removed from the front edge as generations of cleaners before me had scraped their hands on them in an effort to remove the ingrained dirt.

Terry showed me a little dodge. He would take a handful of sand and after washing off the heaviest of the grime and whilst his hands were well lathered with soap, he would pick up the sand and use

this as an abrasive to remove the top layer of skin together with the ingrained dirt. It worked, but what had I let myself in for? I wonder what the Health & Safety people of today would have made of that?

Off we went to the messroom for our sandwiches. I was amazed to find that this eating place was not much cleaner than the locomotive we had just left, before it had been cleaned! Terry made some tea in a white enamelled tin plate can with a wire handle and a cup for a lid – the engineman's billy can. The boiling water came from a massive copper gas-fired water heater. I noticed that the tap was dripping badly into a tray full of spent tea leaves. This apparatus had obviously been 'on the boil' since Queen Victoria had been on the throne. It was in an appalling state.

Terry's next move was to find an old newspaper. He spread this out in front of him and used it as a table cloth. The tables were covered in a brown linoleum-type of material. There must have been some nasty bugs hiding on them because generations of men had carved their initials in the fabric and these in turn had become full of dirt.

I didn't have a billy can so Terry allowed me to share his. He explained that every footplateman had a can in which to make tea. It was an essential item. I would buy one as soon as possible.

It's July 12 1964 and BR Riddles Class 9F 2-10-0 No. 92117 rests in the shed yard at Toton alongside one of the elegant Midland Railway swan-neck water columns. These were originally fed from the Derby Canal which was some distance away, but from 1956 they were supplied by the nearer Erewash Canal. Toton Down Sidings North signalbox in the background (known as 'the shed box') enjoyed a commanding view of the MPD yard. *David Jones.*

I looked around the messroom and noticed that the walls had been painted black with tar paint on the bare brick work to about five feet in height. From there to the ceiling it was painted with whitewash - or greywash. Heat was supplied by two massive pot-bellied cast iron coal-fired stoves. There was one at each end of the mess room.

Footplatemen would bring in coal as needed from locomotives stabled just outside the door. They were not as eager to take away the resulting ash! There must have been at least a half-hundred weight of it around the base of each stove. The tables at the far end

and near to the fire were occupied by drivers and firemen. I was told that we could not sit anywhere near them because of the stink of the mineral oil that seemed to follow we cleaners everywhere.

The drivers and firemen were the elite and they certainly showed it. They regarded us as the lowest of the low. I thought that maybe they had been born on the footplate and had not started at the bottom of the tree!

Lunch time was over and we returned to the Class 8F 2-8-0 in No. 1 Shed to resume the task of getting filthy. I gazed at the lifeless

Above, left: Towards the end of Toton's steam days, A pair of very weary BR Riddles Standard Class 2MT 2-6-0s stand alongside No. 1 shed at Toton. In 1954, the MPD had an allocation of 138 engines; in 1965, one year before closure, this had fallen to just six. *David Jones.*

Above, right: Until the late 1950s, MPDs across the country were recruiting young lads to do the demanding cleaning and labouring jobs required as the first steps on the footplate ladder. John Woolley embarked on this path in October 1954. This picture shows one of the next - and final - generation of BR steam cleaners. Lee Edmonds - known back then and still in 2013 around Long Eaton as 'Eggy' - rests in the ashpit for the camera. This really was a filthy job which BR found it increasingly difficult to recruit for as steam declined from the mid-1950s. *Mick Boyd/Lee Edmonds.*

Stanier; she looked completely immobile. How could this massive lump of metal be capable of any movement at all, never mind haul a heavy freight train? It seemed to me impossible and was beyond my comprehension. The afternoon soon passed and before I knew it, it was 4.30pm and time to go home. The Stanier looked just a little cleaner for our efforts.

I'd enjoyed my first day to the full. The joy was short-lived however. When my mother saw the state that I was in she turned pale. "Good Lord" she exclaimed. "You'd better get yourself cleaned up before your dad gets home or he will have a fit!" I took her advice but couldn't remove the grime, firstly from under my finger nails or subsequently from around the bath. When dad came home he asked me how my first day had gone. I replied that I'd loved it and that I was happy with my choice of career. Off I went, still stinking of oil to see a couple of friends before dad used the bathroom!

First pay day and learning from the fitters

The first two weeks really flew and my first pay day arrived. The method of payment was a strange procedure to say the least. First, I made my way to the stores and asked for my paycheck. This was an oval brass disc and around the edge were the words 'Toton Motive Power Depot'. Stamped in the centre was my pay number - 944.

I then took the paycheck to the pay office at the other end of the block. I handed this to the pay clerk and in return he gave me an oval tin which had my number painted in black on the lid. I eagerly opened it and counted out the princely sum of two pounds and

Top: A last 'brew' around the forge fire, just before 'knocking off time' in the blacksmith's shop one day. From the left: Jimmy Murphy, Colin Parks, Jack Corden, Bill Yaxley, Roy Allsopp, Melvyn Rowthorne and Harry Beatson. *Mel Rowthorne Collection.*

Above, left: A Stanier '8F' 2-8-0 is apparently rerailed at Toton using hand-powered hydraulic lifting and traversing equipment.

Above, right: Midland '2F' 0-6-0 No. 58171 has its tender lifted, seemingly by a powered hydraulic rig, in the Toton shed yard. Both scenes appear to be training excercises. Both: *Ray Richmond Collection.*

14 shillings (£2.70). That was a pretty good wage for a young lad although I could have earned about £5 carrying bricks on a building site! The tin was then discarded into a bin, to be recycled and used again the following week. I suppose this method of payment saved a fortune in envelopes. The days went by and, as they passed, I was beginning to learn more and more about the job. Sometimes the fitters would request the assistance of a couple of cleaners when they had to strip down parts of the locomotives. It was an ideal situation for a young cleaner to ask questions. The fitters would gladly impart their knowledge providing that the questioner showed interest and enthusiasm.

They explained about lap and lead. Lap was the amount that the valve covered the steam inlet port to the cylinders. This was variable and could be controlled by the driver so that steam could be cut off

Passenger power at Toton. Heading north on the main Erewash Valley running lines between the MPD and the up yard on the left is Stanier three-cylinder 'Jubilee' 4-6-0 No. 45557 *New Brunswick,* with a St Pancras-Manchester express, on May 10 1958. The coaling plant marks the location of the MPD in the middle distance and gives scale to the sheer scale of the size of the marshalling yards, which were nearly two miles in length. *T.G. Hepburn/Rail Archive Stephenson*

Above, left: Toton's concrete mechanical coaling plant, built in the 1930s, which dominated the Long Eaton skyline until it was demolished in the late 1960s, after the depot closed to steam in 1966. A wagon is on its way up (or down!) the side of the plant during hopper filling.

Above, right: The ash disposal plant, whose twin skips raised ash from the pits and tipped it into wagons for disposal. *Both: R.J. Essery Collection.*

Above: Freight power from Toton MPD in the early days of the Beyer-Garratts. LMS 2-6-0+0-6-2 No. 4980 passes Long Eaton's second station (and some vulnerable lineside washing, flapping in a trackside garden!) on the Erewash line, on August 27 1932 with one of the Toton-London Brent coal trains for which these monster engines were designed and built. The locomotive is leading with its rotary bunker clearly shown. This town centre station (close to today's Tesco supermarket) served Long Eaton from 1863 to closure and demolition in 1967. Sawley Junction, rather further away from the town centre on the line towards Derby, was thereafter renamed 'Long Eaton.' This latter station is still open today. *T. G. Hepburn/Rail Archive Stephenson.*

during admission to the cylinder, at a pre-determined point along the piston's stroke. Lead was the point along a piston's stroke when steam was admitted for the opposite stroke. The fitters explained that lead steam had two purposes. Firstly to cushion the piston as it slowed down, nearing the end of its stroke and secondly to allow early expansion of the steam so as to obtain the best out of the power available.

These properties were controlled by the driver using the locomotive's reverser. The process was called 'varying the cut off.' In full forward or reverse gear, the steam would be cut off after the piston had travelled about 75% along its stroke. In this position, the locomotive was at its strongest but also at its slowest and most inefficient. This was the position for the reverser when starting a heavy train.

As a train accelerated, the driver pulled back on the reverser, towards mid-gear. The cut off was sooner as a consequence and the piston travelled the rest of the stroke under the power of expanding steam. This was, to all intents and purposes, the locomotive's 'gearbox' and I found out later that a driver who understood this principle was the best mate to have. Those who didn't understand cut-off, wasted coal, water - and the fireman's back!

Toton's fitters were great men and never tired of my questions. They explained the locomotive's motion and taught me the names of all the moving parts and the important relationship between components. They would ask me questions such as: "If the right big end is at the front, and the left big end is at the top, and the locomotive is in forward gear, where does she receive steam?"

The answer was that the right hand cylinder was open to lead at the front and exhaust to the rear and the piston was at the front of the cylinder. The left hand piston was half way along its stroke and receiving steam from the rear and open to exhaust at the front. I knew that they were impressed by my answers, especially from a lad so young. This gave me great encouragement and heightened my interest even further.

The Beyer Peacock 'Garratt'

There were many types of locomotive based at Toton. The largest was the famous Beyer Peacock articulated Garratt. They were built at Gorton Works in Manchester and were the most awesome beasts imaginable. They were articulated locomotives with four sets of motion. The wheel arrangement was 2-6-0+0-6-2. They could be described as two locomotives coupled together, with a common boiler.

They were hated and feared by many firemen who had nicknamed them "Birth Controllers". This was because when a firemen had worked a long, hard shift on a voracious Garratt, all he wanted to do when he arrived home was go to sleep!

Drivers, however, loved them, assuming they had a strong and experienced fireman. They just sat back and enjoyed the tremendous power under their control. They were not so eager however, if their mate was young and inexperienced and they might be called upon to assist in feeding the beast. The Garratts, it was said, ate coal like a pig would eat cherries!

The cabs were enclosed and therefore comfortable in winter. This was good. What was less attractive was that in the summer they were unbearably hot and a fireman could expect to lose quite a few pounds in weight on a long trip. There were no fat firemen in the Garratt links.

These very large locomotives were specifically built to haul the massive coal trains from Toton to Brent in London. When they were introduced at Toton in 1927 they were immediately run on test. The first coal train from Toton to Brent was driven by Toton Driver W. E. Edmonds (whose son Lee also joined the railway at Toton MPD in the 1960s - see page 12) in the autumn of 1927. The train consisted of 1,450 trailing tons and its average speed was 21mph.

No record exists to say how the first Garratt fireman coped but I

LOG OF 1.5pm TOTON-BRENT GARRATT-HAULED COAL TRAIN

Stations	Miles from Toton	Arrive	Pass	Depart
Toton				1.5
Ratcliffe Jct.	3		1.17	
Loughborough	10		1.39	
Syston North Jct	17½		2.1	
Brentingby	28¾	2.38		2.48
Saxby Station	31¼		3.0	
Ashwell	36	3.15		
Oakham	38¾		3.24	
Manton	42½		3.35	
Wing Sidings	43¾	3.40		3.55
Gretton.	49¾		4.13	
Weldon North	53¼		4.30	
Glendon South Jct	58¼		4.46	
Kettering	60¾		4.54	
Wellingborough	67½	5.15		5.40
Irchester South	70½		5.57	
Oakley Jct	81	6.29		
Bedford	82½		6.35	
Amptill	90¾		7.17	
Leagrave	99¾		7.41	
Luton	102¼		7.49	
Sandridge	111			
St. Albans	112¾		8.19	
Radlett	117¼		8.32	
Mill Hill	123¼		8.51	
Brent Loaded Sidings	126¾		9.5	

Above: A delightful image of rural England in the early 1960s. A vintage tractor is busy haymaking at the lineside as Beyer-Garratt 2-6-0+0-6-2 No. 47976 heads south from Melton Mowbray with a train of iron ore empties, circa 1961. *W.J.V. Anderson/Rail Archive Stephenson.*

would gamble that he had never worked so hard in his life. His name was Ron Workman and he was later the driver on my first main line trip. To give an idea of the sheer size of these beasts, here are a few statistics. The boiler pressure was 190 pounds per square inch (psi). They were superheated and the evaporative area was 2,137 sq. ft. Firegrate area was 44.5 sq. ft. Total weight, including coal and water, was 155.5 tons. They carried 4,500 gallons of water and nine tons of coal. The tractive effort was 45,620 lbs and length over buffers was 87 ft. 10.5 inches.

The Chairman of the London Midland & Scottish Railway Board at the time the locomotives were introduced was Sir Joshua Stamp. He said that the Garratt was a tremendous success. The saving of coal over the journey to London set against the amount used by double heading with two Fowler Class 4F 0-6-0 tender engines was a

quarter. What he didn't say or appreciate (or didn't care about) was that the single fireman used all the coal he would have used on a single Class 4 - plus half a tender more!

What's more, while Beyer Peacock built Garratts for countries all over the world and most were fitted with automatic stokers. The British Garratt was one of the few exceptions. Certainly, I will tell you later of a trip to Wellingborough which is only 67 miles from Toton. We had to take the locomotive to the shed to take on more

Above: 2-6-0+0-6-2 No. 47999 rests on the 'Garratt road' which ran close by the wall of Nos. 2/3 sheds at Toton. It was the only road on which the 87ft 10in Beyer-Garratt articulated locomotives could be moved under cover for servicing and repairs. Its position is made clear in the aerial photograph on page 9. This picture was taken on July 24 1955. *Brian Morrison.*

coal before going on to London. Fortunately, we were booked to lodge overnight at Wellingborough and in consequence we were relieved by a local crew who worked the train forward.

I have in my possession a log of actual timings for a train headed by a Garratt in 1927 from Toton to Brent. Although the trip is not dated, the source was from a sales catalogue published by Beyer Peacock during the LMS trials. It can be safely assumed that these timings were typical of Toton-Brent Garratt workings. Timings are given in the table above. The average speed was 18 mph with a train weight of 1,450 tons. The only brakes on the train were on the locomotive and in the guard's brake van.

The speed may seem to be excessively slow but one has to consider that the only powered brake force on the train was from the locomotive. Also, there is one 16 mile gradient of 1 in 200 and another of 4 miles 1 in 132. To haul a heavy train by steam power up these gradients was no mean feat. Stopping the train on the downward gradients was another miracle they had to perform.

Toton drivers were considered by most to be the very best heavy freight men in the country. Their skills with the Garratts were legendary and I doubt very much that today's drivers with their fully

air-braked freight trains, tight couplings, boundless power and short apprenticeships would ever cope in similar circumstances. And I mean no disrespect to today's enginemen, for different skills exist on the railways of today.

The Garratt man's apprenticeship was long and hard, few of them had served less than 20 years on the shovel as firemen before being promoted to driver. There is no better way of learning intricate gradients than having to supply the power to negotiate them. Well, enough of that for now, we had better get back to cleaning and the early days.

More cleaning and labouring.

Life was not all cleaning locomotives. The humour and companionship amongst the young lads was wonderful. I remember cleaning a locomotive in No. 1 Shed. The locomotive was stabled near the doorway to No. 2 Shed. At that time, polythene bags had not long been available and we marvelled how they could hold water. This meant that they made excellent missiles and believe me, a drop of water wasn't going to do any of us any harm at all!

I was working with a lad called Mark that day. The other cleaner was a lad called Keith and he had gone to the messroom to make us a can of tea. Mark had this wonderful idea. I would stand on the back of the locomotive tender overlooking the doorway. Mark would peer around the corner awaiting Keith's return. At a given signal, I was to throw the bag of water at the doorway.

Mark looked up at me and said, "Get ready John - he's coming!" I raised the bag of water above my head in readiness and waited for

Above: An evocative scene under the coaler at Toton. Class 3F 0-6-0 No. 43798 is keeping company with Garratts Nos. 47969 (left) and 47991 (right). *Colour Rail*

Mark's next signal. "Now!" he shouted. I let rip. And the Foreman caught the lot! I fully expected the sack as Mr. Storey stood in the doorway brushing himself down. I was terrified.

He looked up at me and asked: "What's your name, boy?" I replied: "John Woolley, sir." He asked: "How long have you been working here?"

"Six weeks sir" I replied.

"Well, if you would you like it to be seven, I expect to see my face reflected in that locomotive before you go home."

I could not believe my luck! He was a really great man and knew that boys will be boys. He also knew that I had been 'set up.' Mark did not fare so well, I can tell you. But we remained friends for two years until he went the way of many others and left the service.

Because of the poor wages the senior cleaners would sometimes be given labouring jobs. These included working on the ash pits shovelling ashes into wagons, emptying and filling sand wagons, shed sweeping and, in the winter, the best job of all - attending frost fires. These were placed at strategic points all over the depot to protect water cranes and dead locomotives from the ravages of freezing.

To qualify for cleaning, or labouring on the night shift, you had to be 16 years old. But even at 15 there was plenty of opportunity to wield a shovel on the day turn to earn a few shillings extra. Although I had only been employed for about five months I was fast becoming a senior cleaner. This was mainly due to the turn-over of young lads either leaving the service or being promoted as Passed Cleaners and then Firemen.

I well remember Sam, the Chargeman Cleaner, giving Mark and I our first labouring jobs. We were told to fill a 16-ton wagon with sand from a large heap kept in a remote siding near No. 3 Shed. The siding had the nickname 'Bulgaria' for some obscure reason. Perhaps the name originated from the fact that the location was isolated

Left, upper: MR 0-4-0ST No. 41518 is parked with its rear wheels removed for attention at Toton MPD on July 1 1956. A survivor of 28 0-4-0STs built for shunting docks and breweries between 1883 and 1903, No. 41518 was withdrawn in the week ending February 15 1958 and scrapped at Derby. *D.T. Greenwood/Rail Archive Stephenson.*

Left: London Tilbury & Southend Railway Class 3P 4-4-2T No. 41966 awaits its next job at Toton on October 31 1954 - a few days after John Woolley started work at the depot. He recalls that the 'Tilbury Tank' was employed as the shed shunter. *Rail Archive Stephenson.*

and far from the centre of activities and may as well be in another country.

We were only young lads and the shovels we were given were nearly as big as we were! I remember dropping the side door on the wagon and was awestruck by its cavernous interior. Mark and I awkwardly shovelled sand through the door. We worked as hard as we could but had hardly filled the corners of the wagon as lunch time arrived. As far as I was concerned, I may as well have been given the task of baling out the Pacific Ocean into the Atlantic using a teaspoon!

After our sandwiches we started to shovel once more and by mid-afernoon the side door had to be closed so that we could fill the wagon to capacity. This meant throwing the sand up and over the wagon side - about 10 feet.

Sam came to see how the work was progressing and peered through a crack in the wagon door. All he could see was daylight. He passed no comment but asked us to show him how we were using the shovels. We gave him a demonstration. He smiled and said: "You'll be here for a fortnight at that rate! Give me a shovel and I'll show you how to do it." Sam took the shovel from me and dug it into the sand and with a deft swing the sand left the shovel in one lump, ascended the wagon side and dropped onto the wagon floor with a thump.

It was a very fine demonstration. Especially from an old man. We felt quite inferior. Sam explained about the rhythm and how to make the shovel let go of the sand in one lump instead of it shooting off the blade in a spray. Sam's method meant that our arms would remain in their sockets. This would be an improvement. I was already beginning, I felt, to resemble an Orang-utan. We had managed to half-fill the wagon by the end of the day but we were sore and completely exhausted.

The next day Mark and I resumed the task. We were stiff at the start but soon loosened up. Sam's lesson began to tell and the rhythm was coming. We were winning and by the end of the second afternoon the wagon was full. We had blisters upon blisters on the palms of our hands. Mark and I thought that we had done well but Sam had his opinion. He told us that a team of three would be expected to fill a wagon in one shift but let us "off the hook" by saying that as there were only two of us, he would let us off. For the rest of the week Sam gave us respite from the sand and we were given lighter work.

The following week however we were back shovelling sand. As a bonus, Sam gave Mark and me another Cleaner to assist - my

school chum, Les. As a further incentive, we were told that when the wagon was full we could go home. We tackled the job with great enthusiasm and after seven hours the task was done. We were completely exhausted but proud to be going home 30 minutes before the other lads.

These jobs boosted our pay tremendously and I proudly took home to my mother the first white five pound note I had ever earned. This was real money! I was rich! This was living!

In May 1955, I was advised by Sam that I would be going to school to learn about railway rules, regulations, signalling and firing techniques. I would be a Passed Cleaner by the end of May, in time for my 16th birthday. The class was to be run by a man called Lew Crane. He was a very senior Footplate Inspector. Lew was a super fellow and well-liked by everyone. He was tall, slender and gentlemanly. He wore a black suit and waistcoat from which hung a gold chain and pocket watch. He always wore the traditional bowler hat.

The class was normally run by a Firing Instructor but for some reason he was not available. This was possibly because he was also a driver and, given that the summer holidays had started, he was probably needed for footplate duties.

As the course date approached, for which I awaited eagerly, the footplate union ASLEF (the Associated Society of Locomotive Engineers and Firemen) called a strike over pay. Being a member, I was obliged to answer the call, although I was not happy to do so. We were on strike for two weeks. During this time I met Noel Rigby who was a senior Fireman. I taught him to play chess in the strike committee room. We became lifelong friends and I was the best man at his wedding and he at mine.

Incidentally, I was out with Noel for a 'glass or two' one Saturday night in 1956 when I first met Caryl, my wife, and asked her for a date. Looking back, I was wrong to do what I did that night. I asked Noel if he would mind if I left him, to walk my new girlfriend home. Being the man that he is, he didn't object and spent the rest of the evening alone. Mind you, when he started courting, he used me as a "go between" delivering flowers and messages whilst he was working the shifts which made it impossible for him to see her. This made the scores even, I felt.

Noel's father was a senior driver at Toton and as a consequence of knowing Noel, I became a friend of his also. Although I never fired for Noel's father, he would always proffer advice and guidance, should I ask. He was a grand old man.

It was during the footplate strike of 1955 that I received the most

Above: Judging by the large number of inactive locomotives in the Toton shed yard, and the general lack of activity, this was probably a Sunday. At least a couple of gents in sports jackets in the shot suggests an arranged group visit to the depot. *K.H. Cockerill/J.W. Armstrong Trust.*

Above: With the MPD coaling tower glimpsed distantly through the bridge arch, Stanier Class 8F 2-8-0 No. 48384 plods north at Stapleford & Sandiacre station with a train of Class F empty steel-bodied wagons, bound for the coalfield and pitheads north of Toton, for reloading.
B.W.L. Brooksbank/Initial Photographics.

terrible news that one could imagine. A group of young engine cleaners had gone for a swim in a canal lock at Sandiacre. Les, who had been a school friend and started on the railway the same day as me had been in the party. He dived into the lock, which was about 20ft. deep - and failed to re-appear. The lock was quickly drained and poor Les was found tangled in a coil of wire which had been dumped in the lock.

All efforts were made to revive him, but alas, he was pronounced dead at the scene. Most of the staff at Toton attended the funeral including a good few who had never met him. I know fate is fate but I couldn't help thinking that had Les been at work instead of on strike, he might have been alive today.

Les and I regularly used to go to a dance on Saturday nights in the town of Beeston. We'd try to date the local girls, but without much success. Although we were only 16, we'd call in a local pub and have a glass of beer because we were big lads by this stage and looked 18! On the first anniversary of his death, I took my new girlfriend, who was later to become my wife, to that same pub in Beeston. I ordered two pints of mild ale and placed one on the opposite side of the table. I lifted mine and said: "Cheers, Les" I took a drink and placed the unfinished pint on the table. I walked out of the pub and have never returned since.

Eventually, the ASLEF strike was over and I was eager to get back to work. The whole of the footplate staff assembled in the Meadow, close to the depot and went back to work en-masse. Can you imagine the sight? There were about 500 men assembled and it was chaos trying to ascertain from the Foreman our next turn of duty. I was to report the following day at 9.30am, for cleaning.

I arrived at work next day and soon discovered the bad feeling which had sprung up between the footplate grades and the other staff who were mostly NUR (National Union of Railwaymen) members and not involved in the strike. The reason was obvious. Whilst we were on strike, they'd had little to do and had been placed on bare time. Not only had we lost a small fortune, we'd affected the earnings of the other workers also. They were very bitter about this.

Many long-standing friendships were shattered because of this episode and at the end of it, what did we achieve? Drivers got a one shilling a week increase (5p) while the lower grades got nothing! Strikes never pay. But the effect of this 1955 footplate strike had a far more reaching – and very damaging - effect than we at first imagined. Our goods customers had to get their supplies through somehow and they switched to road haulage, dropping the railways which had let them down. A lot never came back and as a consequence, my promotion was slowed accordingly.

Firing school

Early in June, the two-week course began, in a concrete hut about 10m long and about 4m wide. It had an odd bow-shaped roof and was nicknamed 'The Tabernacle.' There were about six of us in the class.

Lew started by explaining fixed signals and how they were used to control the flow of traffic. We made diagrams of the straight track and junctions and Lew asked us to draw in the signals that we would expect to find along the way. It was a marvellous way to teach us because not only did Lew have an idea of how we had grasped the lessons, it gave us great confidence when we got the right answers.

The next part of the course dealt with rules and regulations. Great emphasis was placed on a section in the old BR rule book - Rule 55. This dealt with the detention of trains on running lines and the very important safety procedures it involved to make sure the train was safe. Lew took us to Sawley Junction Signal Box (which was near the site of the present Long Eaton Station) to practice 'signing the book' as part of these procedures.

In the days before track circuits were in place to indicate to the signalman that a train was standing at his signals, there was a possibility that the signalman could forget that a train was in his section and allow another to enter from the rear. This would mean a collision. The fireman of the train held at a stop signal had to walk to the signalbox and remind the signalman that his train was there. He had to ensure that the signalman thoroughly understood the situation. There were several conditions written in Rule 55 which ensured that there could be no mistake. Failure to carry out the rule 'to the letter' could have disastrous consequences.

This had been proven horribly at Quintinshill on May 22 1915 when there was a multiple collision with the loss of 215 souls and a further 191 seriously injured. Although the fireman had carried out most of the provisions of Rule 55, he did not insist that the signalman place a safety clip (a collar) on the lever of the signal protecting the standing train. This device slipped over the handle and locked the release catch. It stopped the signal being cleared and served as a physical reminder that the track was occupied. The fireman should have

Above: The fireman of Stanier '8F' 2-8-0 No. 48185 is taking a breather and enjoying the fresh air of a sunny day as his train rumbles south through Stapleford & Sandiacre station on a Class J coal train from the Nottinghamshire collieries, bound for Toton yard, just a few hundred yards away at this point. *B.W.L. Brooksbank/Initial Photographics.*

ensured that the lever collar was in place before departing from the signalbox to rejoin his locomotive.

The signalmen at Quintinshill had evolved an unofficial agreement between themselves and instead of relieving at the booked time of 6am., the night signalman would work until about 7am to allow his mate more time to travel to work. Entries which should have been entered 'real time' after 6am in the train register were written instead on a plain piece of paper so that the relieving signalman could enter them, in his own handwriting, sometime later.

The night signalman was relieved by his mate after the departure of the fireman. The new signalman was not thoroughly aware of the situation with the detained train and accepted another train – an express - into the occupied section. This express ran into the rear of the standing train. The wreckage blocked the opposite running line and further collisions and fire in the gaslit coaches occurred. It was carnage.

Lew had no intention of a similar accident happening on 'his patch' and insisted that we got it right 'to the letter'. All of us were shocked at Lew's story about Quintinshill but I made a pledge there and then that I would always insist that the rule was carried out to the full.

A few years later, my train was standing at the down home signal at Cromford, near Matlock in the Derbyshire Peak District. I went to the signalbox to remind the signalman of our presence, in accordance with Rule 55. I had carried out the rule to the letter and was quite happy that all was OK. As I was about to leave the box, the signalman said: "West Ham beat Forest". Not being particularly interested in football, I thought it best to reply in a friendly manner. I said "Oh, I didn't know they were playing!"

Confused, he replied: "Who?"

I answered "West Ham and Forest!" He looked at me and bursting into fits of laughter, explained "I said you were waiting for the Westhouses to Peak Forest!". I joined in the laughter but this serves to show that confusion can often arise from the simplest of situations. You have to take great care to ensure the situation is understood by everyone.

Back in the classroom, Lew was careful to allay any fear and said

we'd be fine and safe just as long as we carried out the rules properly. We felt better for that.

Practical training on the steam engine was provided by a senior fireman by the name of Dennis Brakewell. Dennis had fallen from a locomotive tender and broken his ankle. Whilst he was confined to the depot to convalesce, he was allocated the task of taking us in hand and 'showing us the ropes'.

Dennis showed us how to work injectors, which fill the locomotive boiler with water. I thought at the time that the injector was a wonderful piece of physics. How could the steam from the boiler overcome its own pressure to deliver water to that very same boiler? As far as I remembered from my school days science lessons, two equal pressures became no pressure!

Dennis explained that the steam came from the boiler dome and passed through a cone which increased its velocity as would the cone on the end of a Fire-fighter's hose. After the steam cone (as it was known) the jet of steam met the water which had been allowed to run from the tender to the injector mechanism. The water was forced forward to another cone called the mixing cone.

The mixed water and steam by this time travelling at a great velocity, was forced through yet another cone called the delivery cone. The water now had so much energy imparted to it that it was strong enough to lift the boiler clack (one way valve) and actually enter the boiler which had provided the steam to work the device. This effectively overcame its own pressure. Marvellous!

Dennis explained everything a fireman should know. He told us how the blower worked by creating a partial vacuum in the smokebox. This would, via the boiler tubes, pull primary air through the ashpan and secondary air through the firehole doors thereby drawing the fire.

Dennis explained the different characteristics of each type of locomotive and the best methods of firing each class.

It was during these lessons that I became aware of the different properties of coal. Welsh was the best, I was told. Other types from various mines were different. Coal from Wollaton (near Nottingham) came in massive lumps and needed a lot of work to break up before it could be used. We called them "Wollaton Coffins" for two reasons. One because they resembled the size and shape of coffins, and two, a fireman who was unfortunate enough to have a tender full of these, would probably require the real thing before the shift was up! "Idle miners, they ought to break it up for us" was the comment when we had a tender full of Wollaton.

Some coal made excessive ash and clinker. Clinker was a glue-like sheet of melted and solidified ash and other contaminants, which clung to the firebars and impeded the flow of primary air. This would result in a poor fire, with consequent poor steaming. All coal has the same chemical properties but in differing amounts. The constituents of coal could be remembered by the acronym NO CASH - Nitrogen, Oxygen, Carbon, Ash, Sulphur and Hydrogen.

Dennis gave us a list of tools that a fireman had to ensure the locomotive was carrying prior to departure from the shed. These included four spanners, a bucket for washing in, 12 detonators in a can together with two red flags, two oil headlamps with their red shades, three fire irons which consisted of a rake, a dart for breaking clinker, and a clinker shovel for the removal of the same. In addition, the locomotive had to carry a hand brush, a strong coal hammer, two spare gauge glasses together with their sealing washers, and finally, a good firing shovel. He advised us to pick a light one with a smooth handle.

At the end of the course, came the examination. We all passed with flying colours. I was regraded as a passed cleaner on July 27 1955. This meant that I could be used as a fireman when needed, but that my job would still be predominantly cleaning and labouring.

I eagerly awaited the day when I would be rostered to my first firing turn. It was the passed cleaners job to scan the footplate rosters daily to see if they had been allocated to a firing job. We were well prepared for the task of heaving coal into a locomotive firebox. Sam had given us plenty of practice as labourers. On reflection, perhaps this was the strategy and all the shovelling we had done over the previous year, was good, solid training for better things to come.

First trips and more labouring

Early one Saturday morning, I was thrilled to see my name on the footplatemen's roster for the following Monday. It said: 'J. Woolley 10pm Old North.' This was the life! This was real living! That said, it wasn't much of a job though, just a lowly shunting turn in Toton's Old North Yard. I spent most of Sunday and Monday daytime contemplating my first trip. I found it almost impossible to sleep during the day on Monday because, not only had I been in bed on Sunday night and wasn't tired, I was also as excited as a child at Christmas.

I eagerly turned up for work on Monday night 30 minutes early and had to wait for the driver who was exactly on time. He was a smashing chap called Rusty – well, he did have a shock of red hair. He asked my name and how long I had been firing. I had to tell him that this would be my first turn. He didn't seem to mind this one bit.

There were, on the other hand, plenty of 'old hands' who resented us novices. Some would refuse to take a young lad. This was possibly because they might be obliged to offer assistance. These were the days when the driver was regarded as the last word. No one – not even the foremen - dare over rule them! Fortunately, Rusty was not one of these individuals.

Our job in the Old North Sidings was merely to sort empty wagons into types and trains for forwarding to the numerous collieries on the Erewash Valley. The work must have been monotonous for the driver, but to me, being new to the game, it was an exciting experience.

The locomotive was an old Midland Railway Johnson Class 2F 0-6-0 freight engine. These locomotives were not much of an improvement on Stephenson's Rocket. They were not fitted with superheaters and ran on saturated (wet) steam. The injectors were notoriously temperamental, so filling the boiler could be tricky. They were prone to priming - carrying water from the boiler and over into the cylinders, from where it spewed from the blast pipe and chimney. They would not stand hard work for prolonged periods without going slowly 'down the nick' - struggling for steam and water.

As far as comfort was concerned, it was non-existent. The driver's and fireman's seats were wooden boards placed across steel tool lockers. The boards were not part of the locomotive and any scrap timber lying about the depot would be acquired for this purpose.

Because this makeshift seat was so low, the driver had to stand to work the locomotive. The regulator was upright and in the centre of the cab and the steam brake valve wheel was similarly placed. This made it impossible for the driver to observe the shunter's signals and control the locomotive at the same time. The driver's head would be in and out of the cab like a cuckoo in a cuckoo clock at midnight.

The driver had to spin the steam brake valve wheel anti-clockwise to apply the brake and spin it the opposite direction to release it. The sanders would be worked by the fireman who would pull and push a lever which released sand by gravity, in a trickle onto the rail. They were very primitive indeed. However, these shortcomings would not bother me on such a light job. As far as I was concerned at that time, this was the ultimate machine.

Apart from being too over enthusiastic and being told to slow down and take things easy, the night passed smoothly and quickly. I worked the turn every night that week bar one. I was labouring on Thursday night only. My job that night was shovelling ashes on

Above: In steam days 'lodging turns' were common - enginemen worked a train out one day, slept in a lodging house overnight and worked back the next. This was the MR's lodging house, located just south of the high level goods lines crossing the Erewash Valley main line en route from the down yard - behind today's Asda supermarket. Its 20 rooms were mostly filled night each until closure in 1966. Faster trains, changing attitudes and new rosters meant men could - and wanted to - work 'out and home' in a day. It was demolished c1973. *Keith Reedman.*

Above: The Midland Railway's Johnson Class 2F 0-6-0 saturated steam freight engines had been a long-term fixture in the Toton allocation and John's first firing turn had been aboard one of these veterans on local shunting duties at Toton North Yard. He described them as 'not much of an improvement on Stephenson's *Rocket.*' No. 581 is clearly out of use in this wintry view at Toton MPD. *Pete Salmon.*

the ashpits. The ashpits were not far from the Old North Yard and I watched the little Johnson shunting engine working 'my' turn. I felt somehow envious of the more senior passed cleaner working 'my' job.

At the end of the week, Rusty said that I had done well and that I would make a good fireman one day. I was thrilled to hear these words from such a senior driver.

The following week I was back labouring on days. The coal hopper at Toton was undergoing an overhaul. It was divided internally into two separate supplies. There were two lines passing under the hopper making it possible to coal two locomotives at the same time. These were appropriately named No. 1 and No. 2 sides. The best quality coal (for main line work) was generally obtainable from No. 2 side. No. 1 was for shunters and local 'trips'. The Outside Foreman would direct each locomotive on arrival accordingly.

To facilitate the repairs, the hopper had to be completely emptied. Most of the coal could be removed in the usual way - by coaling locomotives. There was however a large quantity of coal left in the hopper which then had to be removed manually. Locomotives were coaled using a crane and grab in the sidings whilst repairs to the hopper were carried out.

Several of us inherited the job of completely emptying the hopper.

It was the most appalling task imaginable. We had to climb into the hopper and working in semi darkness, shovel the coal and dust through the discharge chute and into a wagon which was placed on the track below.

The Motive Power Superintendent at that time was a super guy called Mr. D. D. Scott. No one ever knew what the initials D.D. stood for. To everyone he was only ever known as 'Mr. Scott.' He was a very fair and understanding boss. He knew that no man could stand more than four hours per day working in that kind of dust and grime. He therefore decreed that after four hours was up, the young lads would be relieved by another shift of cleaners. At the end of each period we would be allowed to take a bath at the lodging house before being sent home.

The lodging house was a place where crews from other depots stayed overnight before working back to their home depots the following day. Men from all over the country frequently stayed overnight. To some it was like a second home. The lodging house was between the Low Level Main Line and Long Eaton Goods Yard – just about 500 yards from today's ASDA store in Long Eaton.

When we arrived, the foreign crews already at the lodging house were not impressed by the sight of us. They resented the fact that these scruffy tykes would be using their pristine facilities. I know this because we heard that they had complained to the Lodging House Attendant. Consequently, he followed us everywhere with a mop and bucket.

For our troubles, the following week, me and a gang of cleaners were sent to the lodging house to scrub it through. This shows how filthy the coal hopper job really was. I had black rings around my eyes for many days.

My first main line firing trip

In the summer of 1955 I was thrilled to see my name on the roster for my first real main line train. The turn required me to be on duty at 12 o'clock lunch time for an iron stone train from Ashwell (the exchange sidings for Cottesmore Ironstone Mine near Oakham in Rutland) to Frodingham (a blast furnace in Yorkshire).

The driver that day was Ron Workman who had been the first

Above: John's first main line trip as a young fireman was on Stanier '8F' No. 48141, running north from Toton through Chesterfield to Rotherham. This is sister '8F' No. 48641, north of Toton MPD and yards, at Stapleford & Sandiacre, with a Class H freight on May 17 1962. The 'Old Cross Dyeworks Ltd' factory and lineside painted sign was a well known local landmark.
B.W.L. Brooksbank/Initial Photographics.

Left: After Nationalisation on January 1 1948, it took quite some time for British Railways branding to appear on the entire national fleet of 20,000 locomotives and some never received new numbers or BR markings. But if locomotives were to be properly managed they needed to be given their new numbers. This led to some historically fascinating short term mixtures of the old and new. That's very much the case here where a Toton MR Johnson Class 2F 0-6-0 has received its BR cast smokebox number of 58153 while still paired with an LMS tender, on August 10 1952. Yet more interesting is that the locomotive is carrying its new BR number of 58153 on the cabside - but in shaded LMS numerals matching the tender. *R.J. Buckley/Initial Photographics.*

Garratt fireman to London in 1927. Ron was a really old hand and was one of the nicest men one could wish to meet. Like most of the old hand drivers of the day, he was tall and lean. He had that gaunt look about his face which I am sure came from years of peering out of locomotive cab windows into the cold, rushing air. The lean frame was the result of years of continual manual labour, long hours and very little food.

I met him in the drivers lobby at 12 o'clock and told him my name. I mentioned that this would be my first main line trip. Like Rusty, he didn't seem to mind one bit. His actual words to me were: "Well son, you will soon learn and in any case, what you cannot do, I can, so don't worry!" I was determined that I would do all possible within my limited experience to ensure that I would not have to call on this great man's skills.

A previous crew had taken a train of empty ore wagons to Ashwell, changed the train for a loaded one and was returning with the train for Frodingham. We would take the train forward to Rotherham.

We walked across to Toton Centre relief cabin which was situated under Toton Centre Signalbox. From there, Ron rang the control to ask where our train was. The Controller told Ron that the locomotive was 48141 an LMS Stanier Class 8F 2-8-0. He added that the train was very close and would arrive on the Down main line within a few minutes.

We were waiting at the main line signal when the train came into sight from around the curve at Toton Junction. The train pulled up at the signal and we climbed aboard. The fireman whom I relieved told me that she was a "good un" and that she was a free steamer and would give me no trouble. He then departed with his mate to sign off duty.

I looked in the firebox and noted briefly that there was a good fire burning and that it was nice and bright. She had a full boiler of water also. The previous fireman had thoughtfully shovelled the coal forward in the tender. We were in 'good fettle'. A grand start with a good locomotive. It couldn't be better.

Ron told me that the climb from Toton to Doe Hill (about 17 miles) was the most demanding part of the journey and was uphill all the way. He advised me to keep a good fire on and the boiler well full as the train was very heavy. "There's no rat holes in these". He said. This meant that they were solidly loaded and exceptionally heavy.

Ron blew the whistle to indicate to the signalman that we were ready to depart. The signalman responded by clearing the home signal. Within a second or two, the distant for Sandiacre which was mounted under the home signal, also cleared. We were 'right away.' Ron eased the regulator open and gently took the strain of the couplings. When he knew that he had the entire train 'on the roll', he gave her progressively more steam. As the train accelerated, Ron began to 'pull her back' so as to increase the cut-off and shorten the period of admission of steam into each cylinder. The locomotive was barking like a wolf hound but she was well master of the train.

I opened the firedoors and started to pile in the coal as Dennis had

instructed me during my brief training. I remember saying to myself: 'four down each side, three across the front, four spread across the middle, three into each back corner and six over the mouthpiece.' The locomotive responded by issuing grey smoke from the chimney. This was a sure sign that you had "got it right" and that there were no holes in the fire, which could draw cold air from the ashpan and into the firebox resulting in poor steaming.

On went the exhaust injector. It sang like a soprano. It was a great tool - not a drop of water was wasting from the overflow below my cab steps. Ron looked across the cab and quickly scanned the water level and the steam pressure gauge. I caught his eye and he gave me a reassuring wink and an encouraging smile.

Still on the down main, we were passing Shipley Gate and were overtaking an old Johnson Class 2F 0-6-0 with about 30 empties in tow on the Down Goods. The driver of the train was an Irishman by the name of John. When he noticed that he was about to be overtaken, he gave his locomotive all steam! Although he had no chance against the mighty Stanier he was not going to give in without a fight. It would have made a great lineside photograph.

Ron explained that John was a strange fellow who now only worked local trips because of his age. He added that he always tried to race the main liners with his little Johnsons but obviously never won. My mate eased back on the regulator to give John the impression that he was winning. The Johnson now appeared to be beating us and was travelling about 1 mph faster than us. She was throwing black smoke and sparks high into the air. I began to feel for his fireman.

Ron looked across at me and smiling said: "OK John, now for some fun, give her another round of coal!" I responded and Ron opened the regulator wide open and dropped the lever down a little to decrease the cut off. The Stanier leapt forward and that was the last I saw of John for the time being.

By this time I was really beginning to find my fireman's feet and my confidence rose to great heights. We were switched to the goods line at Westhouses and the trip was uneventful up the long gradient to Doe Hill (near Chesterfield) and as we breasted the summit, Ron eased her back before shutting off altogether. He partially applied the steam brake then came across to my side and wound on the tender brake as hard as he could. This arrested the train's momentum and reduced our speed to no more than 10 mph.

"OK John," Ron said: "Get the can on and let's have tea." I placed the can of water on the blade of the shovel and placed this over the mouthpiece, just into the fire. The can boiled in about 30 seconds. I added the tea and milk and enjoyed the best cup of tea ever!

The next major junction was Clay Cross. It was a notorious place to have to stop with a loose coupled train. Loose coupled meant that the train was not braked throughout and relied on the locomotive and brakevan brakes to keep the train under control. Ron did not allow the speed of the train to rise above 10 mph and reduced speed even further as the junction was approached. He came over to my side and observed the signals. They were clear. The tender brake was released and the train was allowed to accelerate on the less severe gradient.

As we approached Clay Cross Junction Signalbox, Ron said: "Give him two longs and two shorts!" I hadn't a clue what he was talking about and told him so. Ron explained. "When a train approaches Clay Cross, the signalman has to be told which way we need to travel at Tapton Junction. There are two routes - left to Sheffield and right through Barrow Hill to Rotherham. The Sheffield route is known as the fast line and the Barrow Hill route the slow. If we are on the Goods Line and require to turn right, we whistle two longs and two short. If we are on the Main Line, we whistle one long and two shorts. If the train requires to turn left at Tapton, the longs remain the same but you only whistle one short". What he said next really folded me up with laughter. "Some drivers can never remember so they whistle one extra long with little stutters in between and let the signalman work it out for himself!"

We arrived at Chesterfield on the down goods line and stopped there to replenish the water tank. Whilst it was filling, I climbed into the tender and shovelled about a ton of coal forward onto the shovelling plate. The locomotive had been out all day and the coal was well back in the tender. I also ran the straight dart fire iron along the firebars and loosened the clinker. Using the long and unwieldy clinker shovel, this was then thrown out on to the track side and quenched with water, so as to avoid a fire.

The final job then was to wash and brush the footplate, fill a bucket with warm water and wash up. The last few miles from Chesterfield to Rotherham were mostly down hill and required no more than a few breaths of steam to complete.

We were relieved at Masborough and the locomotive was in as good a fettle as when we had stepped onto her at Toton. I had done it! The sense of achievement was wonderful. The next few years saw

many successful trips like this one - but quite a few rough ones as well, where we'd struggle for steam.

Beyer Garratt No. 47973

It was also in the summer of 1955 that I found myself on the footplate of my first Beyer Garratt. Noel had applied for a day off. He was booked with a driver named Billy Webb. I was advised to take duty at 12 minutes past midnight for Wychnor (Noel's turn).

I duly reported for duty and met Bill in the lobby. I was a little apprehensive when I discovered that a Garratt had been allocated to the turn. The locomotive was 47973 and she was stabled in the Garratt sidings which were outside and adjacent to No. 2 and No. 3 Sheds. We prepared the locomotive and departed to the West Yard to pick up the train. Bill gave me the simplest advice: "Just keep shovelling until the firebox is full."

Obviously, I was only a young lad, and Bill with his wealth of experience had taken the precaution of obtaining a spare shovel so that he could assist if necessary. And it was necessary! We worked together - when my shovel was in the coal bunker, Bill's would be in the firehole and vice versa. We must have shovelled well over a ton into the fire before we even left the West Yard Sidings at Toton. As departure neared, Bill stopped shovelling so that he could watch for the signal to start, from the Yard Foreman. She was now 'all mine!'

The signal to start was given and Bill replied with a pop on the whistle. He opened the regulator and gently took the strain. Looking across at me he said: "OK, John, open the back damper wide and when she comes up to blowing off, put the exhaust injector on."

The train was soon on the move and we moved out onto the Low Level Main Line. As we passed Trent, Bill opened her up a little to negotiate the climb to Sheet Stores. The Garratt's exhaust was beating eight to the revolution. She took the train up the bank effortlessly. As we passed Lock Lane Crossing, Bill eased the regulator and wound up the gear a little.

On Bill's instruction I started to pile the coal into the firebox once more. She had a voracious appetite and I just about kept her going across the branch to Stenson. We were then held at Stenson to allow

Above: At more than 87ft long, the Garratts could not be turned (other than on triangles) and so worked in either direction. With mainly wooden bodied wagons on the drawbar, No. 47993 is running in reverse at Chesterfield North with train of coal empties. *Peter Hughes/Colour Rail.*

Above: In seemingly very clean condition, Beyer Garratt 2-6-0+0-6-2 No. 47998 is in charge of an up coal train near Castle Donington on September 25 1955. *T.G. Hepburn/Rail Archive Stephenson.*

more important trains to pass from the Derby direction. This was an ideal opportunity to build up another good fire.

Eventually, we were allowed to leave Stenson. As we passed the box, the signalman was swinging his right arm across his body. Bill told me that he was telling us to "get a move on" as we only had bare running time to Clay Mills Goods Line. We had to make the distance on time if we were not to stop the Derby to Bristol Mail.

Sure enough, the distant was off for the Goods Line at Clay Mills and Bill hurried the train off the Main Line and out of harm's way. Although Wychnor Sidings were not far from Stenson, being only about five miles west of Burton, I seemed to be working all the time to keep on top of this monster's hunger and thirst. I was grateful when the train finally stopped in Wychnor Sidings. The fire was by now painfully thin. We had only just made it, despite my efforts!

Wychnor was an exchange sidings for Bescot traffic. We were told by the Foreman that our return train was coming from Bescot and would arrive within the hour. We washed and ate our sandwiches.

Our train eventually arrived and whilst the guard examined and prepared the train, Bill and I filled the firebox once more. We must have shovelled at least a ton or so onto the grate before we were given the signal to depart. It was the same scenario on the return journey, the more I shovelled, the thinner went the fire! I could see by Bill's face that he would be pleased when the trip was over and Noel would be back. Even so, Bill never once complained about my inexperience and assisted me whenever he could. He was a grand chap, and because of the enthusiasm I had shown on the trip, he reassured me by saying that I had done well - for a lad!

No. 47998 (straight bunker)

The first 'straight bunkered' Garratt (no rotary bunker to help bring coal forward) that I had the misfortune to come across was No. 47998 on a heavy train to Woodhouse Mill (near Sheffield) from Toton in the autumn of 1955. The driver was a fellow called Eric. The

Garatt had come a long way before we relieved her at Toton.

As I have explained earlier, Garratts ate coal as a pig would eat cherries. Miners loved 'em - they kept them in work! This particular Garratt did not have a rotary coal bunker which was a device for bringing the coal forward to the firing plate as it was needed by the fireman (more about this device later).

Eric, it has to be said, was not the best of drivers. He was a nice enough chap in himself but was regarded as rough by the firemen. This was a term often used to describe a driver who was not happy unless the locomotive was making a lot of noise from the exhaust and the fireman's back was bent as he shovelled to keep up! These were the men who didn't know what the cut-off was for! Or didn't care. For them, the engine was working hard and was either in full forward or reverse gear, with very little variance in between.

Anyway, we struck out from Toton and it soon became apparent that I was in for a rough trip. I should like to be able to say here that by this time I had worked quite a few trains and my experience was growing fast, but I can't. I was by no means a weak lad but on this occasion I just could not deliver the coal to the locomotive's fire fast enough. Eric was hammering the engine and burning it faster than I could throw it in! It didn't help that I had to shovel it twice – once forward in the bunker and then again into the fire.

Eric didn't seem to notice that I was struggling to keep her going. I was fast going 'down the nick.' I was holding back the supply of water to the boiler in an attempt to maintain steam pressure - and that's the spiral of decline. Putting cold water in would have cooled the boiler and lost steam pressure even faster – but there's then the risk you run low on water and that's a major problem. I had to tell him: "Eric, we are going to stick. The boiler is only a quarter full and we're steadily losing pressure!"

"We will be OK" he replied. I couldn't work out for the life of me what he meant. Perhaps he meant that it would be OK for him! We stuck at Codnor Park.

Eric lit his Woodbine whilst I made up a good fire to raise steam pressure again and I also re-filled the boiler. As it 'came round' I took the opportunity to shovel a ton or so of coal forward onto the firing plate. Eric eventually whistled to the signalman to indicate that we were ready to proceed and the signal was cleared.

Eric shot off like a 'rat up a sewer.' No cautious use of the available energy with this chap! He drove the locomotive as if power was boundless. It wasn't. We stuck again, short of the summit at Doe Hill. I set about another 'blow up' and got stuck into another coal shifting exercise. Eric? He lit another Woodbine.

We eventually arrived at Barrow Hill. Eric advised the yard staff that we would have to leave the train and go to the shed for more coal. Whilst I coaled the engine and cleaned the fire, Eric departed to the messroom for a cup of tea. And another Woodbine. A very thoughtful chap was Eric...

This escapade led to my first brush with the Firing Instructor at Toton since I had been passed. He asked why I'd been unable to keep the locomotive going and had stuck twice on the way to Barrow Hill? I told him the whole story. He managed to leave me with the feeling that it was 'down to me'. He was probably just about right. My back, arms and stomach muscles hadn't yet had the time to develop fully. I was young and tired quickly. It had just been too much for me.

It was quite a shock for a young lad to be thrust full bore like this into a man's world. Just over a year ago, I'd been sitting at my school desk, pushing a pen. But I had tried my hardest and done all that I was capable of doing at the time. The Firing Instructor verbally cautioned me and that was the end of the matter. At least he had something to put in his official report, and after all, I was the most junior and least important person involved.

Beyer Garratt No. 47993 and lodging at Wellingborough

A few weeks later I had booked on duty at midday for shed work - disposing locomotives. However, a fireman had gone sick at the last minute and the Foreman was waiting for me in the lobby. He asked if I'd go to Wellingborough and lodge overnight, working back the following day. I was obviously not prepared for this as I needed overnight clothes and extra food. The Foreman agreed that I could rush back home and obtain the necessary.

On my return to the depot I was told that the train stood at Toton Centre. A previous crew had taken the locomotive light from Toton MPD to Stanton Gate Up Sidings to pick up the train, which had been formed there, from coal trips working on the Erewash Valley.

The driver was a chap called Chuck Nurse and the locomotive was a Beyer Peacock Garratt, No. 47993. We stepped on the footplate and the fireman told me that he had built up a good fire to give us a good start. Pleasantries over, Chuck whistled for the road and the signalman responded by clearing the signal.

Everything appeared to be normal as we sailed through Trent but it was not long before I noticed that the locomotive seemed to be having to work harder than one would have expected. Chuck passed the comment that the train seemed very difficult to 'get along.' (So he'd noticed it dragging too). Although the locomotive was steaming reasonably, I was having to deliver the fuel by shovelling continuously.

We were struggling for steam (here we go again) as we approached Loughborough water troughs, where we picked up water and replenished the tanks. Chuck had noticed that I was having to work harder than normal and tried to ease the regulator to conserve energy. The Garratt responded by slowing unacceptably as the train weight took its toll. Chuck had no alternative but to give her steam once again.

He then picked up the spare shovel and we worked together for a time in an effort to fill the firebox. We fought all the way to Syston North Junction and easing the train around the severe curve, stopped at Syston East at the water crane there. Although the locomotive had plenty of water to get us to Brentingby, we needed the stop to fill the boiler and build up another good fire.

Eventually, the signal cleared and by the time we had reached Wet Stones Crossing near Frisby, we were struggling once more. We just about made it through Melton Mowbray where the signalman switched us onto the Goods Line to Brentingby.

It was not unusual to spend half an hour or so at Brentingby to allow the expresses and other more important traffic to pass from the Nottingham direction. In the 1950s, the Nottingham- Melton line via Old Dalby was in continuous use. No one in those days would have believed that the line would close and become a research test track.

I realised that we had used a phenomenal quantity of coal over this relatively short distance and the locomotive had not given us a fair exchange for our efforts. I have often tried to work out over the years why one locomotive would perform differently from another of the same class. Some locomotives were notorious for poor performance and no amount of attention from the maintenance staff would remedy the situation. There were so many critical factors, that any one, or combination, could cause problems. Apart from coal type being responsible, there were others such as blast pipe alignment, boiler tube condition, internal condition of the boiler, steam blows, smokebox door seals and many more things to consider. But, like all mass produced machines, there were the good and the rogues. This Garratt was a rogue with a heavy train.

Anyway, I took this stop as an opportunity to use the rotary bunker to bring more coal forward to the firing plate, where I could reach it with the shovel. The rotary coal bunker was cone-shaped with the wide end towards the footplate. On the top of the bunker were six sets of doors. These would be opened under the hopper and the coal would be loaded before the doors were closed once more. In effect, the locomotive then had a conical cylinder containing coal.

There was a toothed gear wheel all the way around the bunker at

A sunny spell in Toton shed yard on July 24 1955 finds Beyer-Garratt No. 47971 awaiting its next duty in company with a sister engine at the front. The engine is clearly ready for its next job - the rotary hopper doors are wide open and good quality coal is piled high. *Brian Morrison.*

the footplate end. This engaged with a small gear wheel driven by a steam donkey engine. The cylinder was pivoted on its long axis. The fireman, on the footplate, would close the door on the firing plate, release a safety catch and pull a lever which allowed steam to the donkey engine. The bunker would then rotate and this action would cause the coal at the back of the bunker to roll forward from the narrow end at the back to the wide end at the front – and onto the shovelling plate.

The action was not dissimilar to that of a cement mixer. Rotation of the bunker would be stopped when the firing plate was in its correct position, at the bottom. Generations of footplatemen however had not used the bunker as intended. Because the donkey engine was reversible they would rock the bunker from side to side instead of rotating it completely. This would wear the bearing track at the bottom only.

If a fireman then tried to rotate the bunker as it was designed to do, and the track was worn, the bunker would jam - upside down. A crow bar would then have to be used in the toothed ring around the bunker to assist the donkey engine and free it. You guessed it - this happened to Chuck and I at Brentingby! The problems continued. We had a really hard time persuading the bunker to return to its normal position, but in the end, we won the day.

Eventually, with the bunker freed and properly relocated, the fire rebuilt and the boiler full of water, we started away from Brentingby in fine fettle. From there it's a gentle climb all the way to a point between Ashwell and Langham. It was not a gentle climb for the Garratt however. She and I were having a battle - and she was just winning! Looking back on that day, I am sure that the locomotive was overloaded.

As we passed Ashwell, Chuck remarked that we would soon be at Saviour's Bridge. This was an overbridge between Ashwell and Langham and was on the summit of the climb. A train arriving there from either direction in poor condition was 'saved' by miles of down hill running. Hence the name - Saviour's Bridge. We passed it with about 10 chuffs to spare and were pleased to see the signal off at Langham for the goods line down to Oakham. Another chance to recover the old girl.

It's down hill from Oakham and through the tunnel to Manton Junction. From there it's a short sharp climb through Wing Tunnel

Above: Driver Chuck Nurse after the end of steam, driving a Class 44 'Peak', was John Woolley's driver on Garratt No. 47993 on a lodging turn to Wellingborough. Note Chuck is still wearing steam overalls and his greasetop cap. *Courtesy: Chuck Nurse.*

Below: A snap of Harringworth Viaduct, from Seaton. Built between 1877 and 1879, it is three-quarters of a mile long. The VW Golf saloon was the Woolley family car at the time, during a Sunday outing into the country. *Courtesy: Caryl Woolley*

Above: Taking water from a crane in the shed yard at Wellingborough MPD is 2-6-0+0-6-2 Beyer Garratt No. 47988, in May 1956. This was the last year of the mighty Garratts. Only four remained by October and none survived through 1957. None of these massive engines survived scrapping - what an attraction one would be today! The shed itself does survive, in industrial use. *Stephen Summerson/Rail Archive Stephenson.*

and onto Wing itself. We were running under clear signals and soon passed Wing and entered the long tunnel at Glaston. I was working furiously on this long down gradient to build up a fire which would hopefully carry us over the long viaduct at Harringworth, up the heaviest part of the road from Harringworth, past Glaston, through the notorious tunnel at Corby and on to the blast furnaces at Stewarts and Lloyds. From there it would be easy for the rest of the journey.

The viaduct at Harringworth is one of the most spectacular feats of Victorian engineering that you'll ever see. It spans the Welland Valley and passes over the village of Harringworth. It has no fewer than 82 arches and is approximately 60ft in height. It was built by Lucas & Aird of London between 1876 and 1878. It contains 20 million bricks. It is a fact that if the bricks were laid side by side forming a path 5ft. 3in. wide, it would reach from London to York, a distance of 200 miles.

The traffic over this route has nowadays sadly dwindled to a trickle, but the viaduct will always stand as a monument to the great railway age of the Victorians. I would urge anyone interested in railway architecture to visit Harringworth and marvel at this wonderful construction.

As the train came out of Seaton Tunnel on the slight right hand curve, I spotted the distant for Harringworth and was thankful that it was in the clear position. I conveyed this fact to Chuck and he responded by giving the Garratt steam. As the train stretched out and we felt the gentle tug of the brakevan, Chuck gave her the lot and wound up the gear to increase the cut-off.

The sparks were really flying as the train passed Harringworth village. There is a thatched cottage below the viaduct on the Up Side on the Main Street. How it ever survived the constant rain of fire from our steam engines I will never be able to understand. But, the cottage is still there today. I would like to gamble that the owner of that lovely building did not mourn the passage of steam. He must have lived a traumatic life.

As we passed the signalbox we knew that this would be our greatest trial. The severe gradient from Harringworth to Gretton soon started to slow the train. This made us thankful that we had been given the opportunity to have a run at it. As the Garratt slowed, her beat sharpened.

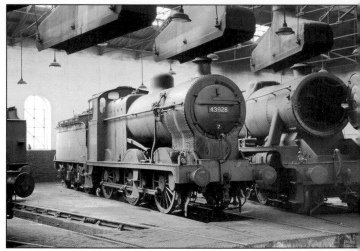

Above: Fowler Class 4F 0-6-0 No. 43928 shares the roundhouse at Wellingborough with a Stanier stablemate on May 18 1958. *T.G. Hepburn/Rail Archive Stephenson.*

The train was really hanging on the drawbar now. It was exceptionally heavy. Gretton signalbox was passed and the roar from our locomotive caused the startled signalman to step back from his lever frame. The noise and vibration probably caused his instrument needles to dance!

We were now approaching the dreaded catch points at the mouth of Corby Tunnel. These were devices for protecting following trains by derailing vehicles which might have broken loose and be running away in the wrong direction, back towards any approaching traffic. Such was the severity of the gradient.

As we entered the tunnel, the Garratt protested by slipping on the water which always cascaded from the roof and on to the track at this point. Flaming cinders the size of walnuts erupted from the chimney. After striking the tunnel roof they rained down on the cab and brought with them acrid, sulphurous fumes. The train slowed rapidly as Chuck eased the power and tried to regain adhesion. He was well aware that the train must be kept on the move, otherwise the catch points would do their work and the train would become derailed. The Garratt regained her feet and stopped slipping - we were on a dry piece of rail at last. I was piling in the coal as fast as I could. We were holding our own.

Corby Tunnel seems endless when you are fighting. The white spot in front (the tunnel end when you could see it through the smoke) didn't seem to be getting any bigger. She started to slip again on another wet spot. The train speed dropped to a crawl. Chuck worked frantically to regain her feet and keep her on the move. She stopped slipping once more and I hardly dare breathe in case she slipped again and we came to a stand in this dark fume-filled hell-hole.

At last we crept out from the tunnel. This was to the credit of Chuck's superb enginemanship. The train was barely moving as we breasted the summit at Lloyd South even though we had full boiler pressure! The train was dead weight. But we had done it. The rest of the way to Wellingborough from Lloyds is mostly downhill. Chuck's main concern now was arresting the train's momentum with the steam brake. A task of which Chuck was a past master.

At Wellingborough we had to come off the train and go to the shed to take on more coal so that the relieving crew would have enough to get them to London. I later estimated that we had burned an average of about one ton of coal for every 11 miles or so over the 67 miles we had come from Toton.

Chuck and I made our way to the Running Foreman's office to sign off and obtain our lodging slip. This was a form which had to be handed in at the lodging house. It was the authority for us to stay and gave the attendant details of our returning train for 'calling up' purposes. I looked at the form and noted that we would sign on again at 5.15am. After a quick shower, a snack and a rest, it was down the town for a glass of beer and a chat with the locals. I wonder if the Dew Drop public house is still there?

It was at this public house that I really upset my mate. It was unintentional, I hasten to add – but it upset him, all the same. I cannot remember how the subject arose but talk came round to the possibility of drinking a yard of ale (two and two thirds of a pint in a yard long glass). I stated that I was sure that I could achieve this without removing the glass from my lips and manage the feat in well under a minute! Chuck did not really believe me. The landlord said that if I managed it, he would pay for the beer, but if I didn't, I would have to pay.

The vessel was filled with beer. I took a deep breath and raised the glass to my lips. The landlord looked at his watch and said

"Go". I downed every drop in 30 seconds flat! It must have been the Garratt that gave me such a thirst. I had won my bet but Chuck was unhappy that I had not told him that I had achieved the feat before. He had failed to have a side bet as others had done in the bar and so lost out. Chuck was a gambling man and he had missed a golden opportunity to make a few bob.

The lodging house at Wellingborough stood on the up side of the track on the top of an embankment not far north of the station. It was a grey forbidding place reminiscent of the 'Bates Motel' in Alfred Hitchcock's thriller film 'Psycho.'.

Chuck and I arrived back about 10pm. We decided to cook a bit of supper. We had a few sausages, a lump of steak, a tin of tomatoes and a loaf of bread. The messroom in the lodge had a great cast iron gas stove and on it was the largest cast iron frying pan I had ever seen. Chuck reckoned that the pan contained the same fat that he had used as a fireman! Certainly it was better than Teflon. This pan had not 'stuck' for 60 years.

We cooked the most delicious supper you could imagine and ate it whilst playing cribbage. This was a card game that was mandatory on the footplate to while away the many hours standing at signals or behind other trains 'on the block.' As part of an engineman's kit there was always a pack of playing cards.

We said goodnight and retired for a well earned rest. The bedrooms were no more than cubicles with dividing walls, as one might find in a toilet block, with a gap underneath. The only furniture was a small cabinet, a Bible and a pot for peeing in.

The beds were spotless, but plain, to say the least. I could never sleep well because of the noise. The trains and engines passed constantly and sang you a lullaby. If that didn't keep you awake, your mates would with their snoring.

The following morning at 4am the attendant gave us a call. After a quick wash and shave it was down for breakfast. I have to say that the cooked breakfast supplied by the lodging house was excellent. There was enough fried food laid on to 'kill a pig'. It was good quality with plenty of cholesterol – but this was unheard of in those days and therefore couldn't do you any harm!

My first drive

We reported to the Running Foreman at the depot. We were to prepare a War Department Riddles 'Austerity' 2-8-0, 90427. These locomotives were as rough as a badger's backside. The ride was terrible. Over 30 mph it was a marvel that they remained on the rails at all. The fore-and-aft oscillation was so bad that the engine and

Below: A section of the Midland main line John Woolley knew intimately - through Wellingborough. On April 13 1961, Class 5F Hughes-Fowler 'Crab' 2-6-0 No. 42799 makes haste with a down Burton freight. *Ken Fairey/Colour Rail.*

Above: 'War Department Riddles 'Austerity' 2-8-0 'No. 90491 rolls past Brentingby Junction with a down iron ore train in April 1964. *W.J.V. Anderson/Rail Archive Stephenson.*

Right: If the MPDs were dirty workplaces for the staff, stations could be almost as bad for the passengers. On a depressing, wet day at Leicester London Road in 1958, Class 2P 4-4-0 No. 40580 pilots 'Jubilee' 4-6-0 No. 45664 *Nelson* with a St Pancras-Manchester train. *Tony Cooke/Colour Rail*

tender crashed against each other and it was rare for the fireman to have to enter the tender to shovel coal forward. The bucking between the locomotive and tender did it for you. In their favour was the fact that the injectors were excellent and they were generally free steaming. We prepared the locomotive and took her (or should I say 'it') off the shed and into Wellingborough down sidings. Our train was already prepared for us and consisted of 60 coal 'empties' from London for Toton.

Chuck said: "Right John, would you like to drive?" I could not believe my ears. I still had very little experience and mentioned this to him, but Chuck just shrugged his shoulders smiled and replied: "Well, you will have to learn to drive some time and I will be watching you. Come and sit in my seat."

Of course I accepted Chuck's generous offer and whilst the guard was walking back to the brake van, I filled the firebox with copious quantities of good, bright coal. This would give Chuck a really good start.

Departure time came. The Yard Foreman gave us the tip to start the train. I gave the 'Austerity' steam and she stretched the couplings. We were away! The 'Austerity' was a very powerful locomotive and we were soon out onto the main line, running at about 35mph with full regulator and the cut off at about 30%.

Above: A highly atmospheric scene at Leicester West Bridge Yard in 1961 as a Midland '2F' 0-6-0 No. 58305 shunts in very grey weather. Black smoke fills the air from an unseen distant factory (or train) in a skyline dotted with churches, chimneys, industrial rooftops - and a couple of power station cooling towers. *Tony Cooke/Colour Rail*

The train was booked to run via Market Harborough and Leicester instead of the more usual route via Manton and Melton Mowbray. The Leicester route was the quickest back to Toton. It was unusual to be booked via this route with a freight train, particularly during daylight hours when the Midland Main Line was busy with express trains. But, because this train was the return of a lodging turn, it had been granted this rare privilege.

It's a long climb from Wellingborough to Desborough but the locomotive was well up to the task. As we passed Kettering we could see that the signals were 'off' at Glendon. This was the steepest part of the climb before the gradient from Market Harborough to Kibworth. Even though I was driving, I took this opportunity to pick up the shovel and give her another good charge of coal. Chuck, of course, was 'well up to it' but I felt it was the least I could do. After all, Chuck was over twice my age.

We breasted the summit at Desborough and I immediately started to apply the brakes on the down gradient to Market Harborough. The bank is very severe between Desborough and Harbro'. It is said that the reason for this was that during the Crimean War, when the line was being constructed, it was imperative that the line should be completed in haste so as to assist the war effort. To smooth out the terrain and make the gradients more acceptable would have necessitated a tremendous amount of earthworks, such as cuttings, embankments and possibly even tunnels. This would have delayed the construction of the line. Consequently, the gradients were left more severe than is normally acceptable. The bank has been known by railwaymen as 'The Crimean Bank' ever since.

There is a dip through the station at Harbro' and as soon as I could sight the signals and saw that we were 'right away', I gave her a breath of steam to stretch the couplings. The power was gradually increased as the 'Austerity' came on to the up gradient towards the North West Bridge. This would ensure that the train was kept tight and that the brake van and the rear half of the train didn't try to catch us up. The rear half of the train was on a down gradient and we going up! We had to keep the couplings tight, otherwise there would be an almighty snatch and couplings could break in the dip. This had happened on numerous occasions at this location. I could

feel the guard's brake as he wound it on a few turns to help us keep the couplings tight. We went through the dip as smooth as satin.

We were soon on the sharp incline from East Langton to Kibworth and still running under clear signals. I picked up the shovel again to help Chuck and shot her another round of coal. He was smiling and happily eating a sandwich. I was in heaven!

The 'Austerity' was banging and clanging like there was no tomorrow. There was play in every bearing. Steam leaked from just about every joint. She was as run down as it was possible to be without failing. Despite this she still seemed to have plenty of power and was steaming freely. We soon breasted the summit at Kibworth and I was able to ease up on the power before shutting-off altogether. As we slowed, the couplings quickly closed up and the train compressed against the locomotive. I dropped the reverser into the drift position, which was round about the 50% cut-off mark.

"They wouldn't coast down a pit shaft!" Chuck remarked.

Now the sound of the engine changed and the banging and the clanging eased somewhat. She started to oscillate and buck furiously between the engine and tender. It was almost as if the train was attempting to climb over the top of the engine. This action caused the coal to shuffle forward in the tender. This would at least save us the job of having to shovel it. I glanced across at Chuck and I must have had a worried look on my face. He smiled and explained: "She's OK John, they all behave like this, that's why we call them Jazzers!" That was another lesson learned.

At Kilby Bridge we were signalled to the goods line and we pulled up at Wigston to fill the water tank and make tea. Chuck walked around the locomotive with his oil feeder in one hand and briefly touching the big ends, slide bars, cross heads and axle boxes with the other, checking for overheating. He removed the big end corks and topped up the oil reservoirs. When he returned to the footplate he remarked that she was running as cool as a cucumber and that this was not surprising , adding that because the bearings had so much play, they were air cooled!

Thirty minutes later the signalman cleared for us to cross the main lines and crawl into Leicester on the down goods. From there it was a matter of 'wait your turn.' There was mostly a train in every block between Leicester and Toton. It was unusual when running on the goods line to ever see a distant signal in the clear position. Toton was always congested.

We crawled 'block to block' all the way home and then stood for a further half an hour at Meadow Lane before finally being accepted onto the Down Hump, where we would leave the train. We had had a reasonably good run and it was my greatest experience so far. Signing off duty at 11.30am I joined Chuck for a glass of beer in the

local club before going home. Looking back, I see and understand how Chuck had expertly guided me through the intricacies of the road almost without me noticing. He was the best there was!

BR Riddles Class 9F 2-10-0 (Franco-Crosti Boiler)

Early in 1955, a strange locomotive appeared on the scene at Toton shed. It issued its smoke from an odd, flattish chimney curiously placed on the fireman's side of the boiler, not far in front of the cab.

It was said that this was the ultimate in steam power and that the design of this locomotive was the way forward. We were told that the new boiler would ensure that the greatest possible thermal efficiency would be achieved. It was the standard in Italy and was well proven. I wasn't very well travelled at that time otherwise I might have argued the point!

The locomotive was fitted with two boilers. The first was of standard design, but slung under the main boiler was a smaller affair. This small boiler was for pre-heating the water from the tender before it entered the main boiler. To achieve this, the path of hot gases through the main boiler was standard, but instead of exhausting to atmosphere from the smoke box at this point, the conventional chimney was blanked-off with a removable cap. The cap was used for exhausting smoke during lighting up purposes only and was closed as the locomotive started to make steam.

With the main chimney thus closed off, the hot gases from the firebox were now drawn down and through the tubes of the underslung pre-heating boiler. These gases were eventually exhausted from the chimney mounted on the right hand side of the main boiler - directly into the fireman's face!

My first encounter with this strange machine came a few weeks later. I had signed on at 5 o'clock in the evening for a special train to Wellingborough. My mate that day was a chap called Charlie. The locomotive was 92024. This would be a very interesting trip.

There were already stories circulating from crews who had experienced this new machine and none of them were complimentary. Enginemen were not at all impressed to say the least. Apart from the side chimney filling the cab with smoke and acrid

Above: On April 12 1958, and working hard with an up coal train, No. 92025 gives a text book perfect demonstration at Kegworth of precisely why the Franco-Crosti Riddles BR '9F' 2-10-0s were so hated by Toton firemen! The exhaust from the cylinders emerged at relatively low pressure right in front of the cab on the offside - and more often than not blew down and around the fireman's cabside, making life unpleasant and difficult. *T.G. Hepburn/Rail Archive Stephenson.*

fumes, the steaming properties were said to be poor. This was mainly due to the fact that the exhaust blast was not sharp enough to draw the fire because of the long passage of the gases from the cylinders, before exhausting to atmosphere through that side chimney.

One comment from a senior fireman by the name of Ivor Eaton summed it up in a few words. "They are certainly as economical on coal as the company say they are," he observed. "But that's because they will not ruddy well burn it!"

He added: "I defy anyone to make 'em steam, they're as cold as a dog's nose!"

With these thoughts in mind I decided to try a thin fire. This was always a good first bet on a poor steaming locomotive as it generated plenty of heat. We departed from the East Yard at Toton at about 6.15 p.m.

The locomotive had a full boiler of water and a nice even fire of no more than a foot thick. She was issuing plumes of smoke from the side chimney and the exhaust beat from the locomotive sounded muffled - it was hardly drawing the fire. The pressure gauge needle was flickering over the 225 pounds per square inch (psi) mark but she was steaming very shyly and not making enough steam for me to put on the injectors with confidence.

As soon as the smoke had cleared from the chimney, I shot her another round of coal. She repaid me by filling the cab with smoke once more. I couldn't help wishing that the designer of this appalling contraption was on the footplate with us to share the fun.

As we approached Loughborough I scooped water from the troughs. Charlie had noticed and remarked on the fact that at that point we should have had a full boiler as well as a full tank of water. Already I was down to half a glass of water because I was robbing the

> "... These gases were eventually exhausted from the chimney mounted on the right hand side of the main boiler - directly into the fireman's face!"

Above: Running rotary bunker-first with an up train of coal empties is articulated Beyer-Garratt 2-6-0+0-6-2 No. 47988. The date is June 27 1956 and the train is about to pass Chesterfield North signalbox.
T.G. Hepburn/Rail Archive Stephenson.

Below: It's July 16 1959 and Franco-Crosti boilered Riddles BR Class 9F 2-10-0 N. 92028 is drawing a long cut of wagons out of the yard at Wellingborough, during a shunt. The picture clearly shows how the exhaust emerged not through the chimney on the smokebox (used for lighting up purposes only) but from an offside exhaust just in front of the fireman's cab windows. The exhaust was directed from the cylinders and through a drum pre-heater mounted beneath the boiler. The idea was to pre-heat the water before it went into the boiler, from the tender, with the aim of cutting coal consumption and boosting efficiency. *Ken Fairey/Colour Rail.*

Above: Framed by the attractive lattice station footbridge at Kirkby is pioneer Stanier Class 8F 2-8-0 No. 48000, which is running light. The picture is rich in the atmosphere of the 1950s steam railway. *John P. Wilson/Rail Archive Stephenson.*

boiler to maintain steam pressure.

Because she didn't seem to respond to my thin fire tactics, in desperation I increased the rate of firing . If anything this made things worse and the coal ended up lying almost lifeless on the firebed. This called for the use of the straight dart to break up and hopefully lift the fire and thereby try to induce some primary air to the fire. Without this it will not burn properly. The reader should know that to use fire irons whilst running was a pretty desperate thing to do and was generally frowned upon……… In such circumstances, any improvement was temporary and by disturbing the fire, the production of clinker was actually increased.

However, we managed to run the train to Syston without losing time. Thankfully, we were held there waiting for a path across the branch to Melton Mowbray. I worked furiously in the time there to 'bring her round'. That's railway slang for filling the boiler and rebuilding boiler steam pressure.

Eventually we set off once more and gained the goods line at Melton in poor shape once again. The fire was almost dead and blanketed with un-burned coal. What more could I do? Charlie remarked that he would fail the locomotive at Wellingborough for poor steaming. I remember thinking that perhaps we wouldn't even get there!

As we left Brentingby, Charlie said that he would thrash her - working the engine much harder than was needed - in an effort to increase the draught on the fire and hopefully make it burn hotter and make steam. It worked to some degree but she still performed far below the standards that one would have expected from a brand new locomotive. We gained the goods line at Langham … just! After another furious attempt at 'bringing her round' I had had enough of this contraption and began to feel an intense dislike for the designers and railway management who had placed us in this predicament.

Eventually we were allowed to leave Oakham. Thankfully, it is down hill from there all the way to Harringworth except for a small climb from Manton to Wing. I took this opportunity to fill the boiler as far as I dare without causing her to prime (carry water over from the boiler into the cylinders) and hopefully gain full boiler pressure.

Charlie gave her plenty of steam and wound up the gear as we ran towards Harringworth under clear signals. It was going to be touch and go whether we would reach Lloyds South. As we entered Corby tunnel, Charlie put on the sanding gear. We could not afford to let the wheels slip and spin out of control on the wet spots otherwise we would surely stall. Miraculously, she 'held her feet' and plodded the train successfully through the tunnel.

We were holding our own for steam but the boiler was only a quarter full as we breasted the summit at Lloyds. I remember

thinking, as we ran down to Storefield, that it was a good job that the wheels were brand new and she didn't slip in Corby Tunnel. The wheels had good contact with the rails. Had the tyres been worn we would have stalled without question. Also, had the bank been half a mile longer, she just wouldn't have made it. It was that close.

I could not get over the appalling performance of this locomotive whose paint still looked and smelled new. It seemed inconceivable that BR could have been conned into building such a white elephant. Even the easy gradients from Lloyds to Wellingborough needed my full attention. But eventually it was all over. We detached the train in Neilsons Sidings and took the beast to Wellingborough shed.

Charlie reported to the Running Foreman and told him that the locomotive was not fit to be on the road. He emphasised that she would never be any good and made me feel a mile high by adding "If my mate cannot make her steam, no one can. He's only a young lad but he has tried every trick in the book, and then some more - all the way from Toton."

In the whole of the very brief spell that the Franco Crosti '9 Freights' were in service, I never once met a footplateman who could 'make 'em go.' When enginemen turned up for duty and saw the dreaded Franco rostered to their work, their hearts fell. They knew what they were in for.

The Francos had gained notoriety amongst the men and it was not long before BR began to take notice. They carried out numerous tests with numerous crews before giving us the benefit of the doubt. They were taken out of service and stored in lines at Wellingborough depot for months, awaiting shops for conversion as conventional Class 9F 2-10-0s. They were a complete and utter disaster!

When the newly converted Francos were pressed back into service they never seemed to be quite as good as the conventional Class 9. The boiler had the appearance of standing on stilts. There was an awkward gap underneath where the pre-heater boiler used to be.

The standard 2-10-0 Riddles Class 9F on the other hand was a fine machine. They rode like a passenger coach and were generally free steaming. I have had some marvellous trips on these locomotives.

I remember one journey with 92052 from Wellingborough to Toton with a driver named Ken Rowlands. Although the train was only 60 'empties', she performed outstandingly. She used very little

Above: This is the locomotive which John Woolley fired on the trip to Kirkby, described below. BR Riddles Class 9F 2-10-0 No. 92054 is making steady progress at Southwaite, Cumbria, with a Carlisle-Liverpool Edge Hill freight in September 1965. *Peter J. Robinson.*

coal and only about 2,500 gallons of water over the whole journey. I spent most of the time watching the cows grazing in the fields! When they were good, they were very, very good. When they were bad, they were acceptable. There were a couple of faults with them however. They were very hot to the fireman's backside! The firehole was cavernous. It sloped forwards so that every time the fireman opened the firehole doors he was scorched off his feet with the heat radiation. My overalls were 'two tone' - scorched brown down the right hand side and blue down the left.

Another fault was the fact that the injector clacks (one way valves from injector to boiler) were prone to sticking in the open position. This caused great quantities of steam to issue violently and with a screeching roar from the injector overflow under the fireman's steps. The remedy was to climb onto the framing and give the clack nut a sharp tap with the coal hammer. The resulting shock nearly always caused the clack valve to pop into its seat. Fitters obviously frowned on this practice because the clack nut became bruised and distorted. But if this happened when you were out on the road, there was no other effective answer.

That said, these faults were a small price to pay for their outstanding performance. I loved the BR Riddles '9F' 2-10-0s.

Riddles Class 9F 2-10-0 No. 92054 to Kirkby.

One afternoon in November 1956, I signed on at 5 o'clock for a train to Kirkby. The driver that day was Ken Stevenson. His nickname was 'Dumper' - I will explain why later.

We had been 'waiting power' for about an hour when the Running Foreman called us and gave us BR Riddles Class 9F 2-10-0 No. 92054, which had been undergoing repairs. We prepared the locomotive for work and departed to the loading point in the Meadow Sidings at Toton.

The climb from Toton to Kirkby is very severe. It is particularly steep from Sleights to Kirkby Summit. With this in mind, I started to pile on the coal to give us a good start. I had shovelled about a ton into her fire and the steam pressure was coming up to blowing-off point (250 psi)

On a Riddles '9F', both the exhaust and live steam injectors were

on the fireman's side of the engine, by the cab steps. Generally, apart from the clack sticking open occasionally these injectors were trouble-free and powerful. To stop the locomotive from blowing-off, I attempted to start the live steam injector to replenish the boiler with cold water from the tender tank. I could not get the injector to work. It just refused to 'pick up' and was blowing off steam from the overflow. OK, I thought, no big deal, I will try the exhaust injector. The same problem existed with this. It was impossible to deliver fresh water to the boiler.

Ken came over to my side of the engine and tried for himself. There was no miracle that he could perform either, however. She wasn't having anything to do with us. I had long since closed the dampers to cut-off the primary air coming up through the firebars in an attempt to dampen the flames, but the fire was still burning furiously. Steam pressure rose inexorably to blowing-off point whereupon both safety valves opened with a deafening roar. We were in deep trouble: a huge fire, both safety valves roaring and no way to get water into the boiler.

When a locomotive is blowing off, water is wasted at a phenomenal rate. We could see the water level dropping in the boiler gauge glass and should this fall too low, the boiler would be damaged when the fusible plugs in the firebox crown melted. There was nothing else for it. We would have to shovel the fire out onto the track and quench it with water.

Anyone who has performed this horrendous task will tell you that "it ain't easy". I was sweating profusely. The searing heat was causing my overalls to smoke! Ken was on the trackside throwing buckets of water over the burning coal as I threw it out with the long clinker shovel. Occasionally, I would throw the shovel onto the track as it became too hot to handle, so that Ken could cool this also.

The boiler water was down to less than quarter full when at last the safety valves closed. The fire was almost extinguished. Ken decided that we had sufficient pressure to run the locomotive to the shed. He advised the signalman to allow him a 'straight run' with no signal checks and we arrived safely on shed a few minutes later.

The Running Foreman was a guy called Nobby and he met us on the ashpit. He was most irate! He wrongly accused us of failing the locomotive on purpose. He assumed that we had failed her so that we would not have sufficient time left in our diagram to complete the turn and deliver the train to Kirkby.

Nobby had brought a fitter with him, who climbed on board and tried the injectors for himself. They both worked perfectly! The boiler pressure was down to 150psi by this time. Nobby gave us another locomotive and we went on our way without further incident.

In our absence, the fitter who could not have thoroughly

investigated our experience pronounced the locomotive fit for work. This was the fuel Nobby needed to write a rude report asking Ken why he had failed 92054 and consequently delayed the train.

92054 was given to another crew - and exactly the same thing happened to them but this time they had to throw the fire out in Toton East Yard! This had happened after Nobby had been relieved by the night Running Foreman. Nobby was therefore unaware of the second incident.

We signed off duty at about 2am and the night Running Foreman passed Ken the report request which had been left by Nobby. Ken was furious. The report was at the very least insulting. Ken showed the report, which had been in a sealed envelope, to the night Running Foreman. Although the two Foremen were colleagues, the night man was also disgusted with Nobby's accusations. He went on to tell us about the second failure and mentioned that at that very moment the locomotive was being thoroughly investigated.

The Foreman asked Ken for the report and said that he would tear it up and explain the next day to Nobby. Ken flatly refused. It was now his turn for blood! We made our way to the Foreman Fitter and asked him if he had found any reason for the injector failures with 92054. He explained that when the fitters examined the water filters, they were blocked with sludge. This restricted the flow of water to the injector, which would not then 'pick up'. He went on to say that there was sufficient water being delivered to the injectors for them to work at 150psi, but at higher working pressures the injectors did not have the weight of water flowing into them from the tender, needed to make them work.

Ken thanked the Foreman Fitter and turning to me said: "Right, John, can you get here tonight before the Shed Master goes home?" I nodded and went home to bath and bed.

I arrived at the shed at 4 o'clock in the afternoon. Ken was already in the drivers' lobby with the report in his hand. We knocked on the boss's door. "Come in," the boss shouted. We entered the sanctified den. I had never been in the boss's office before and found it strange to be standing on the only piece of carpet on the depot. "What can I do for you?" he asked. Ken showed him the nasty report from Nobby and after giving him time to read it, told him the whole story.

The boss picked up the phone and spoke to the Foreman Fitter. The next call was for Nobby. Now Nobby had heard of the second failure and was already regretting the tone of his report request. He would now have to justify his actions and attitude to the boss. Nobby entered the office and we were excused.

We later found out that the boss had asked Nobby why he did not insist that the locomotive was examined more thoroughly. He was reprimanded for not taking our word and for delaying a further train to Wellingborough as a result. There was a written apology from Nobby and a covering letter from the boss to follow. I later saw Nobby and had to ask him. "Nobby, do you really think that Ken and I would have turned away the overtime? Christmas is coming and the goose is getting thin!"

Snowed in with Beyer Garratt No. 47979.

It was the week before Christmas in 1956. I was rostered to sign-on at 2 o'clock in the afternoon, for Buckminster. The job was a 'pick up' goods, collecting wagons and setting them down at various locations along the route. The train started from Toton and was routed via Nottingham calling at Holwell, Melton Mowbray, Saxby and eventually, Buckminster.

The locomotive was another Beyer Garratt and the driver an old hand by the name of Stanley Woods. We had prepared the locomotive on shed and I had been shovelling for ages. A large fire was known amongst the men as a 'drive pile'. I had built one up which would have driven Cunard's Queen Mary from Southampton to New York! We replenished the coal I had used to build the fire under the coal hopper before leaving the shed for the East Yard.

We left the yard on time and passed through Nottingham under clear signals. The climb out of Nottingham was quite severe but the Garratt was easily master of its train and was steaming freely for a change. Now Garratts had a peculiarity. Because they were effectively two locomotives in one, the natural beat of the locomotive was eight to the turn of the wheel. The exhaust sounded more like a muffled roar rather than the staccato bark of a conventional locomotive.

However, because the two sets of motion were unsynchronised and not in any way coupled (wheel arrangement 2-6-0+0-6-2), and because of the slight variation in wheel size, the exhaust beats eventually ran into synchronisation and gradually merged into four

to the turn. Because two cylinders were exhausting at the same time, the consumption of coal rose sharply and burning cinders were tossed high into the air. It was a very spectacular sight at night, I can tell you.

Drivers knew the answer to the problem. They would open the regulator sharply in an effort to produce wheelslip. If necessary, they would repeat the process until the locomotive's engines dropped out of 'sync' and reverted to eight exhaust beats for each turn of the driving wheels.

This locomotive ran into sync on the sharp climb just outside Nottingham, so Stan slipped the locomotive in an effort to knock her out of phase. Showers of sparks and cinders were tossed from the chimney. Daylight was failing and the sparks could be plainly seen raining into the back gardens of the houses alongside the track. We were to find out later that one of the trackside residents had put in a claim against BR for the loss of his garden shed, which had burned to ashes barely a few minutes after our passing!

We spent about an hour at Holwell, where we shunted the steel works sidings, setting wagons down and picking up others. The locomotive was booked to take on water at Brentingby and we did so before going on to Saxby and shunting the sidings there.

At last we arrived at Buckminster and the signalman locked us in the sidings. It had started to snow very heavily. The parcels and fish traffic from Norwich and Yarmouth was prolific. Consequently, we had to wait for a suitable path for our slow train back to Toton.

The time was now about 10 o'clock at night. We had already been on duty for 8 hours. The snow was getting worse and beginning to drift against the locomotive wheels. At last there was a lull in the traffic and the signalman could let us out. Alas, he could not change the points and set the road for our route because of snow drifts.

I climbed off the locomotive with my firing shovel and tried to clear the points. It was hopeless. As soon as I had cleared one end of the crossover and worked on the other, the first was filled again with the drifting snow. The signalman called out his 'snow men' - platelayers on emergency call. They duly arrived but considered us a low priority. They were only interested in keeping the main line open.

We settled down for the night. Our normal food and drink had long since been consumed but I always carried emergency rations. I had in my haversack a tin of soup, an old tobacco tin full of OXO cubes and a tin box containing a dozen dry cream crackers. I shared these with my mate. The OXO drink was delicious and sustaining and tasted even better made with snow water!

The Garratt fared better than us - she had plenty of water and coal. A good job too. It would have been most uncomfortable for us if the fire had been put out.

It stopped snowing at about 6 o'clock the following morning and so at that point, the platelayers proceeded to dig us out. We eventually left the sidings at about 9 o'clock. The progress back to Nottingham

"Paddy acquired a detonator, opened the stove door, threw the explosive onto the hot coals and after closing the stove door, evacuated the hut."

was slow and laborious. There was a backlog of traffic and the lines were congested with other traffic. On arrival at Nottingham we were grateful to see a set of Toton men who had been sent out to relieve us.

The time was 2 o'clock in the afternoon. We had been on duty for 24 hours and still had to travel back to Toton 'on the cushions' home as a passenger. I didn't go to work the following day, I was shattered. Stanley took duty after 12 hours rest! He was a better man than I, Gunga Din!

Bozzy and Mark

During that winter of 1956/57 I was on nights labouring with a few other Passed Cleaners. The weather was very cold with a severe frost. We all knew that there would be a requirement for 'frost fire men'. Fires were lit all over the depot underneath water cranes and dead locomotive injector mechanisms to protect them from the ravages of frost.

Sam was the Chargehand Cleaner when we signed on at 9.30pm. Mark was a remarkable psychologist for a young lad! He told me that Bozzy, myself and he would get the frost fire jobs that night. These were the best jobs of all in a draughty steam shed. We were the very best of friends and loved to work and play together. I wondered how he could be so sure?

Sam was a man who had to show everyone that he was in charge. When he gave an order it had to be carried out to the letter. As the ten or more passed cleaners stood around Sam waiting for him to allocate their duties, Mark dragged Bozzy and I to one side. "Stand close to me," he said. As Sam started to allocate the duties, Mark said in a voice just loud enough for Sam to hear " I hope we don't get frost firing, I hate it!"

Sam passed no comment until he had distributed most of the work, then, turning to the three of us said "Right, you three, get a barrow each and look after the depot's frost fires and woe betide you if you let them go out. You will not pick your jobs with me. You will just do as I say!" We laughed for hours. Mark had us in stitches as he put on a serious face and aped Sam. He placed his hands on his hips, stuck his jaw forward and said: "Now, do as you are told!"

We mended all of the frost fires and decided to walk across to a pond which was adjacent to the depot. We were having the time of our lives skating on the thick ice. We were still little more than boys and a play on the ice wasn't going to hurt anyone. A voice shouted; "Hey you, get back to work!" The voice seemed to be coming from the other side of the River Erewash. It was obvious that whoever it was did not work for the railways.

Bozzy was a little cheeky when he replied: "Mind your own business.". In actual fact, his words were MUCH stronger than that! We carried on playing for a few minutes longer before getting back to the task of 'keeping the home fires burning.' The incident was forgotten.

The next night, Bozzy was a little down hearted to say the least. The voice that he had heard the previous night was in actual fact his father's. He had been subcontracting for a firm on the opposite side of the river and had been working nights also. He had recognised Bozzy's voice but poor old Bozzy had not recognised his dad's. The realisation came at the end of Bozzy's dad's boot when they both got up for tea the following afternoon!

The detonator

The first time that I ever saw a railway explosive fog signal (detonator) used for a purpose other than intended, was in the steam raiser's cabin in the north east corner of No. 1 Shed.

The steam raiser was a person who looked after live locomotives and lit-up dead ones. He made sure that they had water and steam in the boiler prior to crews booking on to take them away. They spent hours between duties in their little hut.

I was on nights cleaning a loco with Mark and Bozzy near their cabin. One of the steam raisers was a chap called Paddy. His cabin stove pipe was blocked by soot and smoke was filling the place. Paddy acquired a detonator, opened the stove door, threw the explosive onto the hot coals and after closing the stove door, evacuated the hut.

We looked on fascinated. After a short while, there was a dull thud, and smoke, ashes and soot shot from the chimney. The stove pipe had been well and truly 'cleared.' Paddy opened the cabin door. The air was thick with smoke, soot and ash. He allowed this to escape before re-entering the cabin and dusting down. The stove was burning brightly once more.

Paddy had given us a great idea for a practical joke. We had noticed that once Sam had given out the duties to his charges, he would retire to his cabin in the north west corner of No. 1 Shed. He would not re-emerge until about 2 o'clock in the morning for his inspection tour.

Sam's cabin had a great pot bellied coal fired stove. The chimney emerged from the shed roof. We had noticed that there was always a glow from the end of his chimney. He must have been as warm as toast in his little den.

We acquired a couple of detonators and about three yards of shot firer's wire. The wire arrived in great quantities with the coal and was all over the depot. It was the wire which carried the electric current to the explosive charge when blasting the colliery coal face.

There was an iron ladder built into the shed wall for access to the shed roof for maintenance. Sam's stove pipe was within three feet of the top of the ladder. We tied the detonators to the wire and climbed the ladder. We could see the red glow at the end of Sam's chimney. The scene was set. We gently lowered the detonators about two feet down the stove pipe and tied them off at the top, leaving them suspended. It was then a scramble down the ladder and back to our locomotive before the detonators were heated to the point of explosion.

We were polishing our locomotive furiously and watching Sam's cabin door out of the corner of our eyes. There was a dull thump. Almost at the same instant, Sam came flying through the door, followed by clouds of dust and smoke. Bozzy remarked that we had cured Sam's limp in an instant!

Sam was dusting himself down and looking around the shed. At the same time the Running Foreman, Mr. Storey appeared. He walked over to Sam and began a conversation. It was impossible to hear just what was being said although both were looking in our direction. We of course carried on with our work as if nothing was amiss. This was probably a great mistake. They could tell by our enthusiastic polishing that we knew something.

Mr. Storey approached us and looking seriously at one and then the other said: "I don't suppose for a moment that either of you know anything about this?" We replied in chorus: "What, sir?"

He didn't explain. He knew that we knew exactly what he was talking about. Mr. Storey nodded his head and spoke again: "I didn't think you would, I never ought to have asked really." He rejoined Sam and they spoke for a few seconds more before leaving him and making his way past us and back to his office. I was sure that I caught a wry grin on his face.

Sam came over to us. "Right, you three, someone has been playing tricks! My office is full of dust and soot. I want you boys to clean it from top to bottom" We spent the rest of the shift under the watchful eye of Sam. The walls, floor and doors were washed. His furniture polished to a gleam. We went home tired that morning.

The next night we told the other cleaners what had happened. We were heroes for weeks after. Mark made great fun out of poor old Sam. "I bet he thought he was back in the Khyber Pass fighting the Indians when the explosion awoke him from his slumbers! Did you notice John, that he appeared to leave his office as if making a bayonet charge?" But, it goes without saying that we never attempted anything like that again, Sam could have had a heart attack.

Fog

In the 1950's, before the Clean Air Act, the winter fogs lasted for days. Toton, being in a valley, was particularly subject to "pea soupers" as footplatemen called them.

Hardly surpising, really. There were hundreds of steam engines in the vicinity all belching smoke. Only two miles away there was Stanton Iron Works with numerous blast furnaces, coke ovens and smelting plants. In addition to all this, most households burned coal as the main source of heat. There were rows upon rows of houses all adding to the pollution. Central heating was very rare and only the rich could afford it anyway.

The drivers at Toton (and any other depot for that matter) coped wonderfully. It was very rare for signals to be passed at danger because of poor visibility. Drivers would learn a route and not only take account of the track, signalling and gradients, but also trackside features such as platelayer's huts, bridges, houses, factories and any other marker which would indicate the train's precise location.

Three memories of these days instantly spring to mind. I remember

> "I stood half freezing at the signal post until the signal cleared before rejoining the locomotive and advising my mate. This was the nature of the job. Nothing unusual at all. It was what was expected."

one November evening taking a train from Toton to Stanton Gate Down Sidings. These were the exchange sidings for the Stanton Iron Works complex. The fog was as 'thick as a bag'. We arrived at Stanton Gate South on No 2 down goods line and guided by the ponds alongside the track, stopped at the gantry of signals.

We could see the gantry post but were unable to see the signal. It was shrouded in dense fog. I ended up having to walk to the signal box to ask whether the signal was clear or not. I have no head for heights and declined to climb the signal gantry steps.

On another occasion, we had passed the distant signal for Foxlow (near Chesterfield) on the down main. It was at caution. We slowed and were looking for the home signal. The weather was absolutely appalling and made worse by the Stanton Iron Works at Staveley. In addition to the thick fog, the locomotive had a blowing piston gland. This made it impossible to see beyond the smokebox.

My mate Ken Stevenson, knew that we must be close to the signal. He reduced the speed to no more than one mile per hour. I had to alight from the locomotive and walk in front, calling frequently to Ken. The signal was found and of course Ken stopped at it without a second thought. I stood half freezing at the signal post until the signal cleared before rejoining the locomotive and advising my mate. This was the nature of the job. Nothing unusual. It was expected.

. I also recall standing behind a train at Stanton Gate North on the up goods. Trains often stood there for hours awaiting acceptance into Toton Yard. The fog was very dense indeed. It is strange to say that even in the most appalling visibility, permissive block was not suspended and drivers had to 'feel' their way to the brake van of the train in front.

The guard of the train in front would place a detonator on the rail one hundred yards behind his brake van to serve as an indicator to any following train. The trouble with that however, was that one had to ask oneself if the guard had been stopped long enough to comply with the rule. It was certainly not 100% effective and many times I have seen a hand lamp waving a caution signal as the guard was walking back to place his detonator.

There could be as many as ten trains and possibly more in the queue between Langley Mill and Sandiacre. Some drivers often stated that they had not bought their houses by driving trains. The real money had been 'earned' waiting for hours, motionless, 'on the block.'

Noel once told me of an incident which happened to him. He had been on overtime and was standing 'on the block' at Langley Mill. The Control had sent out a set of men on the local passenger train to relieve him. He caught a passenger train from Langley Mill to Sandiacre, from where he walked to the depot and signed off duty.

Noel signed on again 12 hours later and was told to walk to Sandiacre to relieve a train 'on the block'. It was the very same train and crew that he had left at Langley Mill 13 hours before! This was by no means an isolated incident and shows how fog and congestion affected the operation of Toton Yard.

Anyway, Ken and I were playing cards and waiting patiently for the train in front to move. I could hear a train approaching on the up main. I was absolutely flabbergasted when a 'Jubilee' drew up alongside. He had been guided by our firelight in the fog. The driver of the express called to us: "Where am I mate?" I answered that he was about 200 yards from Stanton Gate South's home signal. At this the driver shouted: "Thanks pal!" - and off he went! It wasn't the case that this driver did not have a clue where he was, he had just lost his bearings for a second or two in the thick fog and needed reassurance. It's a long block from Trowell to Stanton Gate and I would gamble that this driver considered that he had travelled far enough without sighting the signal. Thank goodness for the AWS (Automatic Warning System) of later years.

The AWS works like this - modern locomotives are equipped with a magnetic receiver which is sensitive to the north and south poles of magnetism. About 100 yards on the approach side of a signal there is a magnetic transmitter in the 'four-foot' (between the rails).

The polarity of the magnet is dependent upon the aspect of the signal. If the signal is clear (green), it is positive (south) and the magnet transmits a clear signal to the locomotive. If the signal is yellow or red, the polarity is negative (north) and a caution signal is transmitted.

As the locomotive passes over these magnets, it sends an indication to the driver of what aspect the signal is showing as he approaches

it. If the signal is green, a bell sounds in the cab and an indicator in the driver's view turns to all black (last signal green). The driver takes no action in these circumstances. If the signal is yellow or red, a horn sounds and the indicator in the driver's view shows yellow and black bars (last signal yellow or red). The driver must acknowledge the warning by pressing a reset button. Should he fail to do this, the power will be cut off and the brakes will be applied automatically, bringing the train to a halt.

Many years later I had occasion to take a high ranking airline pilot on a trip on the footplate. In fact, he was a senior instructor on a Boeing 747 simulator owned by British Midland. He had served his time in the RAF and had also flown for Laker, Orion and others all of his life. I explained how the AWS worked and how drivers coped in the fog. Sadly, he wasn't impressed! He said that it was a credit to the driver that the job was as safe as it was. In a way, I felt deflated. I had always considered that the AWS system was very good indeed.

The pilot said that he would never have the courage to charge headlong into fog at 100mph, not really knowing what was in front. He added that no amount of training would alter his view. I asked him how he coped in thick cloud at three times the speed? He answered: "Ah! But I have radar, constant ground communication and far superior instruments than you have. Further more, I have a first officer who is also a qualified pilot and in any case, I am soon through the clouds" He added that, in his opinion, the driver was not recognised for his obvious skills and was not paid enough.

Test train with No. 70004
William Shakespeare

In the summer of 1958, I was approached by Lew the Locomotive Inspector. He was looking for a couple of fit young firemen for a special test train. I was still a passed cleaner although I had been on the job for four years at this time. It was a long apprenticeship on the footplate, even for a fireman. I was flattered by his request. I was coming up in the world. Of course, I accepted and was assigned with a driver by the name of Harold Mee to an unforgettable week of trials. Well, it should have been a week!

The Motive Power Depot had borrowed two BR Class 7 'Britannia' 4-6-2 locomotives. These locomotives were of BR Standard design with a 4-6-2 wheel arrangement. They were actually express passenger locomotives and as such, the men at Toton took great interest in these visitors.

The CMEE (Chief Mechanical Electrical Engineer) based at Derby needed to conduct a series of trials to experiment with the vacuum brake. The object was to see if the vacuum brake could be made to work as effectively as an air brake. The engineers had modified about 100 16-ton mineral wagons (code named Minfits). They had smoothed out the bends in the vacuum brake pipes in an effort to persuade the brakes to apply more simultaneously throughout the train.

The trouble with the vacuum brake is that it is applied by atmospheric pressure and because the air is admitted through the driver's brake valve to destroy the vacuum, the brake tends to apply at the front of the train first. The air brake on the other hand relies on the discharge of air through the driver's brake valve to apply the brake. The brake therefore tends to apply more evenly as the pressure drops consistently throughout the train pipe.

On the following Monday morning I met Harold at the shed. We found the two 'Britannias' on No. 6 Road (near the entrance to No. 2 Shed) coupled and ready to go. Harold and I were on the leading locomotive (William Shakespeare) together with an Inspector by the name of Cyril Jones. The rear locomotive's driver was David Jones and the fireman was Ken Hardwick. Lew Crane was the Inspector with them. Ken had started on the same day as me, four years previously.

We took the locomotives light from Toton to Ilkeston where the modified train was stabled on a disused goods line. We backed onto the train and were met by the 'boffins' from Derby who had travelled there by road. They had wired the whole of the train with sensors, instruments and a telephone from the brake van to the locomotives. We coupled to the train and the telephones were put in place on the footplates.

The scientists explained that they had devised a new valve called a DAV (Direct Admission Valve) and had fitted one to each vehicle. The idea was that as the vacuum was reduced from the locomotive, the

"I was absolutely flabbergasted when a 'Jubilee' drew up alongside. He had been guided by our firelight in the fog. The driver of the express called to us: "Where am I mate?" I answered that he was about 200 yards from Stanton Gate South's home signal. At this the driver shouted: "Thanks pal!" - and off he went!"

Above: Numerous trials were carried out around and from Toton during the 1950s with the aim of increasing the speeds of the massive coal traffic, to boost line capacity. The one decision that would have solved it - air braking of freight trains - was sadly not taken, so the trials didn't come to much. All sorts of locomotives not usually associated with freight were tried on high speed coal trains to Brent (Cricklewood) including pairs of Britannias. Nos. 70023 *Venus* (pilot engine) and 70024 *Vulcan* stand at Finedon Road, awaiting one such trial on January 1 1952. Sister engines Nos. 70043 *Lord Kitchener* and 70044 *Earl Haig* were also used on such trials, minus smoke deflectors and with air compressors fitted. In 1958, John Woolley was the fireman on No. 70004 *William Shakespeare*, running north from Toton and thence to Nottingham, on rapid application vacuum brake trials - which ended with injuries to technical staff. *Ken Fairey/Colour Rail.*

valve on the first wagon would sense this and open in response. This would admit air to the next vehicle in the train. In theory, each wagon would apply the brakes of its rear neighbour in rapid succession thereby eliminating the more conventional time delay between the application of the front and rear brakes. A quicker and smoother stop was the objective.

They explained that these modificatons would ensure a smoother application of the brake throughout the train. We created the 21 inches vacuum throughout the train required to release the brakes - and made a static test. We could hear the valves snapping open in rapid succession along the train. It sounded almost like a machine gun strafing the wagons from the front to the rear!

After a couple of these tests and reference to the instruments, it was time to leave the sidings for the practical application out on the road. We carried an SN (Special Notice) which told us that the tests would be carried out on the Nottingham-Lincoln line, near Fiskerton. It also told us that we would be held at Nottingham until a suitable gap appeared in the passenger traffic. It stated that no other train was allowed to pass as the tests were carried out.

We departed from Ilkeston at about 10 o'clock in the morning. Cyril happened to mention that the train was the heaviest ever to be hauled on BR to date. I forget the actual tonnage but it could not have been above 1,800 tons which is small in comparison with today - but heavy enough!

We stormed up the bank from Trowell Junction to Wollaton. I remember well the tremendous din from the exhausts of these fine locomotives. As we passed the post office at Trowell there was a small group of people watching us. They must have heard the din as we approached and realised that something unusual was taking place. They were right!

Cyril remarked that the rear locomotive was 'priming' and spewing water from the exhaust either because the boiler was too full, or, the water in the boiler was foaming due to impurities and needed a boiler wash out. This effectively reduced our performance and I really felt sorry for Ken who must have been as 'sick as a pig'. It was his day also. But I had to smile when the small crowd of spectators dived for cover as they were showered with copious amounts of dirty water from Ken's exhaust.

The train arrived at Nottingham and we stood round the back of the station awaiting a suitable path for the actual tests. Cyril had already told me to forget about trying to economise on coal so I had built up a 'drive pile' which would hopefully make up the short fall on Ken's locomotive. I was periodically using the injectors to put water in the boiler and keep her quiet and stop her from blowing off in the station. Eventually the time came for us to depart.

The signal was cleared and Harold whistled his intention to start. At this, our 'boffin' in the white coat with the clip board who had monitored everything we were doing, telephoned his pal in the brakevan. He asked his mate to tell him when the brakevan started to move. Harold gave her steam and we had travelled about 60 feet, taking up the slack in the couplings (that's a full standard rail length) before his mate confirmed that they were on the move also.

We accelerated away and were soon in open country. Ken was still having problems with his priming and our locomotive was having to work flat out as a consequence. We were approaching the point where the first brake test was to be carried out. The speed of the train according to the SN, was supposed to be 45mph. Our actual speed was 41mph and Harold was rocking the valve gear in an effort to get more. At the predetermined mile post, the test engineer telephoned his pal in the brakevan to warn them of the impending test. He put the telephone down and shouted to Harold "Now!" Harold gently started to apply the brake as he would have normally done. But the technician shouted "All on Driver - give her the lot!" So Harold did as he was told – and pushed the brake lever into the emergency position.

Knowing what was coming, I quickly braced my feet on the boiler

John Woolley knew the Erewash Valley line like the back of his hand as a young fireman at Toton. He also knew the 'War Department' Riddles 'Austerity' 2-8-0s pretty well, too. This is No. 90368 at Danesmoor on June 1 1963. *R.J. Buckley/Initial Photographics.*

front. Likewise, Cyril reached up and hung tightly onto the skylight securing handles in the cab roof. The 'boffin' clung to the back of my seat. Harold looked across at me with the look of a worried man.

The locomotive brake bit and immediately she started to slow down. I knew that the train could not possibly be decelerating at the same rate. A few seconds passed (which seemed like a week) and the 'boffin' said: "It looks like it worked."

The words were barely out of his mouth when the train ran into us. There was the most tremendous crash and the coal in the tender shot forward at such a force as to bend the access door securing catches. The doors flew open and in an instant the footplate was under 2ft of coal! The shock caused a ripple effect throughout the train and a split second later it ran into us again with almost as much force as the first impact.

The train ground to a halt. Apart from Cyril's leg, which been bruised by flying coal, and the 'boffin's' bruised arm which he had struck on the back of my seat, we were unhurt.

I looked back expecting to see the train jack-knifed across the track. I was absolutely amazed to see that we were still in a straight line. We were still on the track! A miracle! There was a red cloud of dust and rust drifting across the fields in the breeze. Every rivet and bolt on the train must have been strained to the limit.

The technician tried to contact the brake van on the telephone. He could not get an answer. I jumped off the locomotive and sprinted back to the brake van. The sight that I saw when I arrived, I shall never forget. The brake van stove had been torn from its securing bolts and had smashed through the woodwork of the front end wall, and had come to rest on the veranda. I climbed inside and found the 'boffin' with blood streaming from a cut on his forehead. The poor guard was nursing a broken arm. We arranged for an ambulance and that was the end of the brake tests for the day.

We reorganised when the dust had settled. Harold examined the engines whilst the two inspectors examined the train. We had been standing there for some time and we were delaying passenger operations. We would have to clear the main line and reverse the train at Fiskerton.

Harold reported that a casting had been smashed on one of our buffers. The other locomotive was minus a buffer plate. I recovered this to ensure that it would not be a danger to other trains and threw it on the footplate. Ken, Dave and Lew were all unhurt in the incident. Lew had had the same premonition as Harold and I and had ordered them to brace themselves before the impact of the train into the two 'Britannias'.

The line was at last cleared. The damage to the locomotives was not severe enough to fail us completely and one of the inspectors rode in the damaged brake van and acted as guard. It was now

'at caution' back to Ilkeston with the train for us, and back to the drawing board in Derby for the 'boffins'. The following day, and for the rest of that week, we spent the whole of the time in Ilkeston Sidings conducting static tests.

These trials continued in a less severe form for months, but in the end the CMEE abandoned all hope of significantly improving the vacuum brake and the air brake was chosen as the standard.

Mapperley Branch and Fowler Class 4F No. 43990

In the 1950s the Erewash Valley line was one continuous stream of coal trains coming from the north to Toton for sorting. Equally, there were dozens of empty trains going north to the collieries for reloading. There was a colliery, or a colliery branch line junction every few miles, all the way to Chesterfield. The railway and colliery system employed many thousands of people.

Because of the density of the coal and freight traffic, there had to be three locomotive depots between Toton and Clay Cross just to cope with the work load. There was Westhouses depot within 15 miles of Toton and Hasland within 20 miles or so. The traffic activities had to be seen to be believed. It was like a conveyor belt!

Toton was the main gathering and sorting point for most of the traffic from the numerous collieries. There, they would be formed into full trains for destinations all over the country. But even Toton, the largest marshalling yard in Europe with 55 miles of sidings, could not cope with the volume. Trains would also be formed at Stanton Gate up and down sidings and Codnor Park as well as sometimes full load permitting, directly to destination from the colliery. From this, it can be seen that apart from main line work, there was a tremendous number of colliery trippers working out of Toton.

In the autumn of 1958, I signed on duty at 12 o'clock lunch time for one of these coal trippers to Mapperley Colliery. The driver was John. It was he who had tried to race Ron and I on my first main line trip. We were to relieve the locomotive in the Old North Sidings at Toton. The locomotive had been out since 5 o'clock in the morning and had serviced Mapperley Colliery on the morning turn.

John was a strange character and hardly ever spoke to his fireman. It was not personal; he was like it with everyone. We made our way to the sidings to relieve the day crew. The fireman I relieved was a chap called Eric Allison. Apart from being a senior passed fireman, he was also a Deputy Running Foreman. This meant that he had been selected to act as Running Foreman in times of shortage when the regular men were not available, because of holidays and sickness for example. This was the usual route for drivers to eventual promotion to the salaried staff.

Eric warned me that 43990 (a Fowler Class 4F 0-6-0 goods tender engine) was a 'shy' steamer. I had previous experience with this particular locomotive and knew that she would not stand a thick fire. She liked it 'little and often'. She needed coaxing.

I took the precaution of quickly cleaning the fire and thinning it at the same time. We were in grand fettle when departure time came. The road was level from Toton to Stanton Gate but from there it was a severe climb up the branch to Mapperley Junction. My firing tactics paid off and she shot up the bank as if it wasn't there.

John was just about the roughest driver at Toton. But on this occasion, it was exactly what the locomotive needed. The sharp blast from the exhaust kept the fire dancing and jumping up and down on the firebars which meant it burned nice and bright, making lots of steam. John's face was expressionless throughout the journey. He just stared at the route ahead. It was impossible to judge whether he was impressed by my performance or not.

At Mapperley Junction we ran round and then propelled about half of the train into Manner's Sidings and secured it. We drew the other half back clear of the spring points for Mapperley pit.

The gradient from Mapperley Junction to the colliery at Mapperley was incredibly severe. I have often wondered why it was that nearly all colliery pit heads were on the top of a hill and yet the miners always dug down for their coal? Perhaps they thrived on digging big holes. Anyway, I shovelled just a little extra coal into the firebox to cope with the heavy slog to come.

I mentioned to John that I was intending to run with a thin fire and asked him what he thought of that. He just grunted. The shunter altered the spring points and gave us the 'tip' to start. John opened the regulator wide. After a few protests by the 'Fowler 4' in the form of slipping like Charlie Chaplin on a banana skin, we were on our way.

The '4F' accelerated the train and we were soon on the severe incline. John did not bother to alter the cut-off by more than 10%. The engine was tossing sparks high into the air. I remember smiling and thinking to myself - it's a good job that it's still daylight, otherwise, the man in the moon would get a spark or two in his eye!

The weather was dry and so was the grass and undergrowth on the sides of the banks and cuttings. It was odds-on that there was going to be a fire. There is a farm half-way up the incline known by railwaymen as 'The Donkey Farm.' It was a marker for footplatemen because the gradient eased a little at this location.

John however, did not ease up on either the regulator or the valve gear. As she rapidly accelerated, I could actually see flaming cinders flying from the chimney in broad daylight. The farmer heard us coming - as did everyone else within five miles or so. He was watching us intently as we passed. He knew what the likely outcome would be. He didn't need a fortune teller!

We arrived at the colliery and disposed of the empty wagons. The loaded train was attached and within 40 minutes we were on the way back down the branch. On the steep descent, John held her in check with the tender handbrake and engine steam brakes. The speed could not be allowed to rise above 5mph otherwise we would not be able to stop at Mapperley Junction.

I could see plumes of smoke in the distance and I knew that there was a mighty fire raging. As we approached, the spectacle exceeded my wildest expectations. There were two fire engines in the field close by. I could see men frantically beating the ground with brooms. The hedgerows and fields were well and truly ablaze. It was vandalism!

We would definitely be in trouble when we arrived back at the depot. John would have to explain why he had made so many sparks and not taken into consideration the dryness of the vegetation and eased the locomotive accordingly. The farmer would bare witness as to the ferocity of John's enginemanship. I thought to myself that there was no way I could be held responsible for the incident.

How wrong can you be? Back at the depot, John told the Running Foreman that I was to blame because the fire was too thin, causing the locomotive to issue sparks in excessive quantities! He added that his enginemanship was faultless and that he had used only as much power as was absolutely necessary. It's strange to say that John never mentioned his intention to pass on the blame to me at any time during the last four hours or so of the shift.

It led to yet another brush for me with the firing instructor. I explained about 43990 not liking a heavy fire and asked him to contact Eric the fireman who I had relieved to verify my statement. I also told him that I had made it quite clear to John that I was going to fire her thin to make her steam. I also mentioned the witness:

Above: Sun shines on the smokebox doors in the roundhouse at Hasland on August 26 1956. Visible are: '3F' 0-6-0s No. 47278 and 43211, '4F' 0-6-0 No. 44410, '2P' 4-4-0 No. 40537 and '8F' 2-8-0 No. 48694. *K.L. Cook/Rail Archive Stephenson.*

"Ask the farmer at the Donkey Farm," I said. "He will tell you exactly how the locomotive was being driven."

The instructor told me that he was well aware of John's notorious driving technique and knew that I was not 100% to blame. He conveniently told me to ensure that the fire was nice and thick in future - especially with John at the controls. That advice nicely tidied up his report. He could write at the bottom - Suitable conversation held with passed cleaner Woolley. No further action necessary.

Swanwick Branch runaway

It was Monday March 26 1962. Driver Jack Mears and I signed on duty at 5 o'clock in the morning for a Swanwick coal 'tripper.' The locomotive was a Fowler Class 4F 0-6-0 No. 44270.

We prepared the locomotive and just before leaving the shed we re-coaled her. She would be out until late evening and needed all the fuel she could carry – and then a little more, as we discovered later. The train was coupled on in the North Yard at Toton and consisted of 40 standard BR 16-ton coal 'empties' – the classic four-wheel coal wagon.

The route to Swanwick was north from Toton to Riddings, then we diverged left onto a branch line, passing Ironville, and on to Swanwick Sidings - site of the present Midland Steam Trust. There, we would divide the train before delivering the 'empties' to the colliery.

Access to the colliery was by single line 'Staff Section'. An aluminium staff about a foot long (fitted with a key and inscribed '1 Swanwick Colliery Branch') was the authority to occupy the line. This was issued by the signalman at Swanwick via 'Geordie', the resident shunter. The branch was on a very severe gradient as usual and about three miles long. Fowler 44270 was a fine locomotive. She rode beautifully and steamed like a kettle. We had no trouble at all gaining Swanwick Sidings. I was in for a good day, I thought. The train was shunted into two portions, each of 20 wagons. In no time at all we stood at the branch end with 20 wagons and the brake van leading. All was well with the world. This was about to change!

Geordie delivered the train staff and then joined the guard in the brake van. I had built up a good fire for the slog up to the colliery. The signal was cleared. Jack whistled his intention to start and this was answered by a hand signal from the guard. We were away. The Fowler was making short work of its task. Every time the locomotive passed over a rail joint, the safety valves popped and hissed in sympathy. She was right 'on the mark'. A cracking locomotive!

At the top of the bank at Ripley were a pair of main road crossing gates. We stopped the train short of these to allow the guard and shunter to cross the road on foot into the colliery sidings. There, they would confer with the colliery staff, set the road for the 'empties', examine the loads to come out and work out the weight of the returning train. This procedure usually took between half an hour and 40 minutes.

Whilst they were away, the locomotive stood opposite a farm

house. We were always careful to keep the locomotive quiet at this location so as not to disturb the residents. The farmer would always appear at the fence. He would lean on it and ask: "Can you spare a few shovels full of coal mate?"

The stock answer to this was: "Have you any fresh eggs to spare?" The going rate was a dozen eggs per hundred weight of coal – the equivalent of a household sack of fuel. I would gamble that this farmer had not bought any coal for years. He must have had a chicken run especially for the job of supplying coal.

With the deal done, the exchange was complete and the eggs were safely stowed in the steel locker on the tender of the Fowler. The shunter returned, the crossing gates were opened by the guard, we delivered the 'empties' and attached the return loads.

The method of descending the bank was known as AWB - Apply Wagon Brakes. There was a board bearing these letters at a point just before trains started down the steep bank. The train would be brought to a stand at this board. The guard and shunter would walk to the locomotive and apply the first few wagon hand brakes. The handles would be 'pinned down' to keep the brake applied to the wagon wheels. The train would then be drawn very gingerly onto the down gradient.

More wagon brakes would be applied. The driver could feel the drag of the brakes. When he considered that sufficient had been applied and that he would be able to control the train using the locomotive steam brake and the guard's brake in the brake van, he would whistle for the shunter and guard to rejoin the brake van.

This procedure had been carried out and we were descending the bank. I thought to myself that this driver was pretty confident, because we were travelling faster than I would have expected. Just as this thought went through my mind, Jack applied the sanding gear and rammed the steam brake all on! I was beginning to think that perhaps all was not well, when Jack suddenly put the locomotive into reverse and gave her steam.

"Have you ever been on a runaway, John?" Jack called across the cab. I replied that I hadn't. "Well, you're on a bugger now!" he shouted. The Fowler began to slide, wheels locked, as the braking effort overcame the available adhesion.

> "Have you ever been on a runaway, John?" Jack called across the cab. I replied that I hadn't. "Well, you're on a bugger now!"

There was a strange hissing sound coming from the wheels as she skated along the track. Sparks were flying from the wheels and the smell of burning sand and metal filled the cab.

Jack was fighting hard trying to regain adhesion. But every time he eased the brakes a little to allow the wheels to turn, in order to brake again, the train speed increased and the wheels would lock once more. We were in dire straits. I shot her a round of coal and opened the dampers. She blew off almost immediately. There was nothing more that I could do. The brakes were getting all the steam pressure it was possible for me to make available to Jack.

We were now travelling at a pretty fair rate - and completely out of control. I began to study the passing terrain. I didn't relish the thought of abandoning ship. There were nettles, brambles and saplings in abundance. We would be cut to ribbons.

I yelled at Jack: "What do you think will happen at the bottom of the bank?" I was horrified at his reply.

"One of two things," he shouted back. "The first is that the signalman might be in a position to alter the points and allow us out onto the main line. If he can do that, we will be OK and we'll get the train under control. But that depends on whether the main lines are clear or not. The second is, should the track be occupied, the signalman can do nothing except allow us to run into the sidings. He will abandon the signal box before we smash through the dead end and demolish it!"

I was petrified at the thought of a major mishap. As we came into earshot of the signalman, Jack was whistling continuous short 'pops' - the standard distress signal from a runaway train. The signal at the end of the branch came into view. It was at danger.

My heart pounded hard against my rib cage. Jack ordered that if the signal did not clear within 100 yards we ought to jump for it.

As we came within about 300 yards of the signal, it cleared for the main line. I could see the look of relief on Jack's face. I exhaled loudly. I won't tell you what we said – but I'm sure you can imagine! We shot out onto the main line and eventually stopped a couple of hundred yards past the box. It was then just a matter of shunting the train back into the sidings. The crisis was over and disaster averted.

Over breakfast in the shunter's cabin, we held our own internal enquiry into the incident. It was the conclusion of all that Jack had called "enough brakes applied" too soon. Jack accepted the findings, but as no damage was done, the matter could be forgotten.

Over his second cup of tea, Jack peered at me and said: "Hey, John, if we had abandoned ship, you wouldn't have forgotten the eggs would you?"

All being well, there was much laughter at this.

Toothache!

Between Christmas and New Year 1958 I was rostered to work 12.30 am to Rotherham. The driver was a town councillor by the name of Bill Sharp. He worked this job regularly on a fortnightly basis. This was so that he could be off-duty during the day to attend to his civic duties. The railways always tried to accommodate their staff involved in such public service.

The locomotive that early frosty morning was a Fowler Class 4F 0-6-0 goods engine. I had been suffering the most appalling toothache all Christmas, having broken the side of a filled molar on a nutshell. I met Bill at the shed and hardly dare open my mouth to speak to him in the cold night air. I was in agony.

We prepared the Fowler and took her off the shed and into the North Yard. Bill suggested that I really ought to ask for relief and go home sick. I declined his thoughtful suggestion saying that the tooth would hurt just as much at home.

We departed and gained the main line at Sandiacre. The traffic was light and we were running under clear signals. The locomotive was steaming freely and all was fine and dandy - except for that damned tooth. The pain was getting worse as I put my head out of the window and into the freezing night air for signal spotting.

We were approaching Langley Mill when I noticed a marked and sudden drop in steam pressure. I knew that it was not because the locomotive needed firing - something else was wrong. I opened the firedoor and peered into the flames. It became instantly clear that the brick arch had collapsed, almost extinguishing the fire.

I immediately passed the news to Bill. In these circumstances, the locomotive could proceed if possible but had to be given up at the nearest depot. I started to move the massive lumps of firebrick to the sides of the firebox using the fire iron's long shovel. This would have a triple effect. Although it would allow the primary air from the ashpan to draw the fire, it would also reduce the effective firegrate area. Further, it would spoil the flow of available hot gases through the boiler tubes. We were in trouble and it would not be long before we would be struggling for steam.

We crawled along and stopped at Codnor Park. Whilst I removed some of the firebricks from the firebed and threw them track side and fought to regain steam pressure and boiler water, Bill went to

the signalbox to tell him, and the control, of our plight. He requested a fresh locomotive at Westhouses.

Eventually Bill returned and except for my poor tooth, we were in better condition. The climb from Codnor Park and through the tunnel at Alfreton was quite severe. Bill decided to give it a try. It isn't far from Codnor to Westhouses but it seemed a hellish distance to us that night with an ailing engine. We struggled every inch of the way with our crippled Fowler - but soon Westhouses was in sight.

We swapped footplates with a Westhouses crew and took to a Riddles War Department 'Austerity' 2-8-0. My toothache seemed even worse at the prospect of being shaken up by this 'Jazzer' as they were affectionately called. I noticed that the fire was not as fresh as one would have expected and this was confirmed by the Westhouses crew. She had just completed a turn of duty and although she had taken on coal and water, the fire had not been cleaned. I could see that this was just not going to be my day.

The climb from Westhouses to Doe Hill is steep but short. I could shrug my shoulders knowing that she would do me and that the real suffering would be by the York crew beyond Rotherham. Bill must have read my thoughts and being the person that he was, he said that we would stop at Chesterfield and clean the fire so that the locomotive was fit for the journey to York. Oh, my poor tooth!

On the way down the bank to Clay Cross I made a can of tea and nearly jumped through the cab roof as I tried to drink it. I don't think that I have ever been so miserable in my life. We duly stopped at Chesterfield and filled the water tank. It obviously didn't need filling having done hardly any work from Westhouses but Bill insisted. She took about 50 gallons. Ouch, the pain of the cold air, as I stood on that tender back!

We departed from Chesterfield after cleaning the fire. We were now running hours late. I was tired, hungry, in terrific pain and as miserable as sin. The control had given up on us and we were now a very low priority – if we had any priority at all. We were stopped for all and sundry to pass. After pulling up at about every signal from Barrow Hill to Rotherham, we at last arrived at Masborough around 8 o'clock in the morning for relief. It had been a very long and extremely painful trip.

There was a relief cabin on number one platform on Masborough Station. From there, Bill called the control for our return orders. They asked Bill if we would wait for two hours and work a fitted freight back to Toton. Bill turned and asked if I would be OK? I didn't care two hoots. I would have

> "I was doing well, just the footplate to brush and wash and we would be as clean as a new pin. I had just about finished when this man exploded "PACK IT IN!" He shouted "BLOODY WELL PACK IT IN!" he bellowed. I looked at him like an injured school boy. His face was red enough to burst. "I'VE GOT A BLOODY HEADACHE AND YOU ARE MAKING IT WORSE. SIT DOWN AND DON'T MOVE, OR SAY ANOTHER WORD!" he yelled."

agreed to be shot at that moment.

Whilst we were waiting, I told Bill that I would nip out of the station and across the road to a newsagent's shop to buy aspirin or something to dull the raging pain. I asked the lady behind the counter if there was a dentist close by. She directed me along the road and around the corner. I found the dentist's surgery.

It was a few minutes before the surgery would open. There was a young lady standing on the pavement outside waiting for the dentist to arrive. I struck up a conversation with her and, telling her of my plight, I asked if she would mind waiting a few minutes whilst I saw the dentist. This was assuming the dentist would see me. She agreed.

Within a few minutes the dentist arrived. I approached him with my tale of woe. He smiled and turning to the young girl confirmed that she would be willing to wait. I was in his chair a few seconds later. I explained to him that I had another train to work back to Nottingham and made a request for a shot of gas rather than a local anaesthetic. In less than five minutes I was out of the surgery minus 7 shillings and 6 pence (37p), a tooth and the pain that went with it.

I met up with Bill again. He naturally asked me where I had been. I told him the tale of the patient lady and the kind dentist. It was then that Bill told me that the train which we were to work back had been crewed through from York. The control had managed to find a crew on better hours. We were to travel home 'on the cushions.'

The Sheffield train arrived and, changing there, we boarded a train for Derby. I fell into the deepest sleep that I had experienced since well before Christmas. Bill told me that he had quite a problem at Derby shaking me into consciousness. I made no apology.

Grumpy old hands!

Some of the very old hands at Toton were notorious characters. Bearing in mind that I was 16 years old in 1955, I could and did fire for men well into their 60s. Assuming they had left school and started work at 13, they had commenced their service well before the First World War. They had fired for, and been taught by, drivers whose service went back as far as the 1850s.

It is easy to see then, that the discipline and attitude that we young lads had to endure in the early years with the old hands, had a direct link with Victorian values. Such was the nature of these railwaymen that they considered a man with 20 years service was just a novice. They had spent most of their time either at work or in bed. The modernisation of the world outside had passed most of them by without them noticing.

Noel told me that he was once booked with a driver for a year who would chalk a line across the footplate. He told Noel: "This is my side, that is yours. Don't cross it without permission!" The driver would only speak to Noel when it was absolutely necessary. Noel told me that the year seemed endless. Every day at work was like a week whilst working with this man. Noel is the most easy going and nicest chap one could wish to meet. If a driver could not get on with him, there was no chance for anyone else.

I once fired for a driver whose nickname (behind his back, of course) was 'Nag'. I soon found out why. We had signed on at 5.15am for a colliery trip to Langley Mill. This was the exchange sidings for Moorgreen Colliery. These jobs were very boring and mostly involved shunting the loads delivered by the colliery engine into trains.

Other arrivals from Toton or Westhouses would deliver empty wagons and take the newly-formed loaded trains away to destination. It was considered by most, that the best thing to do was to make yourselves as comfortable as possible so as to alleviate the boredom.

This particular day the locomotive was an old Johnson Class 2F 0-6-0 goods engine. I had resolved that this notorious driver would have nothing to 'nag' me about - I would be faultless. The journey to Langley Mill went as I had intended, without any problems at all. We soon found ourselves in the sidings and had done most of the

Below: Derby Midland was another station very familiar to John Woolley. This was the scene just nine months after he started his footplate career as a cleaner at Toton MPD. On July 24 1955, Stanier 'Black 5' 4-6-0 No 44981 of Bourneville shed (21B) awaits a clear signal with a southbound semi-fast train, while a Fowler '4MT' 2-6-4T shunts empty passenger stock in the adjacent platform. *Brian Morrison.*

> "I hardly dared to move except when absolutely necessary to look after the engine. I was looking for the shunter's signal when a voice bellowed behind me. I nearly jumped out of my skin.
> "WHEN ARE YOU GOING TO SWEEP THE BLOODY FOOTPLATE?"
> he yelled. ....
> ....I couldn't win!"

shunting that was immediately necessary. All well and good.

During a quiet period, I took the headlamps from the locomotive buffer beams. I thoroughly cleaned and polished them and trimmed the wicks before placing them back in position. The next task was to clean the locomotive backhead. This involved the use of tallow which was placed at the highest point on the locomotive boiler, allowed to melt and run down. The tallow was then washed off using the slaking pipe. The result would be a shiny black background for the next task - polishing the brass fittings.

I had accomplished these tasks without comment and turned my attention to the bucket, tools and food locker. I was doing well, just the footplate to brush and wash and we would be as clean as a new pin. I had just about finished when this man exploded "PACK IT IN!" He shouted "BLOODY WELL PACK IT IN!" he bellowed.

I looked at him like an injured school boy. His face was red enough to burst. "I'VE GOT A BLOODY HEADACHE AND YOU ARE MAKING IT WORSE. SIT DOWN AND DON'T MOVE, OR SAY ANOTHER WORD!" he yelled.

I was shocked by this outburst. Was he insane? Had the boredom and the rocking of the old Johnson addled his brain? However, I thought it best to do as he suggested, such was the power and the authority of the man.

We shunted for about another hour or so. I hardly dared to move

Above: On June 4 1962, the lovely little outpost at Barrow on Soar, between Loughborough and Leicester, was known as 'Barrow on Soar & Quorn station'. Even though nearby 'Quorn & Woodhouse' station on the Great Central route closed a few months later on March 3 1963, the 'Quorn' part of Barrow's name was subsequently dropped. The Midland Main Line station is still open today - and of course Quorn & Woodhouse station is beautifully restored on today's Great Central Railway heritage line. Passing the station on a lovely sunny day is Stanier Class 8F 2-8-0 No. 48356 with an up train of standard BR 16-ton mineral wagons. B.W.L. Brooksbank/Initial Photographics.

except when absolutely necessary to look after the engine. I was looking for the shunter's signal when a voice bellowed behind me. I nearly jumped out of my skin.

"WHEN ARE YOU GOING TO SWEEP THE BLOODY FOOTPLATE?" he yelled. I was subjected once more to this man's irrational behaviour. I couldn't win!

It carried on like this for the rest of the shift. Eventually, we signed-off and back at the depot I was pleased to step off the footplate and get away from this horrible man. In the drivers' lobby I scanned the next day's roster. I was pleased to see that someone else would have to put up with him.

I had signed-off and turned to leave the building. With the door held open in readiness for a quick escape, I turned to this man and shouted: "DON'T FORGET YOUR BLOODY ASPIRINS TOMORROW!"

The rest of the crews in the building all burst out laughing. They were well aware of his reputation. I had gone through the door before he could regain his composure and retaliate.

I have already told you about John and the Mapperley Branch. His attitude was that a fireman was just a tool. A means to his end. He would go for hours and hours without speaking. He would thrash the locomotive as if he had a personal grudge against it. Every shift with him was like a week out of one's life. His face was always expressionless so it was impossible to read his thoughts.

When two men are on the footplate for such long hours, one would think that the more pleasant the conversation, the quicker the time passed. It was never so with John, he was like it with everyone, including the ground staff. John had no friends - and he certainly didn't want any at Toton.

Then there was Charles. He would take great delight in making his fireman's life as miserable as possible. Like John, he would not speak unless it was necessary. Mostly, when he did speak, it was to criticise

or humiliate his mate. I well remember asking him a question about the mechanical shunting at Toton. On reflection, I should have had more sense.

I wanted to know how the wagon retarders worked. These were devices for mechanically slowing vehicles which were free running from the hump into a siding. Instead of answering in a civil manner, he took this as a cue to rant and rave at me.

"YOU SHOULDN'T BE ON THE FOOTPLATE IF YOU DON'T KNOW THE ANSWER TO THAT!" I asked in my defence: "If no one tells you anything, how do you go on about finding out?" His irrational response was: "IF YOU WANT TO KNOW ABOUT SHUNTING, WHY DON'T YOU TRANSFER TO THE SHUNTING STAFF?"

I was actually enjoying his odd behaviour. I had long since realised that these men would have to stop short of killing you. So I told him: "I bet you don't know!" He replied "OF COURSE I KNOW YOU CHEEKY YOUNG BUGGER!"

I was enjoying baiting him: "So you must have served your time with the yard staff then?" "NO I DIDN'T" He yelled. "So how did you get to find out?" I asked. This enjoyable conversation could have gone on for hours, but I decided to drop the matter when he began to sulk even more than usual.

There was also an old fellow whose only work was on the pilot engines at Stanton Gate. These 'trippers' were designated numbers 89 and 90 and serviced Stanton Iron Works. He would never make a can of tea. When his fireman brewed up, he would pick up the can and drink directly from it. This had the obvious result of putting his mate off. He would then have a can of tea to himself. Not a bad ploy really. No one as far as I am aware dared to object to his behaviour.

He had another annoying habit which upset the ground staff immensely. Whilst shunting the yard, he would stop the locomotive just fractionally clear of the points which the ground staff had to alter. The result of this action was that the shunter would have to bend his back and look under the locomotive framing to ensure that the points lay in their correct position.

One shunter at Stanton Gate was a grand fellow by the name of John. He had just about had enough of this driver. As the locomotive stopped, John walked into his cabin and returned a few moments later with a piece of paper. He handed the paper to the driver. He looked at it, grunted, and moved the locomotive back about six feet.

Later, I joined the shunters in their cabin for my break so as to avoid my tea being plundered. I mentioned the piece of paper and John told me what he had written. It said: "Your greasy overalls and

Above: This was the destination for much of the coal traffic originating in the Erewash Valley and staged through Toton - Brent sidings, London. This is Brent on June 6 1959 - Stanier '8F' No. 48180 is arriving with a train of vans. The coaling tower marks the position of Cricklewood MPD, which John Woolley knew well. *R.J. Essery Collection.*

Above: BR Franco-Crosti Class 9F 2-10-0 No. 92026 is approaching Hendon with a long Toton-Brent coal train on September 29 1955. *A.R. Carpenter/Rail Archive Stephenson.*

likewise manner make me feel sick to such a degree that I cannot find it in myself to communicate with you except by letter. Please accept this as a formal request to set back 1¼ inches!" That's the way to do it! There was a great deal of laughter.

What about Fred? He had the strangest personality I have ever known. If you had a black coat, Fred would have one blacker! Nothing you could do or say would be accepted as right for Fred. If you wanted Fred to agree that it was a lovely day, you had to say that rain was coming. It was an education to work with this fellow, but was sometimes embarrassing if one was in a conversation within earshot of a stranger. I have seen the travelling public stare in disbelief at some of the things Fred would say.

I remember travelling home as a passenger from Wellingborough. There were two airmen in the same compartment. Fred was saying that to build an airstrip was a waste of land. He had a better idea. Why not have a short conveyor belt rotating in the opposite direction to the approaching aircraft at the aircraft's precise approach speed!

He expounded the theory that the two speeds would cancel each other out and the aircraft would therefore be stationary! The two

airmen looked at me inquiringly. I could imagine what was going through their minds - Does this man really drive trains? Are our lives at risk? No, it's not possible, he can't be a driver! I dropped my eyes, smiled and excused myself for the toilet.

Strangely, when I tried to explain that the aircraft was travelling relative to the ground, and all that would happen in theory was that the aircraft wheels would rotate at twice the speed necessary, he would not have it. I gave up, as usual. There was no talking to Fred.

On another occasion we were working a local trip known as a 'stower.' These trips were little more than a glorified shunt. They would move wagons from yard to yard or siding to siding, effectively stowing them away. It was winter and we had covered the cab with a tarpaulin to keep out the draught.

Later that morning the sun came out and the cab became unbearably hot. I took the sheet down on my side. Fred immediately asked: "What are you doing?"

I replied that I was taking down the sheet to admit some fresh air. Fred erupted "FRESH AIR? FRESH AIR? THERE'S NO SUCH THING, IT'S MILLIONS OF YEARS OLD!" I nearly fell off the

Above: Hasland Beyer Garratt 2-6-0+0-6-2 No. 47986 passes Elstree & Borehamwood, bound for Brent, with an up coal train in 1956. This was one of the last survivors; it was withdrawn in the week ending July 6 1957 and scrapped at Crewe by August 30. *John Day Collection/Rail Photoprints.*

footplate laughing, partly because he just could not see the funny side of what he'd said.

And then there was Ted - a man who knew precisely how the railways should be run. At every opportunity he would be off his footplate and ringing the Divisional Control to say so and give them hell. "You ought to have done this, you ought to have done that! Why did you do this instead of that? I would have done this not that! Why did you delay me? You lot couldn't control your water!" It was a continuous stream of abuse and invective, aimed at men far more educated and experienced than he. Ted could only ever see his train, whereas 'the Control' could see all the traffic in the district and had to take an overall view

Eventually, the Controllers had also had enough of Ted. They wrote to the Shed Master at Toton and complained - bitterly. They had been keeping records of Ted's antics and forwarded them with the letter. With the co-operation of the Chief Controller, the Shed Master came up with a super solution. Ted was confronted with the evidence. The Shed Master told him that he would be relieved of his driving duties for a while so that he could visit the control. Having known Ted, I can imagine that he thought that he was going for a day out as an honoured guest. He had a rude awakening!

The Chief Controller met Ted in the control room and introduced him to everyone. He was shown to a chair and desk festooned with

Above: A very busy scene captured taken from the bank where the bushes are, on the left of the picture at the top of the opposite page. BR Class 9F 2-10-0 No. 92080 is waiting to set back (the fireman is looking back, possibly for a signal to move) whilst sister '9F' No. 92019, in the background, is awaiting departure from the sidings. The Hughes-Fowler 'Crab' 2-6-0 is arriving at Brent with an up freight.
H.D. Ramsey/Initial Photographics.

telephones and told that it was his! The Chief explained that Ted had been given charge of a busy section of line. The Chief told him that in view of Ted's advice in the past, he expected an improvement in performance. He also advised poor old Ted that he would be held responsible for any delays to important trains. The Chief's parting words were "Don't hesitate to seek advice if you are not sure of anything!"

The other Controllers kept an eye on Ted and always put him right before any damage was done to operations. It was a collusion; Ted was not really in charge, but the Chief made it look as if he was and criticised his every mistake. After about a month of this treatment, Ted was allowed back on the footplate. He was, as they say, as cured as a side of Danish bacon!

Ted never complained to, or about, 'the control', ever again.

CHAPTER 2
PROMOTED TO FIREMAN

On February 15 1960, I was at last promoted to fireman and therefore placed in the link structure, which meant that I was given a booked mate for a year. My first driver was a man named Fred Bexon. He was a grand fellow. We were rostered into the 'Bottom Link' which consisted of 12 weeks of work, nearly all confined to the depot.

The bottom links were referred to as the 'Chain Gang' links because of the nature of the work. Our duties were mostly disposing locomotives as they arrived on shed from their work and preparing locomotives for their next turns of duty. It was very, very hard work.

For example, to dispose of a locomotive was no mean feat of strength. We were allowed one hour and 20 minutes to complete the task. If we could dispose of six locomotives in less than eight hours, the rest of the shift was ours and we could go home early.

Practice makes perfect, they say. Providing the locomotives were there to work on, the task could indeed be done in less than four hours. Management didn't really like us to be going home in under half a shift, but tolerated it because of the time saved in locomotive turn round times.

I will run through the elements and procedure for disposing a Stanier Class 8F 2-8-0 to give an idea of what graft was involved.

● **Coaling:** We would board the locomotive under the coal hopper and fill the tender with coal. The driver would then move the locomotive over the ashpits.

Above: A peaceful roundhouse scene of engines simmering at Toton MPD on August 9 1964, as the shadows were lengthening for steam. From the left they are: Stanier '8F' 2-8-0 No. 48178, Fowler '4F' 0-6-0 No. 44106 and Stanier '8F' No. 48168. On the right is an unidentified '4F' with its smokebox door wide open. The tall pipe in front of this engine is connected to the turntable's vacuum tractor. A locomotive on the turntable would connect its front or rear vacuum pipe to the long hose trailing from the top of the vertical pipe, and the locomotive's brake ejector would be used to create a vacuum to drive the donkey engine and revolve the turntable. B.K.B. Green/Initial Photographics.

● **Fire cleaning:** This was the most demanding and back-breaking task imaginable. There were five heavy steel tools for the task.
● **Straight Dart:** A 9ft implement made from 1¼in diameter round steel bar with a loop for a handle at one end and an arrow head point at the other. This would be used to smash the clinker and loosen/ lift it from the fire bar
● **Bent Dart.** Similar to the straight dart but with a sharp bend in it, a couple of feet from the pointed end, so that it could be used to prod and clean the back corners of the firebox which would otherwise be inaccessible.
● **Long Rake.** A 15 ft. tool, again made of round steel bar, but with a flat blade across the end, for raking ashes/clinker from the front of the firebox, through the hole made in the firebed (by removing

Above: The original MR sign adjacent to Toton's No. 3 shed door, warning drivers to stop before entering. It is remarkable that this sign survived until the very end of steam. *Lee Edmonds*

Left: Toton's oldest No. 1 shed, built in 1870 by the MR. *Keith Reedman Collection.*

Lower: Toton's No. 1 shed, from the coaling plant (see also pages 11/127 taken in the 1930s. The ashplant and its disposal wagons are in the foreground, with a rotary bunker Garratt. In the centre are wagons loaded with good quality locomotive coal in large lumps, ready for the coaling plant, and empty wagons which have already been hoisted and tipped into the concrete hopper. At least two other Garratts are stabled in the left distance. The building next to the shed main door was the boilersmiths shop. *R.J. Essery Collection.*

a couple of firebars – a difficult job in itself) and into the ashpan. It was also used when you were underneath the engine, for pulling/ pushing the ashes out of the ashpan and through the dampers, where they cascaded into the pit.

● **Big Bertha.** A chisel like tool made from really heavy metal for smashing the thicker clinker in an extra dirty fire.

● **Bar Hook.** A tool with two claws for lifting the fire bars from the grate, so that ashes and clinker could be raked from the firebed and through into the ashpan.

● **Long Shovel.** A clinker shovel for moving clean fire around the firebox, or if required out on the road in an emergency, baling it out through the firehole to dump it through the cab doors and onto the trackside.

The fireman would first obtain the tools and lean these against the cab side, with the handles uppermost so he could reach them from the footplate. He would start by smashing any clinker on the firebed with the straight dart, to expose about five firebars in the centre of the firebed. He would then use the bar hook to remove the five firebars and draw these through the firedoor and onto the cab floor. The bars weighed about half a hundred weight each but were made of cast iron and were therefore brittle. They could easily shatter.

Using the bent dart, the back corners of the fire either side of the firehole would be poked and cleaned, the ashes being pushed through the hole in the firebed and grate and into the ashpan. Next, the long rake would be used to move all the fire and ash from one side of the firebed and push it through the hole and into the ashpan.

Above: For the moment, a normal working shed - but this picture was taken in May 1966, just five months before Toton MPD's closure to steam. The locomotive is an LNER Class K1 2-6-0 No. 62062. *C.P. Stacey/Initial Photographics.*

Good fire from the other side of the firebox would then be raked across to the freshly cleaned bars. A few shovels of coal would be placed on this to help form the new fire.

The other side of the firebed would then be cleaned and dropped into the ashpan, through the hole in the grate made by the missing firebars. Then you would climb down into the ashpit and all of the ashes would be pushed through the front damper and into the ashpit below. With the fire now thoroughly cleaned, the next task was to rake out the ashes from the back damper. The firebars removed earlier with the bar hook would then be replaced in the grate carrier bars and the fire spread around the entire grate. A good round of coal to start a fresh fire completed the job.

● **Watering and Smokebox Cleaning:** The driver would move the locomotive from the ashpit to the water crane. The fireman would climb onto the tender back, open the filler lid (if it hadn't been running around open) and put in the leather 'bag'. The driver would then open the valve to start water flowing into the tender tank and look after the filling procedure and make sure that the tank didn't overflow.

Whilst the tank was filling, the fireman would open the smokebox door and clean out the char. Char was tiny fragments of partially-burned coal which had been drawn through the boiler tubes from the

Above, left: The shed buildings include the pay office (door on extreme left), drivers lobby (in front of lean-to before the last window on the long wall of the left-hand building) the board room, where engines/jobs were listed (white gable end facing camera), and the first aid room (door with white surround on central brick gable end) *Lee Edmonds.*

Above, right: A happy bunch of Toton enginemen. Left-right: Pete Morgan, Ernie Hart, Denis Fulwood and Phil Warwick. *John Fulwood.*

fire. It accumulated in great quantities in the smokebox. If the wind was in the wrong direction, shovelling out these very dry, abrasive charcoal-like shards was the most horrendous task. This light grit-like substance seemed to get everywhere.

● **Stabling.** The freshly-disposed locomotive would then be driven to the Shed Arranger's cabin. He would tell you where the locomotive needed to be stabled, ready for its next working. The locomotive would be berthed and the task was complete.

Another crew would later board the locomotive and the driver would oil the motion and the axle boxes on both driving and pony wheels. Whilst he was doing this, his fireman would fill the lamps with paraffin, make sure that all the necessary tools were on board,

build up the fire and fill the sand boxes. Dry sand was carried on the locomotive in hopper-like boxes on the framing, by the tops of the driving wheels.

A steam control valve operated by the driver could be turned on to blow a fine stream of sand between the driving wheels and the rail. This would improve adhesion when the rail was wet, oily, or a train was being started on a gradient. The process of making a locomotive fit for the road again after leaving the ash pits was known as 'preparing' and was the opposite of disposal.

Taking all this work – by two men - into consideration, you can see that to turn a locomotive round quickly and efficiently was by no means an easy task. All of the firemen on these links were as fit as fiddles. They had to be! Personally, I was so fit that I could stand at the side of the track on a sleeper end with both feet together, and, still keeping my feet together, I could spring over the rails and across the track to the other end of the sleeper, beyond the other rail. A good five feet! I must say here however, that I would not recommend anyone to try this foolhardy manoeuvre. It makes me shudder to think about it now.

The performance of the depot relied on this gang of very hard-working men to keep the wheels turning. Hence their name: the Chain Gang.

I had been courting Caryl (when I had the time) for a number of years, and now that I was a fully fledged fireman we could make plans for our wedding. We were married in August 1961 and Noel was my best man. He was a passed fireman – which meant he could drive when there was a shortage - and was well on his way to realising his ultimate dream of becoming a fully fledged driver.

My first booked mate, Fred, also came to the wedding. We still have the fruit set he gave to us for a wedding present. My wife Caryl and I spent our honeymoon in St. Ives, Cornwall. We travelled overnight from Derby – by rail, naturally - via Bristol. It took 10 hours! Just one week later I was back at work. The first week's wages which I gave to my new wife was £8.10s (£8.50p). She gave me £2 back for our spending money.

Lucky Len!

One night I was working with Fred on the shed, disposing locomotives. We had stopped work at about 2am, for our break. We were enjoying our sandwiches in the messroom when the Running Foreman came through the door at express speed. His face was ashen as he explained that a driver had been run over and he would need us to man the hospital train to Nottingham. Yes, that's right, we had a hospital train which was in use on the depot until the early 1960s when the footpath from Sandiacre to the depot was widened to create road access for the first time. That road, from Sandiacre to Toton Traction Depot, is still known to this day as 'the Ambulance road'.

We sprinted to the nearest locomotive and quickly coupled it to the ambulance car. The injured driver was loaded and we departed, carrying express lamps on the front of the engine to Nottingham. A quarter of an hour later we were in the station. Already the ambulance crew from Nottingham were waiting on the platform and the injured driver was quickly transferred to hospital. It was only later that we discovered what had happened to the unfortunate man.

His name was Len and he had also been working on the shed that night with his booked mate, Stanley. They were preparing a Stanier Class 8F 2-8-0 when Len told his mate that he was off to the messroom to join us for our break.

Stan still had a little work to complete and needed to fill the water tank. The locomotive required moving about 50 yards to the water crane. Stan, thinking that his mate had departed to the canteen decided to move the locomotive himself. It was in complete contravention of standing orders for a fireman to move a locomotive in steam unless he was accompanied by a qualified driver.

Stan was right - Len had indeed departed to the messroom … but he realised on the way that he had forgotten to lubricate the pony axles. This was a task which necessitated getting under the front of the locomotive. He returned to complete the work but failed to notify Stanley not only of his return, but that he was 'going underneath.'

Len was under the locomotive on his knees oiling the pony axles. The locomotive was standing only 40ft short of a pit. This would have been a much safer and comfortable place for him to work. He had just about completed the task when the locomotive started to move. Len was powerless to do anything. The cylinder taps were open as Stan opened the regulator and the roar of the escaping steam drowned Len's desperate calls to stop.

All Len could do was lie flat on his back in the hope that the locomotive would pass completely over him and leave him unscathed. Unfortunately, there was a pile of ashes and char in the 'four foot' between the running rails at this point and this restricted clearance between the ground and the bottom of the engine – the space Len was lying in. The lowest part of the locomotive was the ashpan and as this passed over Len it fouled his overalls and started to drag him along with the engine.

The terrified driver was dragged along for about 40ft, his body ploughing a furrow in the ashes and char as the engine moved forward. The locomotive eventually arrived at the pit and the engine finally released Len, who fell semi conscious down the pit steps.

Stan alighted from the locomotive to head for the messroom and as he came down the cab steps, he heard Len moaning. The penny dropped as the horrible truth hit home. Stan's first thought was that he had killed his mate. One can imagine how he must have felt at that moment of awful realisation. But, miracles do happen. Len had done the right thing by lying flat and apart from two broken ribs and severe lacerations to his back, he was otherwise OK, with no internal injuries. He was back at work within a few weeks. A very lucky escape.

Limited Clearance!

Compared with today, it's a sobering thought about how dangerous the railways were for their employees in my early years. Nowadays, the railway goes to great lengths to teach and enforce safety. But, I well remember many accidents to staff in those less enlightened

years of the 1950s. Very often there was little or nothing learned from mishaps and regularly no action was taken to ensure that a particular kind of accident wasn't repeated. It was hardly anything to do with the will of the management to reduce personal accidents – they did their best. It was more to do with the design of tools, buildings, materials and the thinking which was mostly of Victorian vintage and handed down the years unchanged. For the staff of the railways of my early days, work was a very dangerous place to be.

Decades later, several incidents instantly spring to mind. The roundhouse sheds were of Victorian design, when locomotives were much smaller and they were not really built to accommodate the larger engines of later years. Consequently, as a locomotive was turning on the turntable in the centre of the building, between the radiating roads, the buffer clearance between the turning engine and the locomotives which had been backed off onto the pits on the radiating roads, was in some cases minimal. This varied depending on the skill of the driver leaving the turntable on whether he could stop the locomotive before running over the 'stops' on the rail ends, and onto the shed floor. If they were good, this left the engine close to the stops, and therefore with maximum clearance at the other

Above: Deeley MR Class 3F 0-6-0 No. 43650 stands in the sun alongside the coaling plant at Toton MPD on March 31 1956. At this time steam sheds were still kept clean and tidy - just look how immaculate the shed yard is here. Yet only a decade later, MPDs were neglected, filthy and with debris everywhere - or, like Toton, closed to steam. When this picture was taken, it would have been hard to believe that around ten years later it would have all gone. *T.G. Hepburn/ Rail Archive Stephenson.*

Right: Another Deeley MR Class 3F 0-6-0 goods engine, No. 43832, is in steam in pretty good external condition at Toton on June 14 1959. The 0-6-0 is standing next to the covered drop pit, where wheelsets were removed for axlebox repairs. This improved Class 3 variant of an earlier 1888 Class 2 design dated from 1903 and whilst withdrawals were heavy after 1955, more than 200 were still in service in 1960. *D.T. Greenwood/Rail Archive Stephenson.*

Above: A lovely comparative study of the conventional BR Standard Class 9F 2-10-0 (on the left) in the shape of No. 92019, with Franco-Crosti boiler No. 92024 alongside. The end of the water pre-heating drum beneath the boiler can be seen under 92024's smokebox door. *T.G. Hepburn/Rail Archive Stephenson.*

end, nearest the turntable. If drivers stopped well short of the stops, clearance by the turntable could be very tight indeed.

I remember a young cleaner named Peter being caught unawares between the buffers of the stabled locomotive he was cleaning and those of a locomotive turning on the turntable. He suffered terrible internal injuries as he was crushed and survived only because there was just enough room to 'roll' him sideways between the buffers without fatally crushing him. He was only a slip of a lad and this saved his life - had he been a larger fellow he would have surely died.

Fortunately, the driver who had backed the locomotive Peter was cleaning off the turntable had done a good job. The engine wheels were touching the stops at the other end. Had he left the engine a mere one inch closer to the turntable Peter would have met his namesake that day at the Pearly Gates. Peter was lucky and recovered to resume work.

There was little management could do except to say that employees should be aware of the danger. Taking more care was the answer. Short of knocking down the shed and rebuilding it with longer pits, what else could be done? Back then, no one thought of designing a board to place over the buffers to serve as a reminder to anyone in the area that the clearance was limited. .

One day in 1957 I was labouring in No. 3 Shed. My task that day was picking up scrap brake blocks from around the shed (where fitters had left them after fitting new ones) and delivering them to a scrap bunker. I was given a special barrow for this task. The barrow was not unlike a packing case trolley with only two wheels. There was a cradle for the brake blocks in the front of the wheels. When it was loaded, one had to press down hard on the handles to lift the blocks clear of the ground. The wheels were the fulcrum for this lift.

I had loaded the blocks and was making my way to the scrap bunker outside at the south end of the shed. When I arrived at the door, I found it partially blocked by a Stanier Class 8F 2-8-0 which had been left on the shed straight, half way in and half way out.

There was just enough room between the side of the tender and

the shed wall to pass the barrow and myself. I was easing the barrow through this very narrow gap when the trolley wheels ran into a hole in the concrete floor. This instantly stopped the barrow and caused the weight of the blocks to overcome my weight. The barrow handles shot up into an upright position but not before trapping my left hand little finger between the handle and the locomotive's tender framing.

Fitters working nearby heard my scream and rushed to my assistance. It took two of them to overcome the weight of the brake blocks and release my hand. The effect of this was to burst the finger wide open and break the bone. The finger needed six stitches and plaster. I was unable to work for about six weeks and I bear a nasty scar to this day. .

In retrospect, there were four main causes of the accident. First, the barrow was of the wrong design and should have had four wheels, like a porter's trolley. Secondly, the locomotive should not have been left in a position where it would restrict the walkway. Thirdly, I should not have attempted to negotiate the narrow gap but insisted that the locomotive be moved. Finally, the shed floor should have been smooth without holes.

What was the outcome? Were any procedures changes or repairs done or new trolleys acquired? No! I was told to take more care. The barrow type was still in use up to the closure of the steam shed. Locomotives were still allowed to stable fouling the walkway. The shed floor still remained in poor condition at this point right up until the shed was demolished. Labourers still used the same route and method. Nothing changed.

Likewise, take the case of Len, the driver who was run over by the 8F. It would have been easy to update standing instructions forbidding the oiling of locomotive pony axles other than when stabled over a pit. Perhaps this would have been too restrictive and may have influenced productivity? In any case, the locomotive was moved without the driver being present. Stan was obviously to blame! Stan could have asked any passing driver to help him move the engine and in the circumstances, they would have obliged without a second thought. They all got something wrong that night and the accident was the result.

Today's railwaymen are never seen walking about trackside without high visibility clothing. At night, this clothing has reflective strips and everyone carries a hand lamp both to see with and to be seen. This is a far cry from the days not so very long ago when the fireman was not supplied with a lamp. Only drivers and guards had these bestowed upon them. High visibility clothing had not been invented and would not have been considered necessary anyway.

It took a long time to get away from the Victorian way of thinking. It's fair to say here however, that when the more enlightened management and Health & Safety thinking required that the men should wear high visibility clothing, there was resistance from the old hands. They stated that they had managed for decades without them so why wear them now? They had forgotten the many men who had died as a direct result of not being seen.

I remember another old driver called Len. He was a First World War veteran and was accommodated on local trips. This was because of respiratory problems caused by mustard gas in the trenches of the Somme. He told me that he could recall when he was a lad, the days when Toton Sidings were shunted using horses.

He told me that to injure a horse was taken as the most serious offence. They cost money! If a railwayman was killed during shunting, that was a different matter. There was another in the dole office queue waiting to take his place. Perhaps he was bitter from his war experiences or there may have been a grain of truth in what he said. I am inclined to believe it was a mixture of both.

I have in my possession an undated booklet (probably 1940s) written and published by the LMS It is entitled 'Prevention of Accidents'. The first two paragraphs of the introduction say it all! They are reproduced here:

"Every year between 200 and 300 railwaymen are killed, and in addition, several thousand meet with accidents which lay them aside for days, months, years or for always.

"Investigation of the accidents occurring shows that a high proportion of them are attributable to thoughtlessness or lack of foresight and care, either on the part of the injured person or others."

The first paragraph shows an obviously unacceptable high number of casualties. The second paragraph places most of the blame firmly on the shoulders of the staff. The word "thoughtlessness" in the second paragraph neatly avoids the issue of the need for safety training, and does "lack of foresight and care" really mean lack of training?

The railwaymen of today are safety and traction trained to a high degree. They are justly proud of the results. The railways are safer today than they have ever been. As a matter of interest and to justify my statement on safety, when the Riddles BR Class 9F 2-10-0 (or any unfamiliar locomotive for that matter) first came to Toton, no driver asked for, or was offered, any specific training. Drivers having passed from firemen would be expected to drive any type of engine. This nearly cost me dearly.

I was disposing of a '9F' and was looking for the handle which allowed the ashes to fall from the hopper ashpan (itself below the grate) to the pit. I was just about to release the safety catch and pull the manual blowdown lever when a fireman opposite stopped me and pointed out the correct handle. Had I have pulled the lever, the full force of the boiler would have been released into the pit. I hate to think what would have been the outcome. Had I not been scalded, I would certainly have had to go home to change my trousers!

Today's managers are enlightened and realise that although training costs money the returns are greater than the expense. There is less sick pay to find and repairs to infrastructure are reduced when accidents are avoided. Also, the legislation is more demanding today. The law told them that they had to improve.

Stanier Class 8F 2-8-0 No. No. 48319 and Frank

It was Wednesday June 13 1962 when I first fired for Driver Frank Winfield. We had signed on at 5.30am for Willesden. The locomotive was a Stanier Class 8F 2-8-0 goods engine No. 48319.

The train was nicknamed the 'The Tin Trunks - they were 40-ton hopper wagons code named 'LHZ.' They were in a flow from the collieries at Mapperley to Stonebridge Park power station. The train was well known amongst the lads as being not only very heavy but also difficult both to drive and to fire. The train was short and heavy – a real dead weight.

The day was warm and dry and the locomotive was in excellent condition. We had a surprisingly easy run to Market Harborough. The train was booked to run via Northampton, where we would be relieved.

From Market Harborough we were booked to have a 'banker' – an assisting locomotive pushing in the rear - to Clipstone. The 'bankers' were based at Market Harborough Shed and if I'm honest I'd have to

Snow-plough-fitted Stanier 'Black Five' 4-6-0 No. 44726 is making smoky progress under clear signals with an up coal train at Trent North Junction, on February 25 1956. *T.G. Hepburn/Rail Archive Stephenson.*

Above: It's a beautifully clear sunny day on June 10 1960 as BR Riddles Class 9F 2-10-0 No. 92164 passes Ratcliffe on Soar, south of Redhill Tunnels, Trent, with an up 'C' class express goods train. Note the immaculately manicured ballast and neatly cut grass banks. Today, this is the location of East Midlands Parkway station - which means the open meadows on the right are now the site of Ratcliffe on Soar power station. *T.G. Hepburn/Rail Archive Stephenson.*

say that they didn't like to work too hard. Many a time in the past whilst climbing the gradient, I had looked back at the 'banker' and could tell by the light exhaust blast from the chimney that they had barely enough steam on to propel themselves and keep up with the train, never mind taking half the weight of the train in front. There was not much 'assisting' going on.

Leaving Market Harborough there was obviously a tremendous amount of work to be done, hence the need for a banker. The gradients were not only steep, but there were also two tunnels on the route which had been designed in hell! Their names were Killamarsh and Clipstone. The up and down lines divided as the train approached these tunnels. There was one tunnel for the up trains and another for the down (northbound) services.

The reason for needing two separate tunnels was said to be that the hill which had been bored by the Victorians did not have sufficient mass to accommodate two tracks side by side in one bore. It was said by the old hand drivers that the owner of the land (possibly Lord Harborough) would not agree to a cutting and that the railway must be hidden from view. This was the only solution. The footplatemen called these tunnels 'the Rat Holes'. It was an understatement!

When the tunnels were approached it seemed a gamble whether the locomotive would fit. In fact, when the Riddles 'Nine Freight' first worked the route, a Toton Driver (whose name I will not mention, although he is long gone) actually stopped short and inched his way through to ensure clearance. He did not trust the Route Availability Book which is a book showing restrictions of locomotives and vehicles over a particular route. This is how tight the tunnels really were - I kid you not!

To give an idea of the quality of the air inside these rat holes, the atmosphere was just a little thicker than the footplatemen's curses! Imagine, the engine was working as hard as she possibly could, with a roaring fire and smoke and steam everywhere…in such a confined space it was nigh-on impossible to breathe.

The crew's gasps only brought more sulphurous fumes to their nostrils and throat. Even the locomotive struggled for air to keep the fire bright. We would wet our handkerchiefs in the bucket and clasp them over our faces trying somehow to gain relief from the rasping pain of the acrid smoke in our throats and lungs.

As for our bankers, perhaps this is why they reserved their steam? Who would take the risk of stalling in a tunnel full of smoke from the train engine and then, in addition, have to put up with the filthy fumes made by your locomotive? It would be unthinkable.

We would emerge from these horrific tunnels and thrust our faces desperately and immediately into the clean air. It would not matter if the air was filled with the biting night frosts or the rains of February. It was welcome. It was so refreshing.

Frank knew from experience that the banker would not really start to assist us until they approached the tunnel mouth. We would supply most of the power necessary all the way through the tunnel and our progress would be slower, and our exposure to the fumes more prolonged in consequence. He also knew that they would 'give their all' when they entered the tunnel to ensure that they passed through as quickly as possible, to minimize their own exposure to the choking air.

But Frank had a trick up his sleeve. He told me to fire the locomotive on the approach to the first tunnel, then close the firehole doors so as to cut off the secondary air. This I did and the locomotive responded by issuing great plumes of black smoke.

Frank explained further. The crew of the banking engine would see this and realise that the tunnel would be full of acrid smoke when they arrived. It was in their interest therefore, to accelerate the train so that they would pass through the tunnels even quicker than normal.

Sure enough, we felt the train accelerating as the banker opened

up. I looked back and noticed that his exhaust had sharpened considerably. Frank looked across the cab grinning broadly. Of course, we were not that inconsiderate and as we entered the tunnel with the banker now pushing hard, I opened the firedoor and allowed the secondary air to clear the smoke.

We had just entered Clipstone Tunnel when I had the fright of my life. The fireman's side boiler water gauge glass exploded. There was a loud bang and the cab was instantly filled with scalding water and steam. There were restrictor valves fitted in the gauge glass taps that were meant to snap shut if this happened, closing off the steam and water. These rarely worked properly, however, and the only protection from the direct blast of boiling water, steam and the flying glass splinters from the shattered gauge, was a thick glass-panelled frame which fitted around the gauge glass assembly.

Although the frame minimised the hazard potential, the steam and water still entered the cab in copious quantities. The air in the cab was already thick with the fumes from our exhaust and this just made matters worse. Water gauge glasses often blew, but I don't think there was a footplateman alive whose heart didn't miss a beat when it happened.

If you think about it, there was only about an inch of boiler steel proecting us from the full fury of nature, and even boilers had been known to explode. One consolation here however was the fact that we were still alive after the bang. That certainly wouldn't have been the case had the matter been any more serious than a simple gauge glass explosion.

I reached for my coat hanging by my seat and holding this in front of me and using it as a shield, I approached the isolating tap for the gauge glass. I threw the coat over the source of the roaring steam and water and was grateful to feel the tap through the coat. I snapped the handle shut and the steam and water stopped immediately.

By this time we were both choking and gasping for air. Frank shouted: "Get down on the floor, John, you'll find some air down here!" I did as Frank suggested and found my head next to his. After what seemed 20 years, we emerged from the tunnel and into daylight. We feasted on the fresh air. It was as sweet as rose water.

The locomotive's brass work had turned green from the acid in the acrid fumes within the tunnel. We were both wet through with water and sweat. We were filthy and coughing profusely. The coat which I had used as a shield was grimy and saturated.

The banker dropped off the back of our train and left us at Clipstone and we soon found ourselves on the steep descent to Lamport. It was business as usual. I fitted a new gauge glass, tidied the footplate, washed up and made a can of tea. Such was the everyday life of a steam engineman.

The spin of a coin

On the way to Northampton, prompted by the gauge glass explosion, Frank told me a chilling story. It was during the Second World War and Frank had been working Garratts to Brent all week and when the Sunday roster was posted, Frank saw that he was rostered to Brent yet again. He had expected an easier turn of duty.

He had been working long hours and experienced long delays in the London area because of Hitler's blitz. He protested to the Roster Clerk and explained that he had done his fair share for that week. "Give me a break from the bombing", he asked pleadingly. The Clerk would not alter the roster.

Now Frank liked a 'pot or two' and went out on Saturday afternoon to a local club. The fact that he was rostered to London the following day was upsetting him. Over his pint he was debating in his mind what to do. He decided that he would toss a coin. If it came down 'heads', he would go to work as normal and work the train to London. If it came down 'tails', he would ring the Running Foreman and report himself sick for Sunday and lose the overtime payment.

The coin came down 'tails' and so he rang the Foreman and reported sick and unavailable for duty. Obviously, the train still had to be covered, so the Running Foreman arranged a replacement driver.

Frank thought no more about it until Sunday lunchtime when he walked into the club again. He was surprised to realise that all of the members were staring at him. Someone said to him: "We thought you were dead, Frank!"

He was then told that the train he had been rostered to work had come to grief at Kegworth. The news had quickly spread to the club. Someone there remembered seeing Frank's name on the Sunday roster and had told the men at the bar the names of the crew. No one knew that Frank had 'gone sick' and a replacement had been called. The obvious conclusions had been drawn.

So, what had really happened on that fatal day? The train had just left Toton and was passing Kegworth on the up goods line when

Above: BR's dieselisation programme started at Toton in 1962 when the first Class 44 arrived. To men brought up on steam they were curious machines. "They won't last," said some of the drivers. "Nothing will replace steam." Within four years steam had gone from Toton. This is 'Peak' diesel electric No. D9 *Snowdon* in front of Toton's new diesel depot. *David Jones.*

Below: Stanier 'Jubilee' 4-6-0 (or '5XP' as Midland men always knew them) No. 45636 *Uganda* passes the neat wayside station at Kegworth with the Sundays-only 3.40pm Nottingham Midland-St Pancras express on May 4 1958. It all looked so....permanent.... yet steam was gone in less than a decade while the station itself closed on March 4 1968. It has since been erased from the landscape. *T.G. Hepburn/Rail Archive Stephenson.*

one of the Garratt's superheater tubes burst. This was effectively a boiler burst, releasing steam and scalding water into the firebox. The firehole doors were found to be open on later investigation, so it may be assumed that the fireman was firing the locomotive at the time of the failure. The full force of steam and hot water at boiler pressure blasted through the firedoors and onto the footplate, filling the cab with scalding water, high pressure steam and fire.

This killed the fireman outright. He must have taken the full force of the blast from the ruptured superheater. The driver was fatally scalded and died soon after at the scene. It was said that as the Garratt passed the signalbox at Kegworth, the signalman could hear the driver screaming. The fireman's surname was the same as mine. Frank had been a very lucky fellow, but if one believes in providence, then it just couldn't have been his turn. It wasn't his time.

Above: A purpose-built diesel depot was constructed at Toton but at many MPDs the new locomotives had to share filthy and increasingly derelict Victorian sheds with the dwindling steam fleet, which caused many reliability problems. A brace of unidentified 'Peaks' make the point - they are standing adjacent to No. 1 shed (left) on what had been known as 'the Garratt roads.' A brake tender is on the right. *Lee Edmonds.*

Right: With a pair of 'Peaks' (and a brake tender) behind, ex-works Sulzer Class 25 D 5281 awaits the call at Toton on July 12 1964. *David Jones.*

The New Order

In 1962 the first Class 44 diesel electric main line locomotive arrived at Toton. To men brought up on steam they seemed a very curious machine to say the least. "They won't last," the drivers said. "Nothing will replace steam," they added. The old hands could not come to terms with this new form of traction.

We all knew that the diesel would eventually arrive; we had been watching them for some time. A Type Two British Thompson Houston had been working the 'Condor' fitted freight through Toton for months. As the train roared through we would drop what we were doing to marvel at this strange sight.

I well remember a very senior driver's comments on seeing a Class 44 approach. "Here comes another bloody sardine can!" Such was the scorn often poured in their direction.

The management at the time asked for volunteer drivers to be trained as diesel instructors. There were a group of youngish men who were not so bigoted as the old hands. Amongst these were three drivers whose names were Bill, Ted and Jack. They volunteered and were duly trained.

It had already been announced that steam was coming to an end and that a new diesel shed was to be built on the site of the old Cory's Wagon Shops at Toton. Diesel training of the main line drivers began in earnest. The end of steam was well within sight.

One of the biggest problems that the newly converted steam-to-diesel drivers had to overcome was the fact that the new traction was very free-running. They would coast for long periods with the power entirely shut off. A steam engine, on the other hand, would

retard under compression when the regulator was closed. This would cause the couplings to close up in readiness for braking.

The newly converted steam drivers, however, would shut off the power of their diesels and after a short period, apply the brakes just as they had done for years. The result would be an almighty bump from behind as the couplings closed and the train ran into the braking locomotive.

The guards in the rear suddenly began to fear the new traction. They complained of being thrown across the brake van every time the driver applied the brake. This was something that they were certainly not used to. To their credit, the new diesel instructors soon identified the problem and they would emphasise this point to the trainees in their training programme. That said, their advice had little effect on the very old hands. You can't teach an old dog new tricks!

Another difference which soon became apparent was that although the diesel brakes were efficient, the drivers could not get used to the fact that the natural retardation of the steam engine was no longer there. This caused drivers to brake more sharply and later, instead of in good time.

Having shut off the power in their time-honoured fashion, they were often surprised at the speed of the train approaching signals at caution or at danger. The steam engine would have done half the job

Right: Class 44 No. D9 *Snowdon* keeps company at Toton MPD with a couple of BR Sulzer Type 2 diesel electrics, paired with one of the heavy brake tenders often propelled in front of a train engine to enhance braking on loose coupled and unbraked goods trains. *Colour Rail.*

for the driver by slowing the train gently and steadily. There was no such luxury with the diesel, and this led to something of a panic to stop when the driver realised what speed he was doing.

Overtaken by panic, some drivers even 'poled' the engine - reversing it and applying power to their diesels as they would have done with a steam engine to arrest the momentum of the train. The outcome of this manoeuvre was major damage to the locomotive and the cost for new traction motors and contactors in the early days was astronomical.

Another major difference between the steamer and the diesel was that with steam one could shut off the power whenever it was deemed necessary no matter what the position of the regulator. The diesel on the other hand demanded a little more finesse and forward thinking. It was necessary to reduce the power gradually in anticipation of stopping the train by placing the power handle to the 'on' position, the lowest setting. This would allow the amperage in the circuit to drop away gradually before the power was shut-off all together.

Above: BR's 'ground zero' main line diesel locomotive - D1 *Sca Fell Pike* **- trundles through Long Eaton (the houses are in Bonsall St) with an up train of Erewash Valley coal from Toton, carried in BR standard 16-ton mineral wagons. The ten Class 44s were all named after British mountains and were dubbed 'Peaks' - a name which strictly only applied to Nos. D1-10. The subsequent Class 45/46 developments eventually numbered 193 examples and all became known as 'Peaks.'** *Colour Rail.*

The old hands found it well-nigh impossible to come to terms with this technique in the early days of the new diesels and would close the power handle from full power to the off position in one sweep! This was exactly as they would have done with steam traction. The result would be an almighty bang in the 'high tension cubicle', the contactor frame for the auxiliaries and the traction motors. This would cause the traction motor contacts to 'flash over' because of the high amperage in the circuit when they were suddenly opened. The contactors would weld together - or at the very least they would

burn badly - and this would cause the locomotive to fail.

Surprisingly, and with some admiration, a good few 'old hands' took to the new form of traction like ducks to water and they made excellent converts. These were mostly the younger men. But, in the early days, for every good diesel man, there were at least two bad ones who had been suckled on steam and simply could not change their ways and adapt.

My own first encounter with a diesel came a few weeks later. A driver named Ken and me took a Class 44 on a train of slack to Stewarts & Lloyds for the blast furnaces of Corby. I cannot remember (and did not record) the locomotive number, as we had all ten of the '44s' and one was as good as another. I do remember, however, that we propelled a brake tender in front of the locomotive.

The brake tenders were pairs of old bogies converted to assist the diesel braking effort. They also reduced brake block wear on the locomotives. They were fully vacuum brake fitted and had a low roof-like body filled with concrete to increase the weight. They were generally propelled in front of the locomotive. I was a little concerned at the tender's 'antics' at speed because they bounced and zig-zagged alarmingly! This fact was eventually realised and after a while an instruction was issued that they must henceforth be marshalled behind the locomotive.

I must say that this first trip was a novelty for me. I could not get over the diesel's easy and smooth running. I was absolutely staggered at the boundless power available.

During the trip I was constantly looking for things to do. I would go into the engine room and examine the coolant levels, temperatures and the pressures of the oil, water and turbo manifold. Ken would check my findings against the instruction booklet for the locomotive so as to ensure that all was well.

I made tea and swept the already spotless floor numerous times. I knew from that day that there was no place for anyone but the driver on these machines. I wondered what the future held for me and all the other firemen when the final curtain was called for steam.

The trip was uneventful. The diesel made easy work of a task which had caused me blood, sweat and tears on many occasions on steam in the past. During the outward journey there was plenty of time to hold a conversation with Ken. I questioned him about his diesel training and asked questions about the locomotive. He was a good man and explained anything I asked. His knowledge was limited: the management needed drivers not fitters. The early diesel courses were built on a 'need to know' basis.

On the return journey from Corby, with about 70 empties, Ken allowed me to handle the '44'. I found it a novelty - and easy. For the first time ever I came home from work as clean as when I went. I was as fresh as a daisy. No aching back or sticky shirt. It couldn't last, I was sure of that.

The introduction of diesel power not only meant that drivers had to be trained, but maintenance staff had to be updated also. The fuelling of the diesels in the early days was done in No. 3 Shed. It was a primitive set-up. The loaded tankers would be placed on a pit in the corner of the shed with the shed shunting locomotive 41966 a 'Tilbury tank' 4-4-2 driven by shed shunt driver, Arthur. The diesel to be fuelled would be placed alongside. The locomotive tanks were replenished by using a small electric pump coupled in the fuel line between the tanker and the locomotive. It therefore took a very long time to accomplish this simple task.

Early maintenance of the diesels was also primitive but was carried out enthusiastically. Most of the fitters had spent their entire career on steam with the exception of the 08 diesel electric shunt engine, which was a simple machine in comparison. The new technology must have been daunting for them. These complicated locomotives would inevitably fail and the lifeless machine would be hauled back to base.

At first the hauling locomotive was often steam but the Chief Mechanical & Electrical Engineer (CM&EE) soon stopped the practice. They made the excuse that there was a fire hazard posed by the steam engine - but everyone suspected that they were worried about the image of the vulnerable diesel locomotive pitched against the absolute reliability of the steam engine.

Fitters and electricians would study the circuit diagrams to try and solve failures. Often a comparatively simple fault by today's standards took hours to resolve. But each incident was a lesson and in a very short time they adapted and learned well. They very quickly became professionals.

The attitude and quest for knowledge by all grades involved in the

Above: BR/Sulzer Class 44 No. D7 *Ingleborough* **rounds the curve near Newton Harcourt (north west of Kibworth) with a train of empty coal wagons in misty weather on November 18 1967. This picture was taken whilst the photographer was waiting for LNER Gresley Class A3 4-6-2 No. 4472** *Flying Scotsman* **to come in the opposite direction on 'The Palatine' special train.** *Brian Stephenson.*

Above: A quartet of 'B1s' stand quietly, but impressively, in the sun outside Leicester (Central) shed early in 1953. They include, left-right, No. 61380 (which was transferring from Colwick to Leicester) whilst 61088 and 61299 are already 38C residents. Though built to Edward Thompson's LNER design, both 61380 and 61299 were built after 1948 by BR, in September 1951 and June 1948. In summer 1962 there was a shortage of firemen at this depot caused by young men abandoning BR for cleaner and better paid jobs then plentiful in other industries - and John Woolley was sent to the GC shed to help out. A very frosty - if not hostile - initial reception by the GC men meant it was not a pleasant experience at first. *Milepost 92 1/2.*

transition from steam to diesel was remarkable. For such a massive undertaking to pass with barely a problem was typical of the spirit and pride of these 'blue blooded' and dedicated railwaymen.

The mixture of steam and diesel power seemed to me to be strange. Fancy having a steam engine belching smoke and sparks alongside one carrying large quantities of flammable liquid! But that is how it was and there was never a mishap as far as I can recall.

The '44s' soon took over as the main power on the Wellingborough, Birmingham and Northampton traffic. Steam was soon relegated to working less prestigious trains. The Class 25 diesel electrics, another early introduction, joined them soon afterwards. They were used extensively on the Stuarts & Lloyds and Birmingham traffic, working in multiple – they were smaller Type 2s whereas the '44s' were Type 4s and more powerful. The '25s' had flexibility however and could be used singly on local 'trippers.'

It is strange that BR in those early days of moderinisation had so many different types of diesel locomotive. One would have thought that the transition would have been an ideal time to standardise the power throughout the network, with fewer different classes. I have heard it said that the engineering contracts went to several companies rather than to just a few.

To me, the Class 20 was the strangest machine of all. The designers must have had steam in mind during its conception. With the driving cab at one end only and driven engine first, the visibility was restricted by the enormous bonnet. This presented manning problems as they needed two men if driven singly and bonnet first.

Obviously, both the manufacturer and the railway management didn't have the foresight to envisage single manning! They ended up being permanently coupled in multiple and nose-to-nose so that there was a cab at both ends. Visibility was then OK and they could be safely single-manned.

The big change

In the early 1960s, the infamous Doctor Richard Beeching, as chairman of the British Railways Board, had been busy deciding the future of the railways. There were to be massive closures of both stations and lines. Protest groups gathered. There was also an outcry from the public when they realised that their beloved - but little used - stations were to close by the thousand.

Toton's work was all freight - and plenty of it – so Beeching's proposals would have little or no direct effect on the depot. It was only when we met men from depots that were directly affected by the savage cuts that we noticed that their morale was at rock-bottom.

It was during the summer of 1962 that I received my first call to work as a fireman at Leicester Great Central MPD. The footplatemen there had heard the bad news that their beloved shed was to be closed within a couple of years.

At that time, work in other industries was still plentiful. Some of the younger men therefore sought and found alternative employment whilst they could. This left Leicester GC desperate for firemen. But the axe was not quite ready to fall and the job still needed to be done – hence my appearance there in that summer of 1962.

I came to work one Friday and was surprised to see my name on the roster for Saturday – 'J.Woolley. 7 am Passenger to Leicester GC for instructions.' I enquired from the Roster Clerk what this entailed? He replied that it was self-explanatory! I was to make my way to Leicester GC and work there for the day under that shed's Running Foreman's instructions.

I pointed out that it would take a minimum of two hours to get there and two hours to get back. This would only leave me four hours to do any work at Leicester, if I was to sign off within my eight-hour shift. His reply was: "OK, you've got a licence to print money! What more could you ask for?"

Even so, I was still not happy and told him that I had arranged to go out with my wife on Saturday afternoon and if I didn't keep the appointment she would probably file for divorce on the grounds of desertion. He retorted: "Well, that's all the more reason to work long and hard to earn the money for the settlement!" My protests were hopeless.

Above: A very rare spectacle sees Stanier 'Black Five' 4-6-0 No. 45101, of 25A (Wakefield) shed, standing outside Leicester (Central) shed in the mid-1950s, adorned with 'The South Yorkshireman' headboard. Presumably having worked in on a passenger roster, the engine has now been turned and is seemingly ready to head back north with the prestigious express, in place of a more normal Gresley 'A3', one of which stands to the right, coupled to a GN coal-railed tender. John Woolley was sent from Toton to work at this MPD on a number of occasions during his steam firing days; compared with Toton it seemed tiny! *Milepost 92 1/2.*

I duly took duty at the appointed time and walked to Trent station. The walking time alone was 42 minutes. After arriving at Leicester Midland, I wasted no time in quickly stepping out across Leicester to the GC shed. By Toton's standards, the depot was tiny. I made myself known to the Running Foreman.

I can still remember the feeling of resentment from both the Running Foreman and the men. This was a new experience for them as well as me. I know that they felt that somehow I was going to be an instrument of their downfall. I was an intruder.

The Foreman introduced me to the driver who would be my mate for the day. I cannot now remember his name but he was a dark-haired stocky fellow in his 50s. He didn't speak to me at all. He just acknowledged the foreman's introduction with a nod of his head.

The first job that we had to do was to dispose of a Gresley 'Green Arrow' 2-6-2 which had just arrived on depot from its previous duties. It was a former LNER machine and I was a Midland man through and through. I was not familiar with this class of locomotive. I had to question the driver on the method employed in removing the clinker. I well remember that it was nowhere near as easy as it would have been with a Midland engine.

This locomotive required extensive use of the clinker shovel to clean the fire and remove the dirty fire through the firehole door. It was very difficult and labour-intensive. I made the fatal mistake of saying so. The driver took this as some sort of ridicule of their methods and locomotive design by a Midland interloper. It certainly wasn't intended as such. It was just a simple statement of fact. But the damage was done.

I had cleaned the fire, emptied the smoke box and completed the other duties associated with locomotive disposal. The driver then told me that we would need to turn the locomotive before stabling her in the sidings. The engine was driven onto the turntable which was in the open air and not under cover inside a shed, as I had been used to at Toton.

I noticed that there was no vacuum motor fitted to the table. It was manually propelled: in other words, it had to be pushed around by hand. It didn't even have a geared winding handle. Instead there was a lever which hinged flat into the turntable floor when not in use. This was lifted out and flipped over to form a lever outside of the turntable's diameter. You then had to put your back to this and

push and strain until the locomotive was turned.

The driver remained on the footplate throughout the operation and adjusted the locomotive's balance by moving it slightly forwards or backwards to compensate for the humps and hollows in the turntable track. The table therefore, had to be man-handled round with brute force with only the strength of the fireman and skill of the driver to accomplish the task.

I found this very strange indeed and somehow felt that the powers-that-be may have been right in deciding to close the place after all! I was in two minds whether to make this statement to the driver who had not spoken to me except when he had to, but decided against it. Within the hour we had completed the first task given to us by the foreman.

The driver then announced that he was going to the messroom for his break. He made a can of tea and didn't invite me to share it. He went to a table occupied by his colleagues and joined them. I was left alone. I knew how they felt about my 'invasion', but I was not there of my own accord. I hadn't volunteered. Yes, I disliked the atmosphere of the place, but I also felt sorry for them as well.

I decided there and then that enough was enough. I would state my case - people who know me would not have expected me to do otherwise. I walked over to their table. They looked at me as if half-expecting a rollocking. I spoke up.

"Look chaps, I'm only here to make a living. I didn't really want to come, I was told that I had to. I'm sorry that things look bad for you, but that is no fault of mine now is it? Why are you sending me to Coventry?"

They had no answer. They knew in their hearts that I was right. A few seconds passed, which I must confess seemed like a week. Then the driver I'd worked with but who had barely acknowledged my presence, let alone treat me like a mate, finally spoke: "What's your name, son?" It was a question he hadn't bothered to ask when we first met. But now the ice was broken and I was invited to join them.

A little while later, the Running Foreman came into the messroom and asked me to go to the carriage sidings, where I would find a locomotive with a driver on board but no fireman. I followed my orders, found the little shunting engine and climbed aboard.

The driver was a lean and tall man with greying hair. He would have been about 60 years old. He couldn't have been more different - he was a real chatterbox! He asked me about myself and about the Midland and passing his well-stewed tea he told me to help myself. I was instantly at home with this old guy.

He told me that he had been at Leicester GC since he was a boy. He had driven 'V2' 2-6-2s, 'A3' 4-6-2s, 'B1' 4-6-0s and all the other fine locomotives on the Manchester to Marylebone expresses. His enthusiasm as he told me these tales was overwhelming. He was a very proud man indeed. I realised even more then, how the younger men in the messroom had felt. This man had seen the best. The

younger men had thought that theirs was to come – but no, their dreams had been shattered by a vandal in the form of Dr. Beeching. No wonder they were bitter.

Time passed very quickly with this old fellow, it was already 3 o'clock in the afternoon. I began to think that perhaps I ought to ring the Running Foreman to ask for relief. The Foreman told me to leave the locomotive and he would send someone to her later. I said goodbye to the old driver and made my way back to the Midland and home.

When I arrived at the Midland station, I scanned the passenger timetable. I was going to be late home. There was no train to Trent for a couple of hours. I noticed a Fowler Class 4 0-6-0 on six coaches standing in the platform. I asked the driver where he was going and he replied that the train was an excursion from Great Yarmouth to Nottingham via Leicester. He had run round the train and was waiting departure time.

I asked if he would be stopping at Trent. He replied that although he wouldn't stop, he would slow down sufficiently for me to get off as it was 15mph through the platform anyway. He invited me onto the footplate for a lift home. Instantly, I noticed that the Fowler was in poor shape. She had no more than half a glass of water in the boiler and the steam pressure was down by about 20psi. The driver told me that he had been struggling all the way from Yarmouth. The fireman invited me to "have a go", commenting that as a Toton man, I was more familiar with the Class 4s than he.

I looked into the firebox and it was obvious that the fire was filthy and burning 'flat' which meant that there was no primary air getting through the firebars from the ashpan to make the flames appear to stand upright. The tender was full of slack with hardly any good lumps of coal at all. The slack had choked the fire and caused the firebars to clinker up.

Below: Restarting a train of coal empties from Trent station on April 12 1958 is Fowler Class 4F 0-6-0 No. 44161. Trent station was effectively 'in the middle of nowhere' with very poor road access and was built as a transfer hub within the web of routes that met at Trent, south of Long Eaton and between Derby and Nottingham. After a few years of rundown, Trent closed on January 1 1968 and was demolished very soon after. Nowadays, you'd barely know it ever existed.
T.G. Hepburn/Rail Archive Stephenson.

The small four-road engine shed and yard at Derby Friargate on September 21 1952. The GN parentage of this line is given away by the locomotives on shed. *R.J. Buckley/Initial Photographics.*

Top: A wonderfully evocative view of Derby Friargate station on February 20 1949 as Stanier 2-6-4T No. 42150 waits to depart with the 11.10am for Crewe. This was a Sunday diversion. Friargate, opened in 1876, was the terminus of the GNR branch from Nottingham Victoria.

Above: Riddles BR Standard Class 2MT 2-6-2T No. 84004 leaves Derby Friargate with a Stephenson Locomotive Society special train on April 21 1956. Closure to passengers was on September 7 1964 and freight on September 4 1967. *Both: R.J. Buckley/Initial Photographics.*

I thought to myself that there were certainly no miracles that I could perform here. I was sure of that. In the very few minutes before departure I scrambled into the tender and proceeded to throw a few hundred weight forward from the back - where the coal was better - to the firing plate.

Meanwhile, the rostered fireman loosened the clinker from the bars and stood it in sheets, upright against the firebox sides. The boiler had gained about an inch of water in the glass and 10psi on the pressure gauge when the guard blew the whistle. The driver eased her out of the station and I gave her a round of reasonable coal.

I scrambled back into the tender to find more good lumps and made these available for the fireman. One had to be careful whilst working in the tender on the move. Many a fireman had been killed by working too high in the tender and had been struck by an overbridge as the locomotive passed underneath. Excellent road

knowledge and sharp awareness were the order of the day.

The driver was 'nursing' the locomotive along and there's no way we could have been keeping time. It was then that I thought of John and Mapperley Bank. I respectfully - and I do mean respectfully – as most drivers resented any advice from lowly firemen, asked the driver to open her up and decrease the cut-off by 'dropping her down a few notches.' He did so and as the exhaust beat sharpened the fire instantly responded and began to burn more brightly and hotter, making more steam.

As we passed Loughborough it was clear that we were in slightly better order than when we had started at Leicester. In an effort to conserve steam, the driver had been working her too light. This had the undesired effect of reducing the draughting and amplifying the steaming problem.

Now that she was being worked much harder she was 'coming

Left: Great Northern Class C12 4-4-2T No. 67398 stands in the sun in the bay platform at Seaton with an Uppingham branch train on October 19 1957. The Uppingham-Seaton branch off the LNWR Northampton-Peterborough line closed on June 13 1960 with the whole route following it into history on May 4 1964. Part of this route at its eastern end now forms the Nene Valley Railway, from Peterborough to Yarwell.
©www.railphotoprints.co.uk - Collection.

Below: A very pleasant general view of Seaton station, viewed from the station footbridge on July 26 1958. This view is looking east and in the bay platform on the left is auto-train fitted Ivatt Class 2MT 2-6-2 No. 41214, on the shuttle service to Stamford. This station is now in private ownership, with the goods yard in use as a scrapyard. The pretty station buildings are in residential use and the lattice footbridge survives, right next to what was the level crossing. There is no public access, however.
R.J. Buckley/Initial Photographics

round' a treat. We were now confident that Nottingham would be reached without having to stop for a 'blow-up.' At Trent the driver slowed and I alighted and waved cheerio. I signed off at about 7pm that night, missing by several hours the afternoon out promised to my wife.

I worked at Leicester GC on many occasions after this and several of the young lads at Toton did the same. But inevitably the axe fell on Leicester GC and it drifted off into history. This was a tragedy repeated all over the country in the 1960s with stations and branch lines closing everywhere. We ended up with a railway that went nowhere. They were very sad days indeed for such a proud industry.

Derby Friargate.

One day in the late 1960s I was rostered with a Toton driver by the name of Harold to work a ballast train for the engineering department. The train was 7 o'clock in the morning Sandiacre to Derby Friargate, via West Hallam. I didn't realise then that Harold and I would be the last train into Friargate station.

The locomotive was a Fowler Class 4 and the train departed from Sandiacre Ballast Sidings with a train of track bolster wagons and a

self propelled crane. At West Hallam sidings, on the Midland, we ran round the train and departed on a very infrequently-used connection to West Hallam Signalbox on the GC.

There, because Harold was not familiar with the route, we picked up a conductor driver, possibly from Annesley. He stepped aboard the locomotive and with hardly a word, took over the controls. It was the same atmosphere that I had experienced at Leicester GC. This man also resented our intrusion and saw us as his downfall.

We arrived at the station and were met by a Permanent Way Supervisor and a gang of his men. The train was positioned in the station and the crane detached. The driver of the crane started his motor and positioned himself on the opposite running line. As the train was slowly drawn back to West Hallam, the track fishplates were removed and the track lifted and loaded onto our bolster wagons.

We departed very slowly from Derby Friargate that day - 60ft at a time. It was almost like a funeral procession. The station buildings eventually disappeared from view. We had isolated it forever from the railway and the proud men who had served it so well. I couldn't help noticing the emotion in that driver's face. I felt sorry, both for him, and the demise of that proud railway.

Dr. Beeching's promises

Many years later I was out with my wife for a drive in the country in the county of Rutland. I wanted to show my wife the marvellous Welland Valley Viaduct at Harringworth. We stopped for lunch at a little pub in the village of Seaton, which is at the north end of the viaduct. The landlord was an ex-railwayman who had worked at Seaton station.

He told me that the whole village had protested to the government when they learned that their railway was to close. The protests were so loud that the government sent an official to a meeting at Seaton village hall and explained that although they would lose the railway, there would be an excellent bus service provided to compensate.

The railway was duly closed and the bus service provided. But this lasted only a short time before being reduced to a token service. The village was thereby denied a meaningful public service. Every family in the village had to purchase a car or be left stranded.

The track has long since been removed at Seaton, but the station platforms, buildings and lattice footbridge between the platforms are still there. Whenever I see it I have a heavy heart and feel a lump in my throat. In my mind's eye, I can see the local from Market Harborough to Stamford standing in Seaton station as we passed over the mighty viaduct with our Garratts, Stanier '8F' 2-8-0s and Riddles '9F' 2-10-0s.

I know that all over the country, village folk and railwaymen could tell similar stories. I wonder why it is, that when the government built a road it was called an investment and when they gave money to the railways to improve services, it was a subsidy? This book is not at all political, but I know (and countless others will agree) that the Beeching cuts were very short-sighted to say the least.

Ken's frying pan

One of the best mates I was ever booked with was called Ken, whose nickname was 'Dumper'. This reflected his habit of leaving locomotives anywhere safe on the depot - but hardly ever where the Foreman had instructed him to leave them.

The reason for this behaviour was that Ken was always in a

hurry. The chain gang men were rostered to dispose or prepare six locomotives and, when the task was done, they could go home. It was in their interests therefore to be as fast as possible. If the water crane or other facility was already in use, Ken would leave his locomotive handy for attention later and start work on the next engine. This meant he could be working on up to three locomotives at the same time!

He would return and complete the outstanding work but by this time he had conveniently forgotten where the Foreman had told him to finally stable the machine. Many a driver had to search the depot for his locomotive after Ken had prepared it. When they eventually found her she would often be blocked in by another and would require shunting out. By this time Ken would be 'on his bike' and up the road - finished for the day.

Ken had an enormous appetite and loved his frying pan. One winter's morning Ken and I signed on for a coal train to Staythorpe power station. We always shared the driving and worked 'day about',

Above: MR Class 4F 0-6-0 No. 43938 approaches Alfreton Old Tunnel with a down train of coal empties on August 11 1956. *John P. Wilson/Rail Archive Stephenson.*

Above: You can almost smell the smoke in this moody and evocative scene at Wellingborough, looking across the Midland main line, with the MPD beyond. It's June 7 1957 and Fowler '4F' 0-6-0 No. 44042 is passing with a goods train, while a shed yard full of stabled engines simmers in the background. A Riddles '9F' 2-10-0 is visible amidst the Stanier engines. *Ken Fairey/Colour Rail.*

driving on alternate days. On this occasion it was my turn to drive.

We had a Stanier Class 8F 2-8-0 that day and the journey to Staythorpe was uneventful. We had eventually disposed of the loaded train and stood on the return 'empties'. The guard and shunter walked along the train examining and coupling the wagons as they went. There was a lull in our activities whilst this was being done.

Ken decided that this was a convenient time to cook his breakfast. Most footplatemen fried their eggs and bacon on the shovel blade. After all, it was perfectly clean, the continual friction of the coal across the blade made sure of that. But Ken had a baking tin which fitted the blade 'to a tee'. He placed his pan on the shovel blade and rested this just inside the firehole. In went the food.

The skill of a footplateman with a frying pan would shame the very best TV chef. Timing had to be impeccable. One would start with the bacon and sausage. When these were at the correct stage, in would go the eggs followed by the bread for frying. At exactly the right moment, the tomatoes or beans would be added. The final result would be a meal fit for a king - and none of it burned. The pan would then be slid off the shovel and onto the driver's seat which he had converted into a table with a newspaper for a table cloth. He would stand to eat. Strangely enough, I still stand and eat my breakfast from the kitchen worktop! Old habits die hard.

Ken was at the final stages of cooking his breakfast that day and, to be honest, I wasn't taking that much notice, I was watching the guard for hand signals in case he needed me to move. Sure enough, the guard signalled me to close up the train. I gave the locomotive steam without warning Ken - and immediately realised my mistake.

The locomotive lurched forward and gave a mighty "CHUFF!" The resulting draught snatched Ken's breakfast off the shovel and it was consumed together with his treasured frying pan by the mighty Stanier! He fished out his pan from the fire with the clinker shovel later on, but it would no longer be non-stick. The fire had cleaned it down to the metal. No one could wish to meet a nicer guy than Ken, but there is a limit. I will not tell you what he said, or where he told me to put my sandwiches. I did offer him a couple when his stomach rumblings started to drown the noise of the locomotive.

Ken soon recovered from this incident and by the time we had arrived back at Toton he was his normal jovial self once more. We called at the local working men's club on the way home. Ken backed a horse called Brothertoft in a selling stakes and won a small fortune. His luck had changed - no thanks to me!

Ken's practical joke

Ken was a man who could not resist a practical joke. These were never dangerous, I hasten to add. I remember working one night to Rotherham with a Fowler Class 4F 0-6-0. The tender was well back and I spent quite a lot of time shovelling the coal forward to the firing plate. The 'Four' was steaming like a kettle and although I had

to shovel the coal twice, this presented no problems.

We were passing Pye Bridge that night and I decided that the locomotive could do with another round of coal. I went for the shovel but, alas, it wasn't where I thought I had left it on the firing plate. At first I thought that perhaps I had left it in the tender, towards the back. I climbed into the tender, but it wasn't there. I began to think that perhaps it had somehow fallen from the locomotive.

I had to report to Ken that the shovel was missing. Ken looked at me as if I was an idiot and 'tut tutting' sternly commented that in that case I would have to fire her by hand! He added that it would serve me right for not looking after this most important piece of equipment.

I scanned the pressure gauge and the water level, both were beginning to fall alarmingly. There was nothing for it but to do as Ken suggested. I began to heave lumps of coal through the firedoors as fast as I could. Obviously, I could not satisfy her appetite by hand and she was losing more pressure.

I thought it strange that Ken was not offering a hand as I would have expected in these circumstances. Just before things became critical, Ken started laughing. I knew then that I had been conned.

"OK, where is it?" I asked. Ken reached outside of the cab on his side grinning like the proverbial Cheshire Cat. His face instantly changed to that of a worried man. It wasn't there!

On a Fowler 'Four' there is a loop handle outside to hold onto whilst walking around the outside of the cab to reach the main framing. Ken had placed the shovel in the loop but it could not have been very secure. It really had fallen from the locomotive this time. It was my turn now to reverse the situation.

"OK, smartypants, you had better start working with me otherwise we'll stick and then there will be some explaining to do!"

By this time we had entered Alfreton Tunnel and knew we would soon be on the short down gradient to Westhouses. There was a depot there where we would be able to obtain a replacement. As we approached the station there was an 'Austerity' for us to pass before crossing to the depot.

Ken slowed and stopped alongside the light engine. He spoke to the crew.

"Excuse me, mate, can we have your shovel? My mate has let his go whilst firing and lost it in the firehole!" The Westhouses crew both laughed and, passing me their shovel, the driver said: "Here you are

Above: Stanier Black Five 4-6-0 No. 45303 stands on the turntable in Wellingborough shed, an MPD well known to John Woolley in his daily duties as a Toton fireman. This was on September 15 1965. Manoeuvring engines in roundhouses could be tricky and dangerous. With boilers crammed full of water, a locomotive could 'go hydraulic' and be impossible to stop. This happened to one of John's shedmates at Toton with a 'Super D' 0-8-0 - it raced across the turntable and knocked another stabled engine through the shed wall. *Hugh Ballantyne/©www. railphotoprints.co.uk - Collection.*

Facing page, upper: Corby's Stewarts & Lloyds steelworks, in Northamptonshire, was a massive manufacturing facility, with an internal railway and a fleet of private steam (and subsequently diesel) shunting locomotives. It was a regular destination for Toton men aboard Stanier '8F' 2-8-0s and BR 2-10-0s. S&L, which used local ore, was nationalised in 1979, becoming part of British Steel, but steelmaking ended in 1980, largely because the expensive local ore was of poor quality. Stanier '8F' 2-8-0 No. 48651 has the sun on its smokebox door as it leaves the exchange sidings.
R.J. Essery Collection

Facing page, lower: Against the backdrop of the towering Stewarts & Lloyds steelworks at Corby, Riddles BR Class '9F' 2-10-0 No. 92132 is at work in rather poor and work-stained condition. *Colour Rail.*

then, mate. See if you can lose this one!"

I was deeply embarrassed - and furious with Ken.

This exchange took only seconds before we were on our way again. I was as busy as a bee regaining the steam and water which we had lost and had no time to 'have a go' at Kenny boy. This could wait until later. We would be descending the bank from Doe Hill to Clay Cross very shortly. He would get it then.

As we breasted the summit and Ken shut off, I walked across the cab. I was just about to speak when Ken beat me to it. He grinned and said "Got you back for the frying pan didn't I?"

It was now my turn to show tolerance. I laughed, and shaking my head, walked back across the cab to my seat and sat down. The incident was forgotten.

The Nurse

Ken and I had worked out to Wellingborough on Thursday July 18 1963. It was about 10 o'clock at night when we arrived. We were relieved by a Wellingborough crew who would take the train forward to London. We reported to the control and they asked us if we would work a train to Toton. Although our diagram showed that we were booked back as passenger, we agreed.

The locomotive was a WD 'Austerity' No. 90590. We were to pick the locomotive up at Wellingborough, take her light to Stuarts & Lloyds at Corby and work a Lloyds to Kilnhurst from there.

Ken and I had our break and prepared the locomotive. We departed light from Wellingborough at about 11.30 pm. The 'Jazzer' was as rough as a 'badger's backside'. Even running light she was bucking and banging in every axle box and bearing. The characteristic 'zig-zagging' that the 'Austerities' were prone to was even more evident on this particular locomotive. The ride was awful to say the very least.

We were running under clear signals on the main line and approaching Kettering. I was surprised to see that the distant signal was on for Kettering South. As we approached the home signal at danger the arm was slowly raised into the clear position. Generally, when a signal was slowly cleared, it was an unofficial indication that the signalman needed to speak to the driver and that he should proceed to the box and stop for a word.

Ken drove the locomotive slowly up to the signalbox. The signalman was on his veranda displaying a red light. Ken acknowledged sight of it with a sharp pop on the whistle.

The signalman told Ken and I that there was a nurse from Kettering Hospital on the station. She had been delayed at work and had missed her last train home to Corby. The signalman asked Ken if he would allow her to ride home on our footplate.

Ken was only too willing to help and we were allowed into the station to pick up our passenger. I alighted from the locomotive and helping the young lady aboard, sat her on my seat. Ken advised her to hold on tight to the window frame and set off.

Because we now had a passenger, I would have to fire the locomotive right-handed. This meant that I would be facing the young lady out of courtesy and as a consequence would have my back to Ken. This would be a 'no no' in normal circumstances. A fireman always faced the driver when firing the locomotive. Some locomotives were left-hand drive and others right-hand. A fireman had to train himself to become ambidextrous so that he could comply with this unwritten rule.

I noticed that as the 'Jazzer' picked up speed it started to oscillate. As the motion increased, the nurse seemed increasingly ill at ease.

Above: It's April 12 1959 inside the roundhouse at Peterborough's Spital Bridge MPD. Stabled around the turntable are consecutive LNER Thompson Class B1 4-6-0s Nos. 61204 (left) and 61205 (right), with Midland-built Class 3P 'Tilbury' 4-4-2T No. 41969. John Woolley visited this East Coast Main Line engine shed having worked through from Toton, via Oakham and Stamford, on an LNWR 'Super D' 0-8-0. *M.J. Reade/Colour Rail.*

solid column of water. This indicated that there was no steam space whatsoever above the top nut: the boiler was solid with water.

Instead of attempting to move her in this condition, Frank asked me to open the dampers, put on the blower and give her a round of coal. The boiler pressure rose quickly and came up to the blowing off point – leading the safety valves to open with a deafening roar. Great plumes of saturated steam and water hit the shed roof smoke chute and cascaded back down onto the engine, bringing with it years of soot and grime.

The Running Foreman was passing and demanded to know from Frank what all the noise was about. It was generally considered unacceptable to blow off, particularly in the shed. My mate replied that until he had blown off at least a third of the water in the boiler he would not attempt to move the locomotive. He was not going to be caught out like Phil. The Foreman accepted Frank's explanation and went back to his office, probably to remove the soot and dirty water from his shirt collar!

The safety valves continued to roar whilst Frank sat patiently with his feet up studying the water gauge glass for about 15 minutes. Eventually the water level dropped into sight in the gauge glass and was more to his liking. By this time the locomotive and the shed floor around it were saturated. I was asked by Frank to 'get the table'. The turntable was therefore rotated into alignment with the road the 'D' was sitting on - and I called Frank onto it. There was a gentle hiss of steam, and with the over-filled boiler now brought under control, the 'Flying Pig' moved forwards as gentle as a kitten.

Our train to Peterborough was booked for relief at Melton Mowbray by Peterborough men. We were often relieved at Melton, particularly on a Saturday afternoon. The main reason for this was the poor passenger service back to Nottingham in the late evening. A crew could easily be stranded until Sunday morning if there were no returning freight trains.

Even though I hated the locomotive, I could just about put up with her over such a short journey. We would be at Melton within a couple of hours and the Peterborough crew would be quite welcome to her from there.

We departed from the East Yard with about 40 mixed vehicles. I gave her a round of coal and, after closing the firedoors, noticed that the chimney did not issue smoke as I would have expected. I realised that there must be a hole in the fire and she was receiving too much primary air through it - hence, no smoke. I shot her another round. Still no smoke.

When the locomotive issues smoke from the chimney immediately after firing, it's a sure indication to the fireman that his technique is right. If there was a hole in the fire, with the bars showing, there would be too much primary air entering the firebox from the ashpan. This would have the dual effect of admitting cold air into the firebox through the hole as well as ensuring that the rest of the fire would not be drawn properly by the locomotive's blast. The fireman would test that his round of coal had completely covered the grate by closing the firedoors and observing the smoke. Then he would open the firedoors sufficiently to admit enough secondary air to burn most of it off. A light grey tinge at the chimney end was the ideal situation.

Even though we were holding our own, the engine was certainly not steaming freely enough to make us comfortable. I knew that my firing was at fault but I could not work out precisely why. I was working all the way to Melton Mowbray but cannot really say that I was her master at any time during the journey.

We stopped in Melton Mowbray station. Thankfully, I would be rid of this wretched locomotive in a few minutes. A driver stepped from the relief cabin and walked towards the engine. Where was his mate? My stomach churned.

The driver climbed aboard the locomotive and spoke to Frank.

"Hello driver, I'm your relief. Control has told me that you are to travel home as passenger, but I'm afraid that I have some bad news for your mate!" Turning to me, he said: "The control has asked me to ask you if you will work the train through to Peterborough? My mate had to be used at New England to work an Edinburgh-King's Cross express."

It was the very last thing that I wanted but I had no option but to agree. Frank said his goodbyes - and then added fuel to the metaphorical fire by adding: "See you Monday John. I think I'll nip for a jar in the Boat Inn before I catch the slow home." The Boat Inn is just outside Melton Station and in the days before management became paranoid about having a half-pint of bitter before travelling back as passenger, almost every footplateman used the Inn. In fact, we had our favourite watering holes all over the country. What better way to replace the sweat after shovelling several tons of coal into a furnace on a hot summer's day?

Frank disappeared through the station exit. I introduced myself to the relief driver, he gave her steam - and we were away. I mentioned that I had been experiencing a little trouble in making her steam. He opened the firedoor and using the shovel to direct a stream of cold air to part the flames, he scanned the firebed.

"Wrong...you've got it wrong!" he told me.

Helpfully, he explained that the Midland technique of having a thick fire at the back and tapering down to the front of the grate, would not work on an LNWR Super 'D'. He went on to say that the fire needed to be dish-shaped - thick all around the firebox sides and thinnish in the middle. He gave me a demonstration. The locomotive immediately responded by smoking nicely from the chimney.

The driver told me that he would look after her all the way to Peterborough just to show me how it was done. I politely declined his offer, saying that one lesson was enough. It was, too. I can honestly say that from that demonstration on I could just about make 'Flying Pigs' really go! Consequently, the run to Peterborough went without any further problems. We detached the train at Peterborough and took the locomotive to Spital Bridge depot, which was just north of the station on the western side of the East Coast Main Line. Here, my driver signed off duty and went home.

I approached the Running Foreman for a service home and after a conversation with the control, he was able to tell me that there would be a train arriving in about three hours destined for Sandiacre. The sidings here were mostly used by the engineers to stable track machines or as an exchange sidings for Taylor Brothers Railway Engineers (now Balfour Beatty). I assumed it must be a train of rails

or sleepers for this depot. I had noticed a number of streamlined Gresley 'A4' 4-6-2 express engines standing on the shed at New England on the opposite side of the East Coast Main Line (ECML). I had never been on the footplate of one of these fine express locomotives. I asked the foreman if he would mind if I visited them. He agreed, but told me not to be more than an hour.

The Gresley streamlined 'A4' 4-6-2s were absolutely beautiful. I sat in the comfortable leather-upholstered driver's seat of a Gresley 'A4'. I ran my hands over the controls. The beautifully crafted regulator handle felt warm, smooth and inviting. Thoughts ran through my mind of what it must be like to be topping 90 or even a 100 mph with 'ten on' from King's Cross to Edinburgh. It would certainly be a better experience than driving a 'Jazzer' with 25 loaded iron stone wagons at 20mph! Perhaps I was based at the wrong locomotive depot? Even if this were true, there was not much chance of my doing anything about it. I had too many commitments at home, plus, in any case, inter-regional transfers were not allowed at that time on British Rilways. I was just dreaming.

Back at Spital Bridge, the foreman told me that my ride home had arrived. I found the train on the Goods Line. It was headed by a Fowler Class 4F 0-6-0 tender engine and comprised four loaded cattle trucks for Sandiacre. The labels on the trucks read: 'Cattle for Sandiacre. To be called for Sunday morning at 7 o'clock" I believe that this was the very last of the infrequent cattle trains to that destination.

I finally signed off duty at 5am. Frank had gone home at 9pm the previous night!

Below: Given that John Woolley was a Toton man, his footplate turns were restricted entirely to the heavy freight work in which his depot specialised - chiefly hand braked coal trains for London, from the Erewash Valley collieries. So when a turn aboard an LNWR 'Super D' 0-8-0 took him to Peterborough, a glimpse of the East Coast thoroughbreds was impossible to resist. After stabling his engine at the Midland's Spital Bridge MPD (where the Power Signal Box is today) he sought permission to cross the main lines to New England shed, where a spectacle like this awaited him. This was the scene at the GN depot in July 1961 - the engines are, from the left: 'V2' 2-6-2 No. 60948, Thompson 'A2' 4-6-2 No. 60514 Chamossaire, 'A4' 60010 Dominion of Canada, 'A3' 4-6-2 No. 60065 Knight of the Thistle and diesel shunter No. D355. John Chalcraft/ ©www.railphotoprints.co.uk Collection.

As the diesels began to overtake steam as the main source of power, steam locomotives began to fall into neglect, with increasing numbers taken out of service. I found myself 'riding' on diesels and was quickly becoming bored and concerned for my future. The Diesel Depot at Toton was well towards being finished and some parts were already in use.

Diesel locomotives would be taken from the steam depot to the new fuelling facilities. The process of 'turn round' improved dramatically. The new diesel depot was going to be the 'bee's knees' and the CMEE at Derby appointed new managers to run it. The new breed would have to have an engineering background.

The first manager at the depot was a super guy by the name of J. V. McKeating. He had an assistant by the name of E.E. Bell. They were sound diesel engineers. During the last days of the steam shed, a notice was posted in the notice case asking for men to act as Deputy Running Foremen and Traction Arrangers on the new depot. Although I was still a lowly fireman, I applied, mostly out of devilment. It was unknown for a fireman to be appointed to a post in charge of drivers.

I become a Deputy Running Foreman

About a week later, I was astounded to receive a letter asking me to attend an interview for one of the new posts. The interview day arrived and I reported to the Chief of Administration. After a short while, I was shown into the boss's office. Facing me was Mr. Bell and his secretary. I had absolutely no idea what questions the new boss would ask. He started by formally welcoming me and thanked me for my application. I was invited to sit down.

Above: BR Sulzer Type 2 (Class 25) No D7523 growls past Ratcliffe on Soar, with the coal-fired power station under construction on the eastern side of the Midland Main Line, with an up class '4' freight on March 27 1965. This is also the site today of East Midlands Parkway station, opened on January 26 2009. Compare this picture with the same scene in June 1960, on page 57. *T.G. Hepburn/Rail Archive Stephenson.*

The first question was: "How do you feel about an engineer for a boss?" I replied that as far as I was concerned, no matter who the boss was, I would still do as I was told. He rephrased his question.

"Yes, but do you think that a Maintenance Engineer could be as efficient as a fully apprenticed operations man?" I answered that as long as the interest was maintained in both aspects of the job and that the new management did not lose sight of the fact that the prime function of any railway was to run trains on time, efficiently, and to keep the customer happy, I could see no problem.

In this new world it had been decided that the old Operating Manager's post would be encompassed by the Diesel Maintenance Engineer. As it turned out, this idea was found to be flawed and Operations Managers were re-appointed.

I remember saying, that with the Diesel Engineer in charge of running trains also, operational problems would be falling on his desk. He would be made even more aware of the necessity of maintaining a reliable traction fleet. Mr. Bell laughed and said: "Are you saying then that the fleet is unreliable?" I answered that failure with steam traction was practically unknown. On the other hand, diesels were proving to be more than a little troublesome. One only had to pick up a daily newspaper to see what the general public

Left: After dieselisation, Toton became famous for its 'Peak' diesel electrics as the Class 44, 45 and 46 locomotives generically became known - even though only the first ten Class 44s were actually named after mountains. Also, where Toton had always been a heavy freight shed, it now became an express passenger shed as the 'Peaks' were used on Midland Main Line London expresses. In the days when diesel fuel arrived by rail, grubby BR green No. D43 shunts the fuelling point in the early years of the new regime. Steam and the 1930s mechanical coaling plant are now history. *David Jones.*

Above: The fan of tracks into the new diesel depot (off to the right) is still laid in clean, fresh ballast which has not yet had time to become work-stained. The first Class 44 'Peak', No. D1 *Scafell Pike* is stabled alongside sister '44' No. D5 *Cross Fell* and an unidentified Brush Type 4 (Class 47). D1 was built at Derby and introduced in April 1959 while D5 followed it into service in November of the same year. D1 worked for just 17 years until withdrawal in October 1976 while D5 (also built by BR at Derby Works) lasted until April 1978. *David Jones.*

thought. The diesels were getting plenty of bad press.

He then asked me an operational question. I suspect he had been briefed by the old Operations Manager. "If you had only one diesel locomotive on the depot and the Operations Controller reported that he had two failures at the same time, one a passenger train, and the other a train of perishable goods, which one would you allocate the locomotive to?" I told him that the answer was obvious. People needed looking after first. One could always compensate the customer for spoiled goods, but people were going places with meetings to attend or aircraft to catch. They needed a reliable timetable. I had a little dig by saying that I would expect the situation never to occur as the engineers progressively got to grips with failures and improved reliability.

We talked generally and Mr. Bell showed me a plan of the new depot. He explained that he needed a conveyor system for small repairs and minor examinations. He asked how I thought this could be achieved. I had noticed on my walks around the depot that there were four through roads. I suggested feeding the diesels through one end and bringing them out of the other. He was impressed and said: "That's exactly the reasoning behind the four through roads. The others from five to fifteen are all dead ends and are for heavy work"

The final question was: "Do you think that as a fireman you could gain the respect of drivers?" I was taken aback with this question although I had expected the subject to come up in some form. I told him that respect had to be earned and couldn't be commanded. If I did a good job, it was just possible that I could break the traditional barriers, I told him. I would have to prove that I was competent. Mr. Bell smiled and thanked me for my time. I did the same.

About three days later I received a letter saying that I had been selected to act as a Deputy Running Foreman and would start in a few weeks time when the new depot was fully operational and the men had been moved over to their new accommodation.

Above: Much to John Woolley's dismay, interest in steam collapsed at Toton once the new diesel depot was complete and at work. "I did not like to see our faithful and hard working steam engines so poorly regarded and treated," he says. The point is made by BR Riddles Class 2MT 2-6-0 No. 78055, stored at the back of the roundhouses in May 1966. *C.P. Stacey/Initial Photographics.*

Right: Cleaner Lee Edmonds had a keen sense of steam passing into history and had himself photographed 'booking on' in the abandoned signing on point, a week or so after the MPD's closure to steam in 1966. Booking on cards are still in place on the right in this rather eerie and sad scene. *Mick Boyd/Lee Edmonds.*

I was obviously elated to be given such an opportunity and reasoned that the sooner the rest of the staff knew, the better. I could then get to grips with the problem of breaking down barriers. The first driver I told of my appointment was my booked mate, Fred. His reaction to the news was: "Well mate I've got to give you full marks for nerve. What do you know about the new diesel depot?" I replied "Nothing, which is exactly the same as everyone else!"

There was mixed reaction from the drivers. Some wished me well; others showed clear resentment. To those who showed animosity, I would say: "Well, the posts were open to anyone's application. Why didn't you apply?"

The new diesel depot duly opened and all of the staff were transferred to the new accommodation. The steam shed fell into disrepair and fell deathly silent. It was a very sad sight to see this marvellous depot begin to crumble. The few steam locomotives which still arrived were left for hours without attention. No one was interested in them any more.

As time went by, the new managers tried to place an embargo on steam. They had become a 'thorn in the side'. A bit of an embarrassment even. It was sad to see. At first the managers failed in their aim, because the steam engine still had a role to play but it was clear to me that this role was indeed becoming less important with every passing day. Even though I had my eye firmly fixed on the opportunities of the future, I did not like to see our faithful and hard working steam engines so poorly regarded and treated.

This irritating anti-steam mood slowly permeated to all levels. Everyone began to treat steam as a nuisance. Drivers would moan if they were given a steamer to work their trains. Diesels were 'in' The only interest now for an increasing number of men was the new depot. Toton Traction Maintenance Depot was born.

Training as Running Foreman

We had been at the new depot for about three weeks when I was told to report to the Shift Running Foreman to begin my training.

The new TMD was to be staffed by two operations supervisors. The senior foreman would be called Shift Running Foreman Grade C, and the junior Shift Running Foreman Grade B. The names were

Left: This was once a busy steam Motive Power Depot. Lee Edmonds recognised the importance of the moment and took the trouble to take a few photographs around the depot to ensure he had a record of this once-important locomotive shed. Here, in this eerily deserted scene, all the engines bar one, whose tender back is dimly visible in the middle distance. are gone. There's a clear view right through the empty shed and there's not so much of a wisp of steam to be seen anywhere - just the vans of the stabled breakdown train. *Lee Edmonds.*

Below: Although John Woolley had loved steam and was deeply disappointed and saddened by the way many of his colleagues simply abandoned locomotives which had served faithfully and well and which were the nucleus of a way of life which was passing into history, he was also a realist. He embraced the new order with enthusiasm and professionalism and this paved the way for him to steadily climb the promotional ladder. This was the new order at Toton on March 25 1965 - the year before the MPD's steam allocation was withdrawn and the shed closed. It's easy to see why those who yearned for a cleaner, warmer and more modern job made a rapid and enthusiastic transfer to the new traction. Compare the airy cleanliness of the new diesel depot with the grimy filth of the steam depot as shown on the opposite page. *William Wright.*

later changed to avoid confusion. The senior man would be known as the TCS (Train Crews Supervisor) while the junior man would be a TA (Traction Arranger).

The principal job of the senior foreman was to be in charge of train crews booking on and off duty, covering shortages and general running matters. He was based in the main building. The junior foreman was solely in charge of fuelling, watering, depot shunting and traction arranging. He was based in a cabin adjacent to the fuelling point. He rapidly became known to one and all by the nickname Outside Foreman.

The Shift Running Foreman who would train me was a great guy called Bill Jacques. He had come through the grades and had previously been based at Rugby. Bill had moved to Toton for promotion about one year before the diesel depot opened.

He knew absolutely all there was to know about running a depot. He also produced the most beautiful hand writing I had ever seen. It was a lovely copperplate. This always fascinated me because my hand writing was pretty straight forward. I mention it because Bill always used to say that "a good hand carries authority and makes the

reader sit up and take notice."

I walked into his office on the first day of training. Bill welcomed me and pulled up a chair beside him. I sat down - and watched. He explained everything he was doing and the reasoning behind his decisions. After the first day I clearly understood that I had a lot to learn. As the week went by, my note book began to fill with the key points I had to understand (and then implement) and the telephone numbers I would need.

Bill would give me imaginary problems and ask me to solve them using the resources actually available. I began to understand more and more. The following week Bill said "OK John, sit in my chair and let *me* watch *you*!" Surprisingly (to me, anyway) the day went without a hitch and I went home elated.

My training carried on for three weeks – and it worked. I began to find it easier and easier to cope as my experience grew. I spent a further three weeks with an old guy called Harry Martinson, to learn the intricacies of traction arranging. At the end of the training period Mr. Bell called Bill and I to his office. The boss asked me how I felt about the job? After I had told him that I felt confident he turned to

Bill and asked him how I had coped. Bill told me that I would be fine as long as I made no hasty decisions.

I was on my way!

The next problem that Mr. Bell gave me was to devise a method of work for segregating locomotives arriving for maintenance from those arriving for fuel and further work. I had already noticed that the depot was running on an ad hoc basis during my traction arranging training. More to the point - I had already worked out a solution.

I came up with the idea that all locomotives for further work would arrive on No. 2 fuel line, while locomotives for maintenance arrived on No. 1. There was a telephone at the entrance to the depot where incoming drivers had to report their arrival. The driver would be told on which line to stable his locomotive by the TCS, who would be armed with a list of maintenance locomotives due to arrive, given to him by the Power Controller at Nottingham. To cover running repairs booked by drivers, there would be a sign at the depot entrance adjacent to the telephone saying: 'Drivers must report any defect at this point.'

The effect of this very simple plan was to improve locomotive turn round dramatically and is still in use today.

Toton Maintenance Depot in its early days was not only for the freight fleet. It was also the mainstay for the Midland Main Line passenger Class 45s. The number of locomotives arriving for maintenance rose sharply as steam was replaced by diesel power. The skill of the Traction Arrangers was paramount if unnecessary shunting was to be avoided.

Above: Carrying the attractive two-tone light-and-dark green livery - and the same British Railways crest as formerly carried by steam locomotives - sparkling BR Sulzer Type 2 (Class 25) No. 7520 awaits work at Toton depot. Derby-built, D7520 was introduced in December 1964 and worked for just 18 years before withdrawal in April 1982. It was cut up for scrap in April 1983. *Both David Jones.*

The depot had four through and 11 dead-end roads. These were constantly being shunted to accommodate the maintenance process. It was becoming increasingly apparent that the co-operation between the running staff and the engineers had to be closer than ever known before. This was possibly the reason for Mr. Bell's first question at my interview. He was a very forward-thinking man. The Maintenance Foreman would predict when a movement was going to become necessary on the depot. The Traction Arranger would then 'work off'

Above: BR Sulzer Type 4 (Class 46) 'Peak' No 149 has just emerged from Elstree tunnel with a down fitted freight on October 12 1963. The Class 46s (D138-D193) were near identical in appearance to the earlier Class 45s (D11-D137) and very similar to the orginal 'pilot scheme' Class 44s (D1-D10). All 56 Class 46s were built at Derby with a maximum speed of 90mph and 2,500hp engines. They weighed 138 tons. As built, the

Class 46s were painted in all-over Brunswick green with yellow warning panels/ends being added thereafter. No. 46009 achieved fame on its last run in 1984 - it was wrecked for TV in 1984 when it was crashed at 90mph into a nuclear flask blocking the track at the BR Old Dalby Test Track, with a train of Mkl1 carriages, to prove how 'indestructible' the nuclear flasks are in routine use. *Brian Stephenson.*

Above: BR Sulzer Type 2s (CLass 25s) Nos D5203 and D5207 approach Elstree New Tunnel after passing the station with an up class '8' freight probably from Toton to Brent on October 12 1963. These handy little Bo-Bo diesel-electrics became the BR Standard Type 2 locomotive and they were common all over the London Midland Region. The first batch were built at Darlington and introduced in 1961 with subsequent batches built at Derby, and the final batch coming from the private sector - Beyer Peacock, who had of course built the Beyer-Garratt articulated locomotives for this route, and this coal traffic. Ironically, the 'Garratts' were built to put an end to the Midland's 'small engine policy' requirement to run the Brent coal trains with two locomotives and two crews - and yet from 1965 the company was turning out small 1,250 horsepower diesels of a type being used in pairs once again on this same traffic! What goes around, comes around. At least these pairs required only one driver and not a crew of four. As built, all bar the final Beyer Peacock batch of 17 locomotives were painted in standard BR Brunswick green, with the subsequent addition of yellow warning panels or ends. The Beyer Peacock batch of 1965 emerged after BR's formal adoption of 'rail blue' livery with the famous white double 'arrows of indecision' and so were some of the first locomotives to carry this livery.
Brian Stephenson.

the good locomotives from the roads in preparation for the move.

At the peak of Toton's diesel operation in the late 1960s and 1970s it was nothing for the fuel line to handle 60 locomotives per shift. I remember one New Year's Eve in the 70s, I was on the night shift when all the locomotives were coming 'home to roost'. I arrived at 10 o'clock at night to find the fuel lines solid with locomotives. There were at least 15 on the fuel line awaiting stabling. The afternoon Traction Arranger apologised for the state of the job but explained that he had been working flat-out all afternoon.

I started work immediately on what turned out to be the roughest shift of my life. At the end of the night, at 6 o'clock on New Years Day, I counted the arrivals. I had stabled 95 locomotives! This was in addition to shunting and resetting the depot for the engineers. At bank holiday times and at the weekends, Toton Depot was not big enough to accommodate all of the locomotives, so we would stable dozens of them in Toton Yard. The Old Bank 1, 2 and 3 roads would be filled solid, from end to end. That would equal a good mile of diesels standing buffer to buffer. Yes, Toton was a very busy place to work. But full of interest.

I was very fortunate indeed to be a Deputy Foreman in those early all-diesel days. The job was full of challenges and I could give this new role plenty of thought whilst I was back on regular footplate duty. Mr. Bell would often give me a problem to mull over. I knew that he probably had his own ideas on how a particular problem could be solved, but he was always looking for greater improvements. It was just possible that I might think of something he had missed. I was honoured to have my opinions even considered by this man and this experience - and being given this wonderful opportunity - taught me a very great deal.

I was invited to many meetings regarding the movement of Class 45s for maintenance. The locomotives had to be taken out of their workings on the Midland expresses and others inserted with the minimum of fuss - and without delays. We came up with the idea of rostering special crews to move locomotives around the region. These were known as ferry crews. Most of their work was done between Toton, Nottingham, Derby and Leicester.

Crews signed on at 0500, 1245, 1500, 1900 and 2230. These were the times when it was decided that most of the locomotives would be available after maintenance: 0500 and 0700 to ferry the locomotives repaired on the night shift, 1245 and 1500 for the day shift and 1900 and 2230 for the afternoon output. The system worked well until the HSTs were introduced and the Class 45s were scrapped.

CHAPTER 4

PASSED FIREMAN

In June 1967 I was told that I was to be passed for driving duties. I was given about three week's notice so that I could brush up on the Rule Book, Operating Instructions and Appendix. This was customary, but it didn't worry me because I had taken a great interest in rules ever since I had started my service 13 years before. I really didn't need to revise – I reckoned I was pretty well-versed.

The day finally came - July 3 1967. The inspector was a guy named Cyril. He met me in the drivers' lobby at 8 o'clock in the morning. His opening words to me were: "It would look fine if a deputy foreman didn't make the grade, wouldn't it?" This remark struck a nerve with me and I replied "Well, if you have come here this morning with a view to failing me, I think we ought to terminate the proceedings now and I will request another Inspector!"

I think this made him realise just what a silly remark he had made. He knew full well that I was keen on rules and had gained a reputation for being 'well up'. But Cyril had to have a go at me because he was one of the men who had resented my appointment to deputy foreman. He was a traditionalist and couldn't move with the times. Never before had a fireman been placed in charge of drivers – and he didn't like it one bit. Also, Cyril had made the mistake of sharing his opinion with Bill - my mentor. By this time, Bill was far more than a colleague and he had become a true friend. He had, therefore, warned me of Cyril's attitude and I was well prepared.

With the pleasantries over, we all went to Cyril's office. He started by opening the Rule Book at page one and asking me a question from each page in turn. This took all morning and most of the afternoon. He was half way through the Appendix Instructions when another inspector came into the office. He had been passing-out three other men and told Cyril that he had passed two, but that one needed further revision.

He asked: "How are you getting on with John?" Cyril replied "Ask him how he thinks he is doing?" I smiled and replied "I don't think that I have put a foot wrong all day, but I don't suppose for one minute that Cyril will call it a day until he can find something

Above: BR Sulzer Type 4 (Class 45) No D25 has just left Redhill tunnel, immediately south of Trent and is about to pass Ratcliffe on Soar with the up 'Thames Clyde Express' for St. Pancras on March 27 1965. This locomotive was built at Derby Works and introduced into service in 1961 *T.G. Hepburn/Rail Archive Stephenson.*

I don't know!" The other Inspector was pretty wise and he sensed the tension between us. He said to Cyril: "Have you had a tea break this afternoon?" Cyril had to tell him that we hadn't. The Inspector turned to me and spoke again. "Go and have a cup of tea John, be back in 30 minutes." he said.

As instructed, I returned a half-hour later - and it was immediately evident that words had been exchanged in my absence. Cyril spoke first: "OK John, you have passed your rules exam. Get off home and tell your wife." I never did find out what had been said in my absence, but then again, I didn't ask.

The next step to becoming a driver was attending the Diesel School at Derby. My Instructor was a great railwayman called Ted. He had been one of the first drivers appointed as a part time Instructor at Toton. He had just been promoted to this salaried post at Derby.

I loved the course, which lasted three weeks. The course had a general approach, rather than focusing instruction on any one type of locomotive. We learned about the diesel engine and how the turbo charger, traction motors, generator, brakes and auxiliaries all worked. It was a new world – and a very long way from the Garratts.

Having completed the course at Derby, the next step was to be trained on a specific class of locomotive. This was done in the classrooms back at Toton. The diesel training varies from depot to depot. The idea being that drivers are trained on a basic locomotive. This locomotive is usually the one most commonly in use at the depot. Every type of locomotive that a driver is trained on thereafter is known as a conversion course. He is instructed on the differences from his basic locomotive so as to widen the number of classes he can drive. My basic locomotive in 1967 was the Crompton Parkinson Sulzer powered Class 44 – the original 'Peaks.' My Instructor was a chap named Eric. He was also a deputy foreman so we had a lot in common. After a few weeks in the classroom I was really conversant with the '44' theory. It was time to start 'running out,' which meant handling the locomotive in traffic.

We ran out with freight trains from Toton. I found it really easy which is hardly surprising when one considers that I had been on the footplate for 13 years by this time. I had served a long enough apprenticeship. Eric was with me constantly. He was assessing and giving further instruction and advice. I was confident that I would pass the next and final examination on the road and become a passed fireman, which meant that I would be called on to drive as required. Eric was a fine Instructor.

The 10.10 Derby to London

The next part of the training was driving expresses. I was thrilled when Eric told me that for the next week I would be driving the 10.10am Derby to London, as far as Kettering.

On the following Monday morning, Eric and I made our way to Derby. I was pleased to see that the train that I was to drive ran into the station spot on time. It had started at Manchester. Eric made himself known and showed his credentials to the Manchester driver. He then vacated his seat for me and, after giving me his schedule, departed to the rear cab for the journey.

I had already studied the weekly operating notice book and made notes of the temporary speed restrictions along the route. The train was booked to depart from Derby at 10.10am and arrive at Kettering at 11.11am after stopping at Loughborough, Leicester and Market Harborough. The locomotive was a Class 45 with a Crompton Parkinson Sulzer 2500 horsepower engine.

The main difference between a Class 45 and a Class 44, apart from a few electrical circuits, was the power available for the driver. A Class 44 (although fitted with a turbo charger) was only 2,300 horsepower. The Class 45, however, was 2,500hp. The 200hp had been gained by fitting the Class 45 with an 'intercooler' - as air is compressed by the turbo charger it reaches a high temperature and expands. Before being admitted to the cylinders it passes through the intercooler to remove some of the heat and contract it again. Now, the cooler air which is still under pressure, has a greater quantity of oxygen per volume. This has the effect of improving the expansive properties of the gases after ignition and the engine becomes more efficient.

Driving a loose coupled freight train compared with a passenger train is as different as chalk and cheese. With a freight train, although the speed is obviously slower, it is usually much heavier and this has to be taken into account when it becomes necessary to stop. I would say that of the two, a freight train requires more handling skill than an express, where you have continuous brakes

> "I thought at that moment of the days of my boyhood watching the 'Jubilees' pass through Trent. I had made it. I had realised my lifetime ambition. I was an express driver. The only difference was the traction. I was in charge of a machine which was 'state of the art' with seemingly boundless power."

throughout the train. Also, the brakes of a passenger train vary very little from train to train, but every freight train is different depending on weight, length, wagon type and brake force available.

The station clock moved to 10.10am. The guard blew his whistle, waved his flag - and we were away. I applied the power and 'picked up' the train. It was 10mph out of the station and as far as Way & Works Signalbox. I watched the train out of the station and past the box. After passing Spondon Junction I wound up the power. The express leapt away. The feeling was exhilarating.

I thought at that moment of the days of my boyhood watching the 'Jubilees' pass through Trent. I had made it. I had realised my lifetime ambition. I was an express driver. The only difference was the traction. I was in charge of a machine which was 'state of the art' with seemingly boundless power.

Passing through Breaston I began to ease back for the 60mph permanent speed restriction through Sheet Stores. We passed exactly on the mark. After clearing Sheet Stores I gave her the lot and the speed increased rapidly. It was soon time to start braking for Loughborough.

As we passed Hathern I had already shut off the power and gave the train a 'good drink' of the brake. The train began to slow as the brakes bit. Passing Loughborough signalbox the train was down to 40mph and slowing rapidly. As I entered the platform, I placed the brake in the running position. Although the brakes were now coming off, I knew that the train would stop before they came off altogether and the customer's coffee would remain in his cup.

We stopped in exactly the right position. I held the train stationary with the direct air brake of the locomotive. We were exactly on time. Two minutes later, we were away again, the next stop being Leicester. I applied full power and had only reached the maximum of 90mph for a few seconds before it was time to think about Leicester.

At Leicester the speed restriction is 10 mph on the approach and into the platform. I remember that it seemed ages before we finally came to stand at the south end. Although the speed was spot on, the contrasts in speed gave me the impression that we had stopped. We were again on time.

The run from Leicester was marred by a 20mph temporary speed restriction at Wistow. I could have done with the speed at that point to assist on the climb from there to Kibworth.

After passing the 'slack', I gave her the lot. I would need to maximise on speed and power and avoid any unnecessary braking if I was to get the time back lost by the slack and arrive at Market Harborough 'on the mark'. As we breasted the summit at Kibworth she was doing about 65mph. She rapidly accelerated to 90 on the down gradient to East Langton. I left the braking to the last minute to negotiate the 60mph permanent speed restriction over the North West Bridge.

I ran into 'Harbro' station about 5mph more than I would have normally allowed. With the brakes hard on but coming off rapidly,

Above: A pleasant view from the London end of a completely deserted Trent station, which was located at the junction of the lines to Derby, Nottingham and the Erewash Valley and served chiefly for interchanges between those lines. This is where John Woolley watched Midland line trains, especially those hauled by Stanier 'Jubilee' 4-6-0s - and dreamed of being an express driver. He realised that ambition. *Colour Rail.*

Above: The Erewash Valley main line from Trent is way over to the left in this view - beyond the three-hipped Carriage & Wagon workshops. EE1 (Class 20) No. 20157 and an undientified Class 08 shunter are marshalling stock at the southern end of the East Yard on May 17 1979. *John Chalcraft/©www.railphotoprints.co.uk Collection.*

we stopped without a shudder in exactly the right spot. Eric spoke for the first time since Wistow. "That was some run John. I bet the Mancunian in the back cab couldn't have done better!" Not surprisingly, I was both flattered and elated at the same time – this was a real compliment.

The time came for the train to depart 'Harbro'. The climb to Desborough is very severe - the Crimean Bank, remember? Eric asked me to estimate what the speed of the train would be when we cleared the summit? I said that she would be probably doing 75-80mph. Eric said: "I bet you as much money as you like that she won't touch 70. Remember, you are at a standing start at the bottom of the bank."

I picked up the train and, as soon as I could do so, without overloading the traction circuits - gave her the lot. As the train approached the top of the bank I knew that Eric had 'been here before'. She was doing 69mph. Strangely enough, on later runs still with eight coaches on, the speed at Desborough was sometimes as much as 75. By closely watching the '45's' performance from Derby, Eric's experience had enabled him to work out within 1 or 2mph what the speed would be at the top of the Crimean Bank. He was some guy was Eric.

On the downward gradient to Kettering, the train rapidly accelerated to the maximum permitted speed of 90mph. I well remember Eric's remarks as we approached Glendon Junction: "This is where we take off!" What he meant was that this was the point at which the down gradient suddenly increases. The locomotive seems to fall away and the driver actually becomes light in his seat for a split second – a bit like going quickly over a humpback bridge in your car.

The train would have easily exceeded the maximum permissible speed coasting with no power on at all had I not arrested her with a little squeeze of brake. Again, we entered Kettering station at 40mph with the brakes hard on, but slowly coming off. This technique of stopping 'with a rising brake' brings the train to a smooth stop, and avoids the sudden lurch which has been known to make standing passengers keel over as the train finally comes to a stand. Again, it's like easing your foot on the brake in your car at the moment you stop. The time was exactly 11.11am.

The Manchester driver rejoined the cab and commented that as far as he could see from the instruments in the rear cab, I hadn't put a foot wrong. Eric and I offered our thanks and made our way back to Toton. After a short spell in the classroom I was allowed to go home.

I drove the Derby-London train for a fortnight on and off and, on

the last day, Inspector Cyril rode with me for my final test. I had driven the mandatory freight train the week previously and had passed Cyril's critical eye OK.

With Cyril aboard, the run was very much the same as the one I have already described. At the end of it we stepped onto the platform at Kettering. Cyril offered his hand which I took and he said: "Congratulations John, you are now a driver!" I cannot actually put into words how I felt at that moment. I had finally achieved my boyhood dream.

My first driving trip in charge

A fact which I have failed to mention thus far is that I have a brother, Dennis. He is 10 years younger than me. When he was about to leave school my father asked him what he wanted to do for a living. Dennis replied: "What's good enough for John, is good enough for me. I am going on the footplate!" I was rather taken by surprise because he had never shown any interest in my job. Or rather, if he had, I had failed to notice. He was as good as his word and he followed me onto the footplate.

It was just before Christmas, 1967. The Sunday roster was posted and I was rostered along with Dennis for 03.00 Toton-Wellingborough. I was a little disappointed because my wife and I had been invited to a Christmas dinner organised by the Running Foremen for the Saturday night beforehand. This meant of course that I would have to remain sober. The dinner was excellent; the orange juice was awful! My wife and I left the 'bash' early so that I could snatch a couple of hours in the 'snore box' before going to work.

I met Dennis at the Diesel Depot and the Running Foreman gave me the details. The locomotive was 44007 a 2,300hp Crompton Parkinson Sulzer. It was going to be an easy trip. The night was foggy, with a visibility of about 100 yards. I guessed that this would be patchy and that once we were out of the Erewash and Trent Valley the fog would clear. We left the shed to time and made our way to the East Yard at Toton. The train was already prepared by

Walter the guard. He gave me the loading slip and I noted that we had 54 loaded coal wagons, 20 of which were vacuum-brake fitted. After the mandatory brake test, I allowed enough time for Walter to walk back to his brake van before whistling for the road. I was given the signal to start by the Yard Foreman and we were away.

On the down gradient between Toton and Trent on the High Level Goods, I made a 'running brake test' as the rules required, to make sure that the brakes were working properly before I actually needed to use them. There was plenty of brake power available. A very nice train indeed. Being Sunday morning the traffic was light and we were running under clear signals. As I had pondered, by the time we had reached Syston, the weather had almost cleared.

Dennis made a can of tea. It may seem amazing, but we had hardly spoken from Toton. Perhaps Dennis thought that I would need all the concentration that I could muster, this being my first trip in total charge, and he didn't want to distract me from looking for signals. Certainly, when a man takes charge of a train for the first time, the feeling is very strange indeed - and it actually takes some getting used to. It's the final test of a long apprenticeship. How you perform on this occasion is an indication of how well you have listened and learned to all the good advice you have been given over the years by all those experienced men passing on their craft. 'The buck stops here' is a phrase that springs to mind. I certainly seemed to be concentrating more than usual even though I was as familiar with this route as I was with my own back yard!

The train was booked to run via Melton Mowbray and Manton. This route is known by local railwaymen as 'over the Alps' because of the stiff gradients involved. There is a dip at Melton Mowbray Junction where many a loose coupled train had been broken in two when a 'snatch' occurred as the power was applied for the climb, snapping a coupling. The technique for negotiating this was to slow the train at Asfordby to about 15mph and then stretch the train's couplings by applying a little power as the locomotive dropped into the dip. The guard would assist in keeping the couplings tight by applying a few turns on his brake. Thus by the time the climb started, the couplings were all stretched and there would be no 'snatch' as the slack was suddenly taken up.

The power was gradually wound up as the locomotive came onto the rising gradient. This accelerated the train through the dip to the maximum speed of the curve of 20mph and kept the couplings tight. As the rear of the train started to climb out of the dip and the locomotive approached the station, the power would be eased back.

If you got it right the train slipped through as smooth as silk. If you got it wrong there would be an almighty snatch on the locomotive drawbar. In the latter circumstances, at best, the guard would have something to say at destination about being thrown around in his brakevan. At worse, the train couplings would break under the shock.

On this occasion we slipped through as if the dip wasn't there. Dennis looked across the cab and smiled. It is amazing how all that experience on steam locomotives with loose coupled trains with limited brake power taught men the intricacies of the many 'humps and hollows' along a route. Today's drivers have tremendous power available. The modern air brakes are also wonderfully efficient. The couplings are mostly kept tight and the guard in most cases rides 'up front' with the driver. The necessity of knowing all the little undulations in the track is not quite as crucial as it was for us.

There are many places along that route where similar techniques had to be used. These are notably: through Manton to Wing, across the viaduct at Harringworth, through Storefield, Glendon Junction, Kettering and between Burton Lattimer and Wellingborough where the track is like a switch back. A golden rule whilst driving a loose-coupled freight train is that either the couplings are kept tight by having power on, or the couplings are closed by having the brake on. Coasting without doing either is confined to dead flat track.

Apart from signal checks at Syston, Manton, Glendon and Kettering, we had a reasonable run. We had been chasing and catching one of our colleagues who had left Toton a little earlier. It was not long before we found ourselves in Neilsons Sidings at Wellingborough where we left the loaded train. I was feeling easier with the whole situation. I began to wonder why I had felt so apprehensive - if that's the right word. We were soon in the Up Sidings on a train of 60 'empties', enjoying our sandwiches.

The time came to depart. The train was booked back via Market Harborough and Leicester. I thought back to that long-ago trip I had enjoyed with Chuck Nurse and my first main line steam drive over

Below: This is the famous MR level crossing signalbox at Oakham - prototype for the famous 'Airfix' plastic construction kit built by tens of thousands of railway modellers over the last half century. Passing through the station in an easterly direction on the line from Melton Mowbray and Leicester are English Electric Type 1s (Class 20) Nos. 20177 and 20188 with coal bound for the Ketton cement works on April 28 1983. *John Chalcraft/©www.railphotoprints.co.uk Collection.*

that very route with Chuck with 'WD' 2-8-0 No. 90427. I remembered that back then I had been a very young hand indeed and realised that although Chuck had allowed me to drive and operate the locomotive, he had nevertheless steered me over the route almost without me noticing. I wondered whether I could emulate Chuck's achievement? I decided to try.

I spoke to Dennis, "OK Den, it's your turn". He looked at me and replied: "Hey John, thanks. You will have to watch me though, I am not thoroughly conversant with the road". I smiled at Dennis and said: "That makes the two of us!" We laughed and changed seats.

To my surprise I quickly discovered that Dennis had more skill than I had given him credit for and he handled the train very well. Apart from a little advice at Market Harborough and from Kilby Bridge through Knighton and Leicester, he did the job perfectly. We were relieved at Toton at midday. After signing-off duty it was off to the local pub for a pint before lunch.

Some years later, Dennis applied for an engineman's post in Liberia (West Africa). He was successfully appointed and was soon driving 4,000-ton iron ore trains from the mines at Nimba to the sea port of Buchanan. He worked hard and made his fortune before leaving for England once more because of the military takeover by General Doe. Liberia had lost it's stability and was not really safe.

The Route Card

In my day as a young passed fireman, it was very rare to be rostered for driving on weekdays. There was a large spare capacity of drivers to cover leave, holidays and sickness, for example. The only chance of being considered was if you had plenty of routes on your route card. The more routes you knew, the better your chances of securing a driving turn as you were of greater use to the roster clerk.

As a fireman, I had taken quite a lot of interest and whenever I worked over a new route, I would take notes and question the driver. I was always eager to learn. I must say that when Cyril had passed me out and I was requested to make out a route card, the running foreman was very impressed with my wide range of routes. I signed for all of the routes which I had worked over as a fireman.

The route card is a document which lists all the routes and yards that drivers at a depot are likely to work over. It reflects the depot's sphere and influence. The driver initials and dates the routes of which he has a thorough knowledge. The card is verified and countersigned by an Inspector every six months. I still have mine and when I look at it now I realise just how much the railways

Above: The 11.08am St Pancras-Nottingham powers away from Loughborough on May 29 1978, with Class 45 No. 45110 in charge. The Brush Works is still in there in the background today - but all else has changed. The '45' and Mk 1 stock are long gone, as are the goods warehouse (and Class 08 shunter!) on the right and lovely little MR signalbox just beyond the last coach. The station platforms were extended north in time for the 2012 Olympic games. *Gavin Morrison.*

have changed – by which I mean cut back. My card shows routes including Whitemoor via Sleaford, Ashwell to Cottesmore Ironstone Mine, Northampton via Market Harborough and numerous colliery branches all of which are now closed.

It wasn't until the diesels took over that Toton crews worked to Whitemoor. I was a passed fireman riding on these turns. I quickly learned the route and signed for it. A driver called Joe Meakin taught me the finer points and it became a 'good payer' for me. I would often be driving over the route when more senior men would be second manning because they didn't have the necessary route knowledge.

I remember well my first trip as a driver to Whitemoor. The turn was on duty at 1400. It was November and the locomotive was Class 44 'Peak' No. 44001 . The weather was fine with clear skies when we set off. It was not long before darkness fell and with the sudden drop in temperature it began to get foggy.

The route to Whitemoor across the Lincolnshire Fens is almost flat with a few exceptions. The trouble with the route was that in places there were few markers to indicate your exact position and in this featureless landscape it was easy to misjudge your position in fog.

I had experienced no trouble until I was approaching Whitemoor. In the distance I could see a green colour light signal and momentarily assumed that I was running under clear signals. At virtually the same instant I suddenly realised that something was wrong - I was a signalbox short! I shut off the power and applied the brakes. As I did so I passed an oil-lit distant signal which was at caution but poorly illuminated and almost invisible.

I had 'read through' the signals and the green light I could see through the mist was actually for the train in front of me in the next section. I of course stopped at the home signal as if nothing was amiss and reported his distant nearly out. This experience left a funny taste in my mouth, however. From that moment I became suspiciously and acutely aware of the dangers of mixing modern, very bright colour lights, with Victorian, dimly visible oil-lit signals.

The colour light had obliterated my signal in the Lincolnshire mist.

A few days later, I met Joe and told him what had happened. His response was "Well, you stopped on your side of the signal didn't you?" I replied that I had.

"Well then, it shows that you know the road doesn't it?" He added: "I thought that I had told you of that danger when you were learning the route, it happened to me once and like you I stopped as well."

I brought up the subject with Cyril the Inspector. His response was that although he accepted that 'reading through' was a possibility, special note should be taken by a driver to allow for this when working over a route with mixed signals. I knew this of course but thought that perhaps a little updating wouldn't go amiss. His statement did not alter my view that to mix signals was more than a little hazardous.

I must say in retrospect however, that perhaps I was over-enthusiastic and it was asking too much to alter signals on a line that was destined to close anyway.

Arthur

One of the last booked mates I was rostered with was a grand fellow named Arthur Fisher. He was a shortish man with a ruddy complexion. He possessed a great sense of humour and a vast knowledge of his job. Arthur was happily married but had no children. He loved life and never missed an opportunity to join his friends, along with his lovely wife at his local pub.

Because he was in the top link at Toton and at the peak of his career, and also his wife was employed as a supervisor at a local factory, Arthur was comparatively wealthy. Both he and his wife adored foreign holidays.

We booked on duty one night at 2230 for the 2315 to Northampton. The locomotive was Class 44 'Peak' No. 44004 Great Gable, a 2,300hp Crompton Parkinson Sulzer. After an uneventful trip to Northampton we stood on the return train and Arthur and I changed seats. The train consisted of about 60 coal empties. The '44' wouldn't even know it had a train!

The return journey was running effortlessly and without much applied thought from either of us. Arthur and I were chatting away to pass the time. During our conversation the subject came around to holidays. He told me that he had booked a holiday in Yugoslavia and mentioned that he was on a night flight. He said that his wife was horrified at the thought. Arthur had told her that her concern was irrational and that all would be OK.

We had passed Leicester running under clear signals when the first unusual event occurred. I wasn't working the locomotive hard. We were on almost level track and the train was quite happy at about a quarter power. I was sitting back completely relaxed with my arms folded when the engine speed suddenly dropped to a tick over. At the same time, the traction motor ammeter dropped to zero and a red light appeared on the fault panel.

The red light indicates 'engine stopped', but the engine was still running. Before the reader says 'If the engine stops, surely the sudden silence would become immediately apparent to the driver.'

I will explain that the light was originally there to warn the driver that the rear locomotive had shut down when working in multiple. The driver could never hear the rear locomotive. The 44s were built with multiple potential but this facility was deemed unnecessary and removed.

I was pretty fresh from diesel training and instantly recognised the fault. The main generator separate field fuse had ruptured. This had caused a relay to drop out and shut down all the auxiliaries except the vital triple pump which pumps cooling water, fuel oil and lubricating oil to the diesel engine. The pump was now running direct from the batteries. It was the only fault on a Class 44, where a red 'engine stopped' light would show but the engine continued to run.

Because the vacuum exhauster and the compressor had stopped, the brakes were beginning to bleed on. I allowed the train to slow from this gradual application of the brake, without touching the handle, until I was close to a telephone. We came to a stand at a signal near Sileby. I asked Arthur to advise the signalman that we had failed but would probably be able to fix her within a few minutes.

Whilst Arthur had gone I shut the engine down and operated the battery isolating switch. I quickly removed the fuse from the panel and tested it. It was open circuit so I fitted a replacement. I had the engine running normally again in about two minutes. We advised the signalman and restarted the train.

Now, when one thing goes wrong, as everyone knows in any walk of life, it is quite likely to be followed by another! Because the locomotive had been shut down and the cab doors opened to the night air, the temperature of the cab had dropped dramatically. Arthur therefore switched on all the cab heaters. He was like a greenhouse plant and could catch a chill in Dante's Inferno. I found the heat overpowering as we approached Barrow upon Soar.

Arthur mentioned that he was going through the engine room to the other cab to retrieve his bag and coat in readiness for going home. Whilst he had gone I opened the side windows to allow a change of air. I was feeling drowsy and needed to reduce the cab temperature to stay awake.

We were just approaching Loughborough when Arthur returned. "Crikey, John! It's cold in here. Have you switched the heating off?" Before I could answer, he walked across the cab and pulled down the switches above my head. We had just come out of the over bridge south of Loughborough signalbox and come into the signalman's vision. I switched on the cab lights and looked at the switches. Arthur had switched on red headlights! We had passed the signalbox before I could switch them out again.

A train running with red head lights is a danger signal to approaching trains from the opposite direction – had they been seen, the approaching driver would have made an emergency stop. Fortunately for us there were no other trains in the vicinity, so all was well.

I looked at Arthur and said: "Well mate, I bet the signalman saw the red 'uns! He will be onto Hathern like a shot!" Sure enough, Hathern's distant signal was at caution. I gathered the train and

Above: The Class 44 'Peaks' were John Woolley's first main line diesel locomotive and they became symbolic of their home base at Toton - especially the first 10 'true' Peaks' actually named after British mountains. They were versatile too and worked on both express passenger and freight duties. This is No. 44008 *Penyghent* passing Ratcliffe on Soar Power Station, south of Trent, in charge of the 1440 Toton-Whitemoor freight on May 17 1979. *John Chalcraft/ ©www.railphotoprints.co.uk Collection.*

A very typical (and typically very neatly aligned) line-up of front ends outside the shed at Toton on July 8 1976. The locomotives are (from left) Class 20 No. 20195, Class 47 No. 47332, Class 45113, Class 44 44002 *Helvellyn* and Class 40 No. 40114, *Gavin Morrison*.

stopped at his home signal. The signal slowly cleared and the signalman stood on his veranda displaying a red hand signal. I popped the horn in reply and drew the train up to his box.

The signalman spoke "My mate at Loughborough reckons that you were carrying red headlights. He must be going daft!" I tut-tutted and shook my head. The signalman spoke again: "It must have been a reflection or something. Anyway driver, sorry for stopping you, I will tell my mate at Loughborough to get his eyes tested! You're right away". As we restarted the train I looked at Arthur and remarked that we were lucky to get away with that one. Well, I thought, that's enough for one night. I was wrong.

We eventually stood on Toton's down hump where we would leave the train. To explain what happened next I will have to describe the layout. At the point where we would uncouple, the locomotive was standing on a set of trailing points. These could be set from the hump to the arrival road (which was the line we stood on) or for a siding known as 'the box side.'

The box side was a couple of dead end roads where wagons could be stabled awaiting orders. They were on a rising gradient from the points to the dead ends. Wagons stabled in the sidings needed the hand brakes applying hard to stop them running away.

The shunter had uncoupled the train and Arthur had gone to the rear of the locomotive to place a lamp on the bracket. This indicated to anyone that the train was complete and that the locomotive was running light. The signal was cleared for the depot. I dropped the window and looked back to see where Arthur was. He was just beginning to climb the locomotive steps.

What I saw next made my heart leap. There was a wagon running away towards us from the box side and would collide with the locomotive cab steps. I reached around the door pillar and, grasping Arthur's coat, yelled a warning and snatched him inside the cab and out of harm's way. Arthur tripped and fell in the door well. A split second later the wagon collided with the locomotive! It sheared the hand rail fixing bolts, bent the door frame, removed the cab steps, became derailed and bounced clear of the locomotive. The wagon came to rest between the Shunter's cabin and us.

Arthur was shaking but apart from a few grazes to his shins caused by his fall in the door well, he was OK. Vandals were seen running from the scene and the shunters gave chase. Unfortunately they escaped. We took the locomotive to the shed, reported the damage

and made out the necessary reports for both failure and the wagon incident. Arthur was given first aid and thankfully, apart from being a little sore, he had fully recovered. He remarked that he would have been crushed between the wagon and the locomotive for sure had I not yanked him into the cab.

A few weeks later Arthur and his wife flew to Yugoslavia for the holiday he'd been telling me about. They never arrived and I never saw him again. I was absolutely shattered when I picked up the Daily Mirror and read the casualty list for the Ljubljana air crash. Arthur and his wife's names were amongst them.

Single Manning

As I have said before, I could see no place for a second man on a diesel and I began to fear for my future. The unions also recognised this but had a duty to protect the interests of the redundant firemen. I was actually dead wrong to fear anything. The majority of the drivers were well into their 60s and management realised that to make all the young men redundant on a 'last in first out' basis would leave them with no drivers at all in the very near future.

The solution was to offer the older drivers a chance to retire early. A large number took up the offer and retired from the service. Many of the senior second men (passed firemen) were made up to drivers and promotion actually improved. Those second men that remained who were employed before the Single Manning Agreement between the trade unions and management, were allowed to ride out on their booked trains. This was unless alternative bona fide double manned turns could be found for them. This protected their earnings and also gave them experience on the road.

The management offered a few hundred pounds to any second man who would 'sell their star' and forfeit their rights to earnings protection. I didn't sell mine but many did. To be quite honest, promotion was so fast that I was foolish not to have taken the money. Only a few years passed before all the men who had commenced service prior to diesels were promoted to drivers.

But the truth was that I just didn't fancy spending the rest of my days driving diesels. For me, the glory of footplate work had disappeared with the steam engine. When the last steam locomotives went I decided there and then that my future would be in the salaried grades as a Running Foreman.

A Stressful Sunday Afternoon - Do it yourself!

It was a lovely summer afternoon in 1970. Deputy Running Foremen were rostered to cover for the Running Foreman one Sunday in four. This gave the regular men a break and allowed the young 'up and coming' chaps to gain experience. It was my turn and I signed on at 1400 to relieve the day shift foreman.

The job on a Sunday afternoon was generally quiet. There was nothing outstanding to be done, nothing unusual at all. I settled down and expected a quiet shift. The last ballast engineering trains arrived around tea time. I fuelled the locomotives and stabled them. There were no other trains to come. We would not be 'winding up' again until early Monday morning.

I had noticed that there were four Class 45 express locomotives which had been serviced on the day turn. Using the two shed shunt crews, who had also signed on at 1400, I rearranged the shed to make these easily accessible. I knew that they would be required for express work and ferrying to either Derby, Nottingham or Leicester. There was also a ferry crew on duty at 1400 for this purpose.

The ferry crews were always under the direct orders of the Divisional Power Controller. He rang me at about 1600 and ordered three of the '45s' away; two to Nottingham and one to Derby. There was a '45' at Derby that required maintenance at Toton. The move therefore, would be three '45s' to Nottingham, detach two, one to Derby and exchange it for the locomotive for Toton.

The ferry driver was a guy called Jack. He was a cricket fanatic and played for his local team. He had completed the ferry move by about 1800. After Jack had eaten his sandwiches he asked me if it would be possible to finish early so that he could catch the tail end of an evening match.

By this time the job had become very quiet indeed. I had shunted the shed, setting it for both the maintenance staff start of work at 2200 Sunday night and for the beginning of freight operations early Monday morning. The job was 'straight up' - meaning nothing outstanding for a few hours.

I spoke to the Power Controller (the ferry men being his crew remember?) and he said: "OK John, I see no problems. As far as I am concerned I have finished with ferrying". However, there is one thing that a Running Foreman must always work towards, and that is to ensure that should anything unforeseen happen he has the resources 'up his sleeve' to pull the job round.

With this in mind I spoke to the shed crews and told them of Jack's request. One of the drivers was confined to the depot because of ill health, but the other was a main line man and he agreed to cover for Jack should it become necessary.

Jack went off to play his cricket at about 1930. He must have been the last man! Now, fate takes over. At about 2015, my last main line driver until 2200 slipped on a patch of oil on the fuel line and badly sprained his ankle. I arranged for an ambulance and asked his mate to accompany him to the hospital for an X-ray.

I started to fill in the necessary and comprehensive accident report forms. The telephone rang. It was the Divisional Power Controller. "John, I have a request from the driver of an express at Chesterfield. When he gets to Toton Centre he will require a fresh engine, his is low in power."

The only driver at my disposal now was one confined to the depot. For this problem, he was about as useful as a rubber spanner. There was only one thing that I could do. I rang the shed man and told him to prepare the last remaining passenger 45 as a matter of urgency.

Having rushed through the accident forms, I rang the power box at Trent to enquire about the express. "He's just passing Ilkeston". He replied. I was expecting to be relieved at about 2100. We had an agreement between ourselves to relieve one hour earlier on a Sunday night. My wife and I had been invited to a friend's house for late dinner.

My wife arrived to pick me up at 2045. She was just in time to see my Roster Clerk and I disappearing off the shed in charge of the '45.'

The express arrived at the up main signal. I was waiting to uncouple his locomotive. This done, the driver shunted her out of the way whilst I backed my '45' on to his train. The express driver walked over to his fresh locomotive whilst I was coupling it. I came from between the locomotive and first coach. 'Hooking on' is a filthy business and my hands were inevitably covered with a thick coat of grease and grime.

The express driver viewed us with suspicion. We were not dressed as footplatemen. I could read his thoughts so I said: "Well mate, you've really let us down tonight. My mate and myself had just got changed and we were about to nip off for a pint when your call came." The driver replied "Sorry mate - not much I could do. She's had it! I reckon the turbo charger has ceased. She's smoking badly and as weak as a kitten!" With the brake test complete, the express departed four minutes after coming to a stand which ain't a bad show really.

We arrived back on the depot with the crippled Class 45 diesel at 2115. After scrubbing up and handing over to the night Running Foreman it was off for dinner. My wife was immaculate; her husband rather less so with a large patch of grease on his jacket shoulder. I could hear the night foreman laughing as we drove out of the car park.

It was then that I hoped at least Jack had won his cricket game. In similar circumstances, I was sure that he wouldn't get a chance for a return match. It would be 'belt and braces' for me from now on!

Below: Awaiting the call of duty inside the depot at Toton on April 26 1984 are, from the left: Class 31 31288, Class 31 No. 31124, Class 25 No. 25048 and Class 20 No. 20049, Class 45 No. 45131 and Class 56063. *Gavin Morrison.*

The Supermarket

In all the years up until 1967, I had never once been late for work. There had, of course, been times when I was ill and unable to attend - but these were very infrequent. On these rare occasions, I had always let the foreman know in good time, so that he could arrange cover for my rostered turns of duty. Perhaps 1967, being my 13th year of service was unlucky for me.

I was rostered for a Sunday engineering ballast train at 0200. Having set the alarm clock, I retired to bed about 1900 and fell into a deep sleep. I awoke without the alarm, switched on the light and looked at the time. To my horror it was 0230! The alarm clock had failed. I rushed down the stairs and rang the foreman. "Sorry" I said. "I am afraid my clock failed, I can get there in 30 minutes if you still need me!" Foreman Harry told me to get to work as soon as possible because the train was standing.

It was a rush for me to make it in 20 minutes - but that is as long as it took. The foreman greeted me with a stony face. He passed a 'Please Explain' form through the window. This form is the first step in the railway's discipline procedure. I was rather disgusted when it was handed to me. Surely, on this first occasion I'd been late, a verbal explanation would have been enough? Being only just awake and in the heat of the moment I wrongly treated the form with the contempt that I thought at the time it deserved. The fact that a whole gang of engineers were waiting on site for the train didn't occur to me.

"Please say why you were 50 minutes late for 0200 Sunday morning". I read the words and smiled sarcastically. I would have thought the answer to that question was obvious. I wrote in the reply box: "I am sorry I was 50 minutes late for 0200 Sunday morning. The reason is that I was out shopping in a supermarket and couldn't get out for the crowds at the checkout!" I handed the form back to the Foreman who looked at it. Still stony-faced, he placed it in the out tray for the boss.

I had fully expected him to laugh, tear it up and call it a day. I had misjudged Harry. It was two days later that the duty Foreman told me that the boss would like to see me. I knew full well what for and I was already regretting my flippant reply to the 'Please Explain.'

I knocked on the boss's door. "Come in. Oh, hello John, sit down". I could tell by his extreme politeness that I was 'in for it!' He reached into his drawer and took out the form. "What's this all about?" The boss spun it around and pushed it across the desk and under my nose. He sat back in his chair, folded his arms and awaited my reply.

I looked down at the piece of paper. "Look boss, I can't tell you how sorry I am about this, I only did it for a joke!" He looked me straight in the eye. "So you think it's funny to delay a train and all

Above: Even after the end of steam, coal traffic from the Erewash Valley heading south continued to dominate Toton and this carried on until the mid-1980s. This scene at Langley Mill makes the point clearly that coal was still king at Toton. Class 56 No. 56128 (in large logo blue livery) leads an up merry-go-round past Moor Green Colliery exchange sidings on the Midland Main Line, on August 28 1984. *Gavin Morrison.*

those men, do you?" I was lost for the right words - if there were any - and lowered my shaking head. I was done for. He spoke again "We've made extensive enquiries and our findings are.....". He paused and I just knew I was going to regret the end of his sentence. "There are no supermarkets open at 0200 on a Sunday morning." He looked across at me as if to take particular notice of any reaction. I didn't think that, even then, a smile was appropriate so I remained stony faced and didn't move a muscle.

"Now look," he said, "Go back to your foreman, Harry, ask him to make out a fresh form, apologise to him for your sarcasm and for the fact that you have caused him the pain of repeating his paperwork. Bring the new form back to me and we will resume the interview."

I did exactly as he asked. Harry the foreman was as stony-faced as ever and just nodded at my apology. I was back 'on the carpet' in five minutes flat. I passed the new form over to the boss. He looked at it and said: "That's better. Now, as a deputy foreman you do not have any special privileges. I do not expect this sort of thing ever to occur again. You can go now, the matter is closed, but this form will go onto your service record for two years in pencil. If you 'come it' again, I will go over it in ink." I thought he'd finished as I headed for the door, but he spoke again.

"Oh, and by the way - get yourself a new alarm clock!" I heaved a sigh of relief as I shut the door.

That episode taught me an extremely valuable lesson that I would never forget. From that moment on, I would never mix humour and business. Well, not when it really mattered. Somehow, in that incident, the content of my reply to management became known to the men. I suspect it was a young administration clerk called Derrick who betrayed me. The reply was viewed with great delight around the depot. One particular colleague of mine by the name of Keith asked if he could see the boss's official letter which stated what I had said, together with a request for the correct reply.

I really needed the matter to be forgotten as quickly as possible, but to satisfy his curiosity - and hopefully draw a line under the matter - I said: "Here you are then, here is the letter from management, keep it. I never want to see it again." He kept that letter - and showed it to me on the day of my retirement!

It was in May 1972 when the big moment came. I had been interviewed on several occasions previously for the permanent post of running foreman but had always been 'pipped at the post' by someone with more seniority. In fact, after many disappointments, I had approached the boss and asked him if I would ever be promoted. I remember that he said that I was still a young man with plenty of time ahead of me.

Finally, the time came, even though there were several other applicants. I sat nervously in the staff mess room waiting for the call for the interview. I had studied long and hard for this opportunity and I knew I was well prepared. The interview was routine, thank goodness. There were no surprises. I remember that rather than being a technical interview, I was given the chance to talk generally about the job. I was asked what ideas I had in mind to improve the job.

Anyone going for an interview for a post such as this had to give consideration to methods and improvements. You had to have something 'up your sleeve' to impress. I remembered that one of the boss's hobby horses was to improve the punctuality of freight trains. So I think he was impressed when I laid plans out for the monitoring and trouble shooting of pre-selected trains.

The simple idea was that a list of a dozen or so trains would be drawn up on a weekly basis. Every element in the locomotives' movement would be recorded and set against their booked timings, from the driver signing on duty to the departure of the train. If a train was late for any reason the causes could be identified and put to rights.

Of course, similar tactics were already used but late departures were looked at in retrospect. My idea was that all late start causes would be dealt with 'real time'. I explained to the boss that the impact of the 'real time' method would sharpen up the responses of the staff involved. As far as the locomotive was concerned, the running foreman would monitor punctuality to the depot outlet signal. Beyond that, he had no control.

The Yard Master would monitor signalmen, the locomotive's running time to the yard, the preparation of the train and its departure time. A late start would mean a conference there and then between the parties involved, to determine the cause and take action to remedy the problems for the future. The boss would have on his desk each morning the previous day's performance data together with any action which had been deemed necessary.

I didn't hear a thing about the job for two months. No one knew who had been appointed to the post. There were rumours of course (there always are) but it seemed strangely quiet. It was years later that I discovered the reason for the long delay. The boss had to convince the Divisional Management that such a young man could do the job.

It was July 31 1972. I signed on at 1245 for a coal tripper to Langley Mill. My driver that day was a grand chap by the name of Arthur Heath. I didn't know then, but Arthur would be my last mate. The Running Foreman told me that before I started work I was to see the Chief Clerk. I knocked on his door and he invited me in. "Hello John. Can you hang on a moment whilst I fetch the boss?" He disappeared through the connecting door. Although I strongly suspected it was going to be good news, I couldn't help going over recent events to ensure that I had committed no crime!

The boss and the Chief Clerk reappeared. The boss started to speak. "Congratulations John, you've made it! You are a Running Foreman Grade B as from today. You will be paid at the appropriate rate once you have completed your training for the Train Crew Inspector's position". This position (as I have already explained) was the senior shift foreman's job. I had already trained for this whilst learning about traction arranging (the position which I had been

appointed to).I explained to the boss that I wouldn't need training and that I could take over immediately. He insisted that although I showed plenty of enthusiasm it was customary to learn the finer points and I would have at least two weeks training.

The short interview was terminated and the boss sent for the Shift Running Foreman (later renamed Train Crew Inspector). The boss spoke to him: "Harry, I can now tell you that John has been appointed to the position of Running Foreman Grade B (later called Traction Arranger). He is no longer a footplateman. Can you find another man to cover his turn?" Harry, nodding his head, said: "No problem, what is John doing today?" The boss answered, "I am going to give him the rest of the day off so that he can tell his folks and get his thoughts together."

He smiled at me. "Get off home now then John and well done. Come at 0600 tomorrow and start the two weeks training with Harry." He glanced at Harry. "Look after him for the next two weeks and keep him out of trouble." It was as simple as that! I remember coming home and telling my wife. She was, of course, delighted. I loaded my golf bag into my Austin A40 and went for a round with a friend. I couldn't keep my mind on the game and lost easily.

The training went without a problem. I had been appointed to the relief position. My regular mate (Traincrew Inspector) was a lovely man named Les Matthews. He had once been a shedmaster in London, I cannot remember which one - but one famous person would know the answer.

Les's Story

I had taken over and was working well with Les. During a quiet period one Saturday afternoon, Les was reminiscing about his experiences. He told me that there was a young fireman at his old depot in London who had a habit of bringing his guitar to work.

He would often entertain the men in the messroom, sometimes standing on the messroom tables to do so! He was also known to have played his guitar on the footplate. At times he even serenaded the passengers waiting on the stations. Les had warned him about this on numerous occasions. It was a very serious breach of regulations.

The Beeching axe was about to fall on the depot and most of the young men were looking for alternative work. There had been a directive issued by top management at the Railways Board level that Depot Managers should do all possible to encourage the men to stay with the railways. They could envisage a mass exodus which would leave a railway without engine crews to run it.

This young man had put in his notice. Les was obliged to try and get him to change his mind and so he called him into his office. "Do

you think that you are doing the right thing? There will always be a job for you on the railways, you cannot say that about any other industry." The young man replied " Look Guv. I am going into show business! I am going to become a professional musician".

Les laughed and told the young man that he would never make it. "Your future lies on the railways," he added. The young man's mind was made up, however, and he duly left the service.

Some weeks later, Les was at home and his daughter was watching a TV pop music programme called 'The Six Five Special' which was very popular at the time. There was a young man performing and Les recognized him straight away.

"Do you know who that is?" he asked. His daughter replied "His name is Joe Brown, he's all the rage at the moment".

"Well, I never," thought Les. "He was right!" The rest is history.

Crewe for training!

It really never occurred to me that I would need professional training. The boss called me into his office one morning in the Summer of 1972. He greeted me and said: "Well John, I am going to send you on a six-week course at Crewe for supervisory training". The course was for the NEBSS certificate (The National Examination Board in Supervisory Studies).

He added: "I also want you to enroll at night school for a GCE English Language course. I know that you know your job as it stands, but you will need to further educate yourself and obtain professional qualifications if you are to progress up the ladder."

Webb House at Crewe is a beautiful building. It had once been an orphanage and was founded and named after the great Crewe locomotive engineer F.W. Webb. It had now become a training school for railway staff and a wide variety of courses were available, covering just about all aspects of railway work.

The Principal, Mr. Jackson, met me at the door. He was an upright, dark and imposing figure of a man. He had been a Major in the British Army before working for the railways. All those years of holding a position of authority and discipline showed in his face. I

Left: Eight Class 20s were briefly reclassified as Class 20/3 in 1986 for working the Peak Forest aggregate traffic - this is the renumbered 20306 under repair at Toton. This plan only lasted a few weeks after which the eight locomotives concerned reverted to their original numbers - in this case, 20173. August 4 1986. *Gavin Morrison.*

Below: 'Peaks' everywhere. On April 20 1986, one of the electric train heating (ETH) fitted Class 45/1s, No. 45133 was under heavy maintenance inside the depot at Toton. *Gavin Morrison.*

never once saw him smile. The course at Crewe would be residential from Monday to Friday and in three blocks of two weeks, known as stages 1, 2 and 3. The period between each block was to be used for revision and application at job level of the lessons learned in previous stages. Stages 1 and 2 of the course were all theory. At the end of the four weeks students would be assessed and the best would go on to Stage 3.

The final two weeks at Crewe would be spent writing up a project report on a subject set by the student's local manager. At the end of the six weeks, there would be a further assessment and the chosen few would be sent to a college at Darlington for a further - and final - two weeks. At the end of this final stage, there would be a full day of examinations followed by an interview with a top railway manager, who would challenge the viability of your project report.

I thoroughly enjoyed Stages 1 and 2. I learned how to manage men, study problems methodically, write reports, conduct time and motion exercises and generally approach the job in a more professional way.

Getting results through people!

It was a very warm summer's day during Stage 2. The lecturer had opened the windows to allow the light breeze to cool the classroom. We were half way through the afternoon and the lecturer was teaching us 'How to get results through people.' This involved (amongst other things) understanding your men. He was well into his lecture when the gardener started up the lawn mower.

As the mower passed by the open window, the lecturer's voice was drowned. He realised this and waited for the mower to get out of earshot before continuing. He resumed his lecture only to hear the lawnmower returning. The lecturer paused once again as the mower passed the classroom window.

This scenario was repeated several times and I could see that the lecturer was getting a little irate. The pupils could see the funny side and each time the mower passed and the lecturer paused, the class giggled. At last the poor teacher had had enough. He turned to the class and said:"Let me give you a practical demonstration on 'Getting results through people.' He leaned out of the window and hailed the gardener. The gardener drove the lawnmower to the open window. The class was in uproar when the lecturer then yelled: "P*SS OFF WITH THAT BLOODY LAWNMOWER!"

Stage 3

I was delighted when I was accepted to go forward to Stage 3. Back at the depot the boss, who had obviously been advised of my progress gave me a project to look into. It was to do with the flow of coal from Harworth colliery, in West Yorkshire, to Didcot Power Station in Oxfordshire.

I looked at the problem and, armed with the lessons learned at Crewe, I broke the job down into elements and brainstormed these one by one. The report was written and I have to say that there were no really new ideas forthcoming. The project however served its purpose. It showed that at least I had a grasp of the supervisory techniques taught at Crewe.

It was then back to Crewe for Stage 3. Also on this course was a lifelong friend of my school days. His name was John. He was a locomotive maintenance supervisor at the Depot. When we arrived at Crewe I was told that I had been nominated as the 'Student Principal'. On every course there was always a student elected to this position. His duty was to ensure that things ran smoothly in the evenings when the lecturers had gone home. The holder of this position had the rare privilege of having his own room.

When the rooms were allocated and John realised that we would not be together, he said to the receptionist: "We want to sleep together!" What he really meant was that because we were friends it would be nice if we could share a room. The receptionist eyed us with suspicion. She allocated us a room together – but with a third person! Normally there were two to a room. I was mightily embarrassed, to say the least.

It was during Stage 3 that I met one of the funniest men of my life. He had been a signalman 'somewhere down south'. He told me of one night in the signal box when he noticed that an approaching oil train had a derailed tanker a couple of wagons behind the locomotive. He could see that it would strike the signalbox as it passed and would probably demolish it. He rushed to the frame and slammed all the signals to danger. He then had no time to evacuate the box so he dived behind the lever frame for cover.

The offending vehicle struck the box, as predicted. There was an almighty crash as the front was torn away. When the dust had settled he climbed from behind the frame and looked around. The instrument shelf was leaning at a precarious angle. It was then that he thought about the signalbox cat! The mouser had a basket on the shelf and had been asleep prior to the incident. At that moment, the cat peered over the rim of the basket, pulled its ears back, yawned, stretched its front legs, turned around and lay down again to resume its sleep. It was used to the noise of trains thundering close by the box and the box shaking as they did so. She hadn't turned a hair. The puss was oblivious to the surrounding mayhem.

At the end of Stage 3 at Crewe I was told that I had achieved the standard necessary to progress to Stage 4 at Darlington. A few weeks later I found myself at 'Favourdale' which was the name of the railway college there. This course was more concentrated and much more difficult. Everyone had to study long and hard, late into the night. We had sat the examinations and the course was finished except for the closing interview with a high-ranking manager.

I was pleased when the chief instructor told us that we would attend for the final interview in reverse alphabetical order. My name being Woolley placed me in first position. I would be able to get it over quickly - and then relax a little.

Thankfully, the interview went without a hitch. It was some weeks later that the boss told me that I had passed with flying colours. I was given the certificate and the £25 reward that went with it.

I enrolled for the English Language course at the local night school and passed that also. The certificate from NEBSS is equal to City & Guilds. I used this to gain access to a course run by the IWM (Institution of Works Managers).

| Toton train sheet | | July 2 1979 |
Loco Class	Off depot	Train
47	0102	0153 Didcot.
45	0128	0200 Northfleet.
37	0217	0215 Sheffield.
47	0253	0344 Didcot.
47	0227	0315 Fletton.
37	0346	0428 Tinsley.
45	0419	0445 Northampton.
2x20	0422	0458 Corby
25	0438	0506 Bescot.
45	0444	0514 Hallin.
2x20	0453	0510 Clipstone.
45	0459	0530 Wellingborough.
47	0456	0549 Eastleigh.
47	0538	0609 Northampton.
45	0608	0636 Severn Tunnels.
1x20	0610	65 Tripper.
2x20	0641	0712 Whitemoor.
08	0642	Ratcliffe fly ash prep.
25	0624	0642 Kirkby Summit.
45	0654	0720 Ridham Dock.
2x20	0705	0736 Northampton.
45	0724	0800 Lloyds or Corby
1x20	0735	Ballast.
2x20	0803	0820 Rufford.
45	0805	68 Tripper.
45	0821	0849 Stoke.
47	0916	1007 Didcot.
56	0923	0940 Langley Mill.
2x20	1043	66 Tripper.
56	1100	1150 Fletton.
47	1050	1141 Didcot.
40	1118	1220 Teeside
25	1115	1145 Worthington.
2x20	1128	1145 Clipstone.
45	1144	1215 Lloyds.
2x20	1213	1300 Rufford.
45	1218	1250 Northfleet.
47	1224	1315 Didcot.
47	1310	1401 Didcot.
47	1408	1439 Whitemoor.
45	1430	1510 Fletton.
2x20	1510	1541 Lloyds.
45	1520	1551 Acton.
2x20	1639	1710 Lloyds.
2x20	1710	LD to Spondon for Tinsley.
47	1712	1744 Northfleet.
45	1738	1744 Ridham Dock.
08	1745	LD Ratcliffe for ash prep.
45	1941	2009 Severn Tunnels.
2x20	2002	2033 Northampton.
45	1913	1945 Northfleet.
45	2056	2128 Westbury. F.O.
2x20	2105	2136 Whitemoor.
45	2149	2221 Westbury. M.W.O.
47	2104	2155 Didcot.
2x20	2158	2230 York.
47	2146	2237 Didcot.
2x25	2210	2238 Walton Jct.
2x20	2244	2315 Northampton.
56	2318	0010 Fletton.
37	0003	0054 Margam.
45	0021	0048 68 Tripper.

From this, I went on to gain passes in Production Organisation and Economics. That period of my working life placed me in a sound position for the events which were to follow.

Traction Arranging

Toton Diesel Depot was, by this stage, massive. Although the building is still the same size today as in the 1960s, the work carried out there is only a fraction of what it was.

The Midland Main Line express passenger '45s' and '46s' were maintained there. Toton was the mainstay of the passenger business until the locomotives were withdrawn from service and replaced by the HSTs. The freight business at Toton was also thriving and its massive fleet of locomotives were maintained and stabled at Toton. The Traction Arranger's job was one of the most demanding posts at

the depot. There was a constant stream of locomotives arriving. All needed fuel, water and sand, for example.

There was a constant stream of departures. They had to be arranged in meticulous time order. In the accompanying table, I have listed the freight locomotive allocation sheets as it was in July 1979, to give an idea of the activity.

The depot required constant shunting to facilitate maintenance and operations. Every move had to be considered carefully but quickly. It was the busiest depot in Britain - possibly Europe.

The Traction Arranger worked very closely with the Maintenance Foreman and the Power Controller in Nottingham. Locomotives needing maintenance would be advised to the Traction Arranger prior to arrival. The passenger '45s' and '46s' always took priority. As I have said, they were the mainstay of the Midland passenger service prior to the introduction of the HSTs and so it was imperative that these were kept running and returned to service as soon as possible.

Every time a locomotive arrived (at times about one every five minutes) the Traction Arranger checked his maintenance list. If it was a locomotive for maintenance, he would decide, along with the Maintenance Foreman, how to deal with the locomotive in question. Toton is a depot which has mostly dead end roads. It would be easy to stable locomotives and block in another which was really needed first. It was like the game of chess.

One had to think before every move, otherwise the drivers on the fuel line who disposed of the locomotives would have to move them over and over again. The turntables of the steam days were sadly missed. It would have been easy if all the locomotives could have been backed off onto their individual roads. This of course would have been impossible because of the sheer size of the fleet maintained at Toton.

How did we know where all the locomotives were on the depot at any one time? Well, we devised a shed plan on an A4 sheet of paper. It was a schematic diagram which showed all roads on the depot both inside and outside of the Maintenance Depot. As the locomotives

Top: Class 31/1 No. 31298 heads north with a freight, past the site of Stapleford & Sandiacre station (closed on January 2 1967 and subsequently completely cleared) on June 7 1976. A Class 47 is in the background, near the signalbox. *Gavin Morrison.*

Above: A loaded MGR coal train from the Erewash Valley passes under the double carriageway A52 bridge and enters Toton yard on July 8 1976. *Gavin Morrison.*

arrived they were first written in pencil onto the fuel line in their correct order. The maintenance list was studied against the new arrivals. If they were maintenance locomotives we would confer with the Maintenance Foreman and decide where best to place them.

The Maintenance Foreman would estimate how long it would be before the locomotive was fit for work or would require moving for further maintenance. The Traction Arranger would use this as a guide for stabling the good locomotives. It was close co-operation that ensured that shunting was kept to a minimum.

If the locomotive was a good one (ready for further work) I would decide where she should be stabled. The plan then would be updated. The locomotive would be erased from the fuel line and shown in its new position on the shed plan. Departure times would be written above train locomotives and the Traction Arranger would check to make sure that they departed on time and would erase them from the plan as they did so. The plan therefore reflected the position of the depot real time.

I enjoyed the job immensely and was astounded when a staff reviewing committee decided that the job was under graded. As a result of their findings I was regraded to Grade C on the October 2 1972 (I had only been on the staff three months). The old steam title of Running Foreman was dropped and I became known officially as a Traction Arranger. This title had been used by us from the onset to differentiate between the two running foremen on shift.

CHAPTER 6
THE NEXT MOVE TO OPERATIONS

I was basking in the glory of my regrading together with the real wage that went with it when I learned a new phrase from the boss. I met him in the maintenance shed whilst he was on one of his morning walkabouts. "Hello John, how are things going? Are all the trains covered for power? Are there any moves outstanding for the maintenance section?". I was able to reply that everything was under control. "Good," he replied. "Now then John, I don't want you cresting. I think it's time for a change, come and see me at the end of your shift."

At 1400 I saw the boss in his office. "Boss" I said, "what do you mean by 'cresting'?". He replied: "Your railway career is much like a surfer. Whilst he's riding the wave, he's on top of the world but eventually the wave runs to nothing and he starts to sink." He added, "I don't want you to consider that the wave that you are riding at the moment is the biggest you will ever encounter. There are many more waves in the ocean and you should strive to ride the biggest you can find. You have ridden your particular wave now for two years. Don't let it run out or you will sink."

The boss went on to explain that I ought to consider a move into the Traffic Operations Department. I was told that such a move would broaden my knowledge of the job and increase my promotional prospects. There was a vacancy for an Operating General Purpose Supervisor at the same grade as my own. I was told to apply. I was appointed and took up the new position on April 1 1974.

For a man who has known little else but locomotives and locomotive men, the move into the traffic department was daunting to say the least and I had been appointed on April Fools day! I knew nothing about wagons, traffic, yard shunting or anything else about the operations. At the time, TOPS (Total Operations Processing System) was being introduced on the railways.

Above: An atmospheric night shot looking down into the sidings from the up hump, in 1951. The hump room is behind the photographer, the control tower is on the right, from where the operators would send rafts of wagons into one of the many sidings, to make trains up for onward despatch. The retarder enabled a highly-skilled control room operator to regulate the speed of 'cuts' of wagons to ensure that they neither collided too heavily with vehicles already stabled there, nor stopped short through too little momentum. *Roger Lymn.*

This computer controlled operating system was completely new to everyone. It dawned on me that because of its introduction I was on the same footing as the old hand operators. No one knew anything about it. I made up my mind there and then to learn the system quickly and thoroughly. This was going to be my lever to gain the respect from the new team of men under my command.

The first day's training in my new position was spent walking around the vast Toton Yard complex and meeting the men. They treated me with suspicion. Some would say outright "What does an ex footplateman know about train operating?"

I had to admit that they had a point but in my defence I would say something like "Well, I know very little yet but I do know an awful lot about locomotives and their men. I intend to try and unite these with the operating function and break down the old traditional barriers. As I see it, we need team spirit if we are to compete with ever-improving road transport"

Toton Yard

Toton Marshalling Yard was then the largest in Europe. There were 50 miles of track in the sidings and 100 roads. The main traffic was

coal from the numerous collieries in the Erewash Valley and beyond. The collieries in those days had many single wagon load customers. The colliery trip engines would bring trains of wagons into Toton, destined for many locations throughout the country. These would have to be sorted and made up into train loads for forwarding to the next point of distribution along the line.

For example, any traffic for the London area would be shunted into massive trains and sent to Cricklewood (Brent Sidings). At Cricklewood, the train would be reshunted and the wagons delivered to their final destination by the trip engines working at the London end. It was time consuming, slow and very labour intensive.

There was a constant stream of trains arriving from the collieries. These would be cut (uncoupled) into 'sorts' by the shunting staff and at the same time, the shunter would chalk on the wagon the number of the road in the sidings which corresponded to the final destination. There were 37 roads in the Up sidings (Loaded Side) and all of these would have an allocation.

For example, 20 was Stuarts & Lloyds works at Corby. 24 was London, 35 was Whitemoor in Lincolnshire. 8 was Derby. 3 was Stoke and so on. The shunting locomotives would then propel the uncoupled wagons towards a hump.

Top left: The down hump room, which sat on the very apex of the hump, and from which shunting locomotives slowly propelling rafts of wagons at very precise slow speeds, up the hump, could be controlled. Shunters 'on the ground' would uncouple groups ('cuts') of wagons as required and would chalk a number on the lead wagon, indicating which siding they should go into. As they rolled down the hump, the control tower would note the number and quickly select the siding for each cut, using the control panel. (see next page) *Colour Rail.*

Top right: The hump room control panel. *Keith Reedman Collection.*

Above: The down yard and control tower, from the hump. *Colour Rail.*

The panel operator (person in charge of shunting) would watch the wagons as they arrived on the hump and read the chalk mark. Wagon information would be sent by teleprinter to the hump control tower. Using this information, the wagons were gravity shunted into their allocated roads. The wagon's speed would be controlled by the use of hydraulic rail brakes called retarders. When there were sufficient wagons in a road, a brake van would be run behind to

Right: The down hump, looking past the hump room (left), control tower (right) and sidings beyond. The diesel shunter shows the lines via which trains for dividing and remarshalling were drawn, before being propelled up the hump.

Below right: The control room in the tower – on the left, the retarder panel, on the right, the panel to select sidings for 'cuts' of wagons. In the centre, the supervisor's desk.

Below: A close-up view of the retarder control panel, whose levers worked the hydraulic equipment which could 'squeeze' wagon wheels as they passed to slow them down as they rolled down the hump towards the sidings.

Lower, right: the panel controlling points leading to the many sidings, and the panoramic view from it. In the days when Toton handled one million wagons a year, these control rooms would be very busy. *All: Keith Reedman Collection.*

complete the train. At its peak, no fewer than 4,000 wagons were shunted over the hump in 24 hours – that's an average of over 160 wagons an hour! If the massive yards were not to be overwhelmed, the same number of wagons had to leave in newly formed trains. A similar situation existed in Toton Down Sidings (Empty Side) where the returning empty wagons would be sorted for dispatching back to the collieries. Toton was a very busy place. In those days Britain would have closed if Toton had stopped work!

Shunting Derailments.

The process of 'Gravity Shunting' whereby wagons (either individually, or in 'rafts') run free down a gradient was a very skilful activity. There was always an element of risk involved. A slight misjudgement by any of the staff employed could - and often did - result in a mishap.

Although these accidents were very rarely threatening to the safety of the shunting staff, some of the derailments were spectacular and the damage to the infrastructure had to be seen to be believed. The Health & Safety Works Inspectors of today would have condemned the operations outright. There were many things that could go wrong. I will relate here just a few of the common causes of the chaos I have witnessed.

Most of the trains arriving for shunting had a vacuum-braked fitted portion at the front of the train. This 'fitted head' of continuous brakes gave the driver of the engine extra brake power and control. The additional brake power also allowed more tonnage to be conveyed on the train than if he had only the brake power of the locomotive available. Behind the 'fitted head' of the train would be

Left: Judging by the number of suits and gaberdine 'macs', this was some kind of officers' visit to Toton. Operation of the retarders on the down side of the hump is explained. The operator using the control room panel shown opposite could 'squeeze' the wheels of passing wagons using the long, moveable horizonal I-beams clearly shown in the 'four foot', to control their speed. This is the down yard retarder. *Colour Rail.*

Below: Two views of an accident south of Toton yards in 1962. BR Riddles '9F' 2-10-0 No. 92100, with a train of iron ore, passed a signal at danger descending 'the Lickey' to Toton Junction and collided with a train departing from the West Yard to the Low Level Goods (see trackplan, page 141). The view on the right shows No. 92100 minus its left hand smoke deflector. The 2-10-0 has been rerailed and shunted clear. The breakdown train is standing on the Up High Level Goods Line and a rerailed wagon has been shunted clear on the Up Low Level Goods. The signal is the one passed at danger by the '9F'. The picture on the left shows the breakdown crew hard at work clearing up the mess at the point of impact. Both pictures were taken from Toton Junction box. *Signalman Peter Salmon.*

the loose coupled, hand-braked wagons with no continuous brake.

The train locomotive would be uncoupled. This would apply the brakes on the fitted portion. The shunter would pull the brake release on the vehicles and uncouple the wagons ready for shunting. The vacuum brake on a wagon relies on the atmospheric pressure of approximately 15psi (pounds per square inch) to apply the brake. This is achieved by the locomotive creating a vacuum the equivalent of 21 inches of mercury by extracting the air from the brake pipes and cylinders of the vehicles. This releases the brakes. The brakes on the vehicles are then applied when the driver allows air to enter the system, through his brake valve. This partially (and ultimately completely) destroys the vacuum on only one side of a cylinder which contains a floating piston.

The atmospheric pressure acting on only one side of the floating piston and against the vacuum on the other side applies the brakes. Once the train locomotive is uncoupled, the brakes on the fitted vehicles would be 'hard on'. One side of the floating piston would be open to atmosphere whilst on the other a vacuum remained. It was necessary to then move the vehicle to destroy the vacuum left by the train locomotive on the opposite side of the brake cylinder. This would equalise the atmospheric pressure and release the brake, allowing the wheels to turn once again.

Often, the shunter would pull the brake release and listen to the air as it entered the system. When the hissing had ceased and the brake blocks appeared to be free of the wheels, he would repeat the duties on all the vehicles in the fitted portion.

Occasionally, he would not totally destroy the vacuum and therefore he did not release the brake properly. The brakes would be left slightly applied. Then the shunting engine would start to push the wagons up towards the summit of the hump so they could roll down the other side - but the driver of the locomotive would not notice the additional resistance. He would assume that the weight of the train was responsible. The wagons would pass the summit of the hump, gravity would take over and they would start to free wheel down the sharp incline to their allotted sidings.

Now, because the brakes were only partially released and the

gradient became less severe towards the 'retarders' (manually controlled hydraulic rail brakes), they would come to a stand at the bottom of the hump instead of running over the retarders and into their siding – in other words, out of harms way. The retarder operators could mechanically stop a following shunt. However, if the busy panel operator did not notice that the vehicles were slowing and that they would stop short of the retarders, he would fail to place the shunting signals at danger.

The next shunt would therefore follow and the next cut of wagons would come over the hump and start freewheeling towards the obstruction. All that the shunting staff could do now - apart from applying the hand brakes on the wagon which rarely had any significant effect - was to look on powerless as the impact approached.

An almighty collision would occur at the bottom of the hump. The wagons would attempt to mount one another and they would skew across the track. The permanent way would be damaged. There would be tonnes of coal strewn across the railway. Delays to operations would be inevitable. Reports and explanations would be demanded. Steam cranes and hydraulic lifting equipment would be called for together with the staff to operate them. The buck stopped on my desk. It was a scenario that was repeated almost weekly.

Occasionally, the shunting would be going as smooth as silk when the retarder operator would call over the Tannoy system: "OFF THE ROAD" I would look down the hump to see wagons sprawled across the track. The shunting signals would be placed at danger and I would make my way to the site to investigate. Obviously there was always a cause. Sometimes however, the cause was not at first apparent.

I remember one such incident when the wagons were 'On Merry England.' The wagons had attempted to negotiate two roads at once. In railway terminology it's called 'splitting the points.' The previous shunt had been slowed sharply on the retarders and the coal had moved in the wagon. A piece of coal had fallen from a wagon and dropped into a set of points. When the points were reversed for the following shunt, the coal 'held them off' stopping them from changing

Top: The intensely busy Toton operation which John Woolley inherited had changed only in scale and modernity over the years. Top: LMS Fowler 0-8-0 No. 9531 passes Toton South with an up coal train comprised of various sizes of wooden-bodied wagon, all loaded with very good quality coal in large lumps. There is a single tank wagon, eight vehicles behind the tender. *R.J. Essery Collection.*

Above: Class 37 37016 also heads an up train of empty ballast wagons, bound for Loughborough, at Toton South. In the background of both pictures is the Carriage & Wagon workshop and both pictures seem to have been taken from a footbridge known locally as 'Long Tom's bridge' over the railway. *John Chalcraft/©www.railphotoprints.co.uk Collection.*

properly and leaving them set for nowhere in particular. It was as easy as that. More cranes, more reports....

Then there would be those occasions when the Retarder Operator would misjudge the speed of a wagon. The result would be that it (or them) would enter the road at too great a speed. There would be an almighty dull thump as the vehicles met violently and one could judge by the sound that the wagons had become buffer locked. This piece of railway terminology means exactly what it says. The wagon would jump on impact and the buffers would climb over its neighbours buffers and lock. They could not then be conventionally separated. More lifting gear. More reports.

Some simple derailments involving just one wagon would be dealt with there and then by yours truly. We had special steel ramps that we would place under the offending wheels. The shunting engine would be attached and the wagon would be drawn up the ramp and it would drop back onto the track. This did not obviate the need for reports however. The track had to be examined by the platelayers and the wagon had to be examined by the Carriage & Wagon maintenance personnel; both were costly and required formal explanation.

I became quite adept at rerailing wagons and soon gained respect amongst the older operators. I knew that I had won them over when they started to ask me for advice. In general, taking into account the thousands of wagons which were shunted over the humps weekly, I think we did pretty well to get away with just a few derailments. Management obviously did not take this view and in their true railway tradition any derailment was unacceptable and avoidable.

I would gamble however, that had they taken my desk over for a month, things would not have improved one iota.

Main line derailments.

I was often called upon to cover for the Movements Inspector. His job was varied and very interesting. His duties included:
- Visiting signal boxes to ensure that the place was safe and clean and examining the signalmen on their rules and regulations.
- Examining yard staff and guards on their rules.
- Planning engineering operations alongside the engineers.
- Studying weekend diversions to ensure that all the signal boxes in his area were manned at the proper time.

Above: A busy 1980s scene in the up yard at Toton, with the MPD yard in the distance, marked by the line of stabled Class 20s. In the yard two Class 58s and a Class 56 owned by the Coal sector are going about their business with merry-go-round coal trains in HAA hoppers. Note the large number of red-bodied house coal wagons. The breakdown train stands ready for the next derailment. *John Woolley.*

● Investigating mishaps and identifying the causes and recommending action to avoid repetition.
● Taking charge of engineering operations at the weekend to ensure that a safe method of work was always employed.
● Examining large loads to ensure that they were safe to travel over the route to their destination.

This would often involve issuing a certificate called BR29973. This would inform the drivers, guards and signalmen along the route of the restrictions placed on the load. The restrictions on the form would show the route the load had to travel over, speed restrictions over various points and crossings and any other detail to ensure that the load was handled safely.

The Movements Inspector would be 'On Call' every other week when not on duty. When he was at home and on call he could not leave the house without informing the control how he could be contacted. This was in the days before the mobile phone. In effect, the Movements Inspector was at work 24hrs a day, 7 days a week, every other week.

Coal train at Bennerley

I was in bed one early morning in 1977. The telephone was ringing. At that time in the morning it was obvious who the caller was. I picked up the phone. "Hello, John Woolley here".

"Hey John, we've got a right pile up at Bennerley. The on call manager has asked me to give you a ring. Can you attend please?" I was soon in the car and at the site of the derailment.

The sight I found was spectacular. The track from Shipley Gate to Bennerley is on a falling gradient and after the canal bridge there is a right hand curve and a steep embankment. The cows grazing in the field at the bottom of the bank that morning must have had quite a shock. A train of coal bound for Toton running on the Up Goods Line had come to grief on the curve.

The locomotive and about half the train had successfully negotiated the curve when the driver felt a sharp pull on his drawbar. He looked back in horror. The rear half of the train had become derailed. The train must have been travelling at about 30mph. The couplings had snapped and the rearmost 20 wagons or so had ploughed down the bank and into the field. Fortunately, the train was fully braked and didn't have a brake van at the rear. There were no human casualties, the guard was in the rear cab of the locomotive - lucky chap!

At this location there are four lines of way (Up and Down Goods and Up and Down Mains). Thankfully, the only track affected was the Up Goods. There would be no delay to traffic. Freight would be run via the Up Main. Diversion arrangements were not necessary and we could get on with the clearing up exercise and the investigation

into the cause. The front half of the train and the locomotive was disposed of into Bennerley Open Cast Sidings. The driver was interviewed by the Traction Inspector. The driver had not been speeding and stated that he had done nothing out of the ordinary. The Permanent Way Inspector examined his track and although severely damaged by the derailment, could find nothing to account for the mishap in the first instant.

In his defence and to justify his statement, he remarked that the front portion of the train had passed the point of derailment without incident. The Carriage and Wagon Supervisor examined the offending vehicles and although these also were severely damaged he passed them as fit for the road at the time of derailment.

The incident was baffling. In such cases, when a derailment's cause cannot be identified, the Chief Mechanical Engineer's Scientists are called in to see if they can solve the case. Obviously a cause must be found, otherwise, how can we justifiably state that the railways are safe? The driver was re-questioned and the track was re-examined. It was noted that the track's camber on the curve was slightly less than might be expected but was not a danger in itself. The driver went through his actions at the time of the derailment and said that he was braking for a caution signal at Bennerley when the signal turned to green. He released his brakes and applied power. He mentioned that he did feel a slight pull as the couplings tightened just before the derailment.

The slight pull that the driver mentioned would have been quite severe on the wagons which had become derailed. It would be even more so if the driver had not allowed sufficient time to completely release the brakes on the wagons before applying power. The cause had been determined. There had been a snatch on the curve - technically known as a 'traction shock'. It had already been established that the track's profile was less than perfect. These two factors in combination were sufficient to cause the wagons to jump the track - with the resulting mayhem.

We spent a couple of days retrieving the wagons from the field. The fact that the farmer's cattle had gone off milking was appeased by the gift of several tonnes of bright house coal almost delivered to his back door! All he had to do was pick it up.

Sandiacre

It was the Friday before my annual leave. I had signed on at 0800 and was expecting to finish by lunch time having booked half a day's leave to travel to Cornwall. As is generally the case when you really need things to go smoothly, the telephone rang. "John, can you go to Sandiacre? There is a train derailed across the main line crossover blocking all lines on the Erewash".

The boss was in the office at the time and of course I told him that we had an emergency. The site of the derailment was very near Toton Diesel Depot where the breakdown crane and vans are kept and very near to my office. All the other personnel who would have an interest were also very close to the site.

The boss and I arrived on site a few minutes later. Already there were representatives from other interested parties arriving. My first job was to ensure that all the lines that were affected were protected from further mishap. I placed detonators and flags at all the necessary points and arranged diversions of traffic.

Wagons were strewn all over the railway. A train had been leaving the Meadow sidings and was to cross the Number 2 Down Goods, the Up and Down Mains to Number 1 Down Goods and depart Toton to the north. It was a real mess. Wagons were on their sides. Some of them had mounted their neighbours. The track and points were severely damaged. Cornwall would have to wait.

What on earth had caused this one? The signalman had left his levers just as he had set them. He had done nothing wrong. He was in the clear. The wagons were examined. No broken axles or defects prior to the derailment. The Permanent Way Supervisor and I carefully examined the track at the point where, at first, we thought the derailment had occurred. Apart from a mark where the first derailed wagon had struck the crossover, there was nothing evident which could have caused the mishap

Above: Class 56 No. 56053 passes the very primitive Bennerley Opencast loading point with a southbound merry-go-round train on May 17 1979. *John Chalcraft/©www.railphotoprints.co.uk Collection.*

At first, we were completely baffled. My mind switched to the Bennerley incident. I asked the Traction Inspector to go through every move with the driver. The driver had said that as he left the Meadow sidings and had just passed the Diesel Depot building where he was in a position to sight the signal at Sandiacre, he spotted the signal which was in the clear position and applied power. Everything was normal until he started to cross the main lines. He had felt an unusual tug and looking back at the train, he noticed that the wagons were derailed.

Above: It's June 7 1976 and a pair of English Electric Class 20s pass the site of the former Stapleford & Sandiacre station (closed January 2 1967) with a northbound ballast train heading for the Erewash Valley. The bridge beyond the train is the dual carriageway A52 and the depot is on the other side, to the right. On the left of the flat-roofed Stapleford & Sandiacre signalbox can be seen the reception sidings for the up yard. Compare this picture with those on pages 20 and 21. *Gavin Morrison.*

Above: A lovely view which perfectly captures the beautiful rural appeal of Manton Junction, south of Oakham, where the Peterborough and Corby lines diverge. The Corby line heads off to the right, with the mighty Harringworth viaduct not far away. Brush Type 2 (Class 31) No. 31 218 is coming off the line from Stamford and Peterborough with a loaded cement train from Ketton on August 16 1983. It will shortly head into Manton Tunnel, en route to Oakham, Melton Mowbray and Leicester. *John Chalcraft/©www.railphotoprints.co.uk Collection.*

So, perhaps the derailment did not occur on the crossover at all? I kept the thought to myself and shifted my attention to the point when the driver first came into sight of the signal at Sandiacre. I measured his train from the locomotive and up to the first wagon which had become derailed.

Armed with this information I started to walk the plain track back into the Meadow sidings. There were a few shiny marks on the inside of the rail chairs. These were obviously fresh and indicated to me that the wheel flanges of a wagon had been running derailed. So he had not become derailed on the crossover. He had been derailed sometime before the pile up. I arrived at the point where the driver could first see the signal at Sandiacre.

I added on the length of the train that had remained on the rails and walked back further. Sure enough, at almost the exact point of my calculation, there were signs of derailment. Also at the site I noticed that the track chairs and fishplates were loose and there was a slight dip in the track. I would hasten to add that sidings track is not so meticulously maintained as would be the main line carrying our most valuable commodity, the passenger, but it still has to be kept well within safety standards.

The driver had applied too much power as he sighted his clear signal and created a traction shock throughout the train. This and the track defect in the siding – once again, in combination - had caused the wagon to jump the rail. The driver would not have noticed this because the train was running on straight track. The wagon would just happily bounce along, derailed, on the rail chairs.

In all probability only one pair of wheels would have been derailed at that point. Certainly the slight marks in the track gave that indication. The tight couplings of the accelerating train would have kept the wagon from derailing further and kept it running in a straight line.

Nothing would be felt on the locomotive at this stage. It was not until the offending wagon reached the points at Sandiacre that anything unusual would be noticed. As the vehicle arrived at the crossover the derailed wheels would strike the rail and leap into the air. The rest of the train following would then derail and start slewing across the track. The jack knifing of the wagons would be amplified by the driver, as he applied the brakes very strongly, in his justifiable haste to stop the train. The derailed wagons then ran into the slowing vehicles in front of them, slewing them off the track too and adding to the chaos.

I was home and dry. I called all the other parties to the scene and explained my findings as to what I believed had happened. The Permanent Way Supervisor accepted that the track was not 100% at that location. The driver admitted that he had perhaps applied

his power with too much gusto. It was 50/50. The railway was a safe place to be once more.

The derailment was cleared by about 1800 that evening. The Rerailing Gang and Permanent Way Supervisor did a tremendous job. I departed for Cornwall late but happy in the knowledge that the paper work and the incident had been brought to a satisfactory conclusion.

The long night

I had been working as Movements Inspector one week in August during the long hot summer of 1976. It was Friday evening. I was looking forward to a long weekend with my family. My boss at that time was a super guy called Alan.

After my evening meal, I was planning a trip to the local pub for a few beers with the lads, an early return, an early night then up on Saturday and out with my wife and daughters, Helen and Sarah. The beer was going down well when the landlord answered the ringing telephone. "It's for you John, sounds like your wife".

"Hello sweetheart, what's the matter?" I asked. "Alan has just rang me, he wants you to ring him back as soon as possible". she replied. "OK love I will do it now, thanks for ringing me, see you later".

Alan explained that he was in trouble for an Inspector to take charge of a large engineering job at Manton on Saturday night. He told me that the Leicester Inspector who had been allocated to the job had suddenly been taken ill and passed away. He went on to explain that although he realised that the job was outside my area, I was the only Inspector available who intimately knew the road, having previously signed over the route as a driver. The job was a big one involving several trains loaded with track and cranes and other equipment.

I explained to Alan that I had already had a couple of pints and should not go back to work until Saturday morning to obtain the engineering notices and make a plan of the work, but that I would of course take on the job and that he should consider it done. I rang my wife and told her that I would have to go to work on Saturday morning and again that night. As usual, she took it in her stride and didn't complain at all about missing out yet again.

Arriving at my office on Saturday morning I studied the engineering notice. It soon became apparent that the job I was to take charge of was indeed a very big one. There were seven engineering trains involved. I was to take possession of the line from Manton Junction to Harringworth at 2000 Saturday night. The job involved taking up the Up Main, digging out the ballast trackbed, relaying new track and replacing the ballast with new. The track was to be reopened by 2200 Sunday night.

Some of the trains would come into my section of line from the Harringworth Viaduct end (Down direction) and some would come from the Manton end (Up direction). I drew up a track diagram and worked out the ballast train movements which would be necessary to complete the work. It was most important to arrange things in the right order if there was to be no delay to operations. With the plans worked out and drawn up, I left my office three hours later armed with the necessary information. From my home I would need at least two hours to drive to Manton, make myself known and take possession of the track. I said goodnight to my wife at 1800 and set off on the 40 mile drive.

Manton Signal Box is on the south side of Manton Tunnel. It is a typical Midland style signalbox. The setting is a railway photographer's dream - or at least it was, until modern portacabins were erected adjacent to the box. The box sits on the junction for Peterborough or Corby. Manton Tunnel mouth dominates the scene and the box nestles in a deep cutting. I arrived there at about 1915. The signalman did not know me but had been advised by Nottingham Control that a Toton Inspector by the name of Mr. Woolley would take possession of the Up and Down Main Lines between Manton and Harringworth that night.

I signed his train register at 2000 exactly "Total possession of the Up and Down Main lines between Manton and Harringworth taken by Inspector J. Woolley at 2000." The signalman countersigned my entry to indicate that he knew the track state exactly. The track was now mine and not his. Any movement between these points would have to be sanctioned by me. I informed the signalman at Harringworth by telephone. He would make the entry, on my behalf, in his register.

> "I rang my wife Caryl and told her that I would have to go to work on Saturday morning and again that night. As usual, she took it in her stride and didn't complain at all about missing out yet again"

There was already a train waiting in the sidings at Manton and also a track laying machine. The train was placed onto the Up Main and run to a point just short of the section of track which was to be removed, which was at the mouth of (and into) the north end of the tunnel at Glaston. The machine was placed on the Down Main and instructed to run in the wrong direction to Wing. His task was to lift the track from the Up and load it onto the train standing on the Up short of the worksite.

From Wing towards the tunnel at Glaston the track falls away sharply. It was important that the movement of the tracklayer was restricted so that should it become overloaded or the brakes fail, it could not run away through the tunnel and onto the viaduct at Harringworth, perhaps meeting an oncoming ballast train in the process. I instructed the tracklayer driver to stop short of the severe gradient and await further instruction from me.

On the south side of Glaston Tunnel on the Down, there is (or was) a set of catch points which are there to derail any vehicle running away in the wrong direction. I would have to clip and lock these points so that there was no chance of a derailment. I would be using the track in both directions.

The catch points at Glaston are at a very remote location and difficult to approach unless one walks through the tunnel which is a mile long or more. I didn't fancy the long walk through the tunnel and back so I decided to take the car and park on the main road which runs over the tunnel and walk across the fields.

From where I had parked the car, I could see the track snaking away to the south. I was still about half a mile away from the railway and well elevated. I started to walk across the field and down to the tunnel mouth. The temperature was still very hot. It was a lovely evening and I thought how nice it would have been to be with my wife and daughters outside a country pub. As I approached the tunnel there was a fence to stop animals (or people) from falling onto the track from the tunnel top. The fence was placed well back from the tunnel mouth and through the years a small wood had grown on the railway side. I climbed over the fence and picked my way through the wood. I was thinking about nothing in particular when I was frightened out of my skin! "Hello there". A voice

hailed: "What are you doing in here tonight?" I composed myself "Good Lord! You frightened me to death! I might ask you the same question?"

The man smiled. I could see that he had some sort of electrical equipment set up on the ground. There was a black box, I assumed later to be a tape recorder, a bank of batteries and a dish pointing towards the sky.

"What are you looking for, UFOs?" I asked. "No, there is an owl's nest in that tree over there and she has about four young. I am recording the night noises as she feeds them". Well, it takes all sorts to make a world I thought. "Is your equipment sensitive enough to pick that up from this distance?" I asked. "More than good enough" he replied.

I had to tell him that there would be bulldozers coming through the tunnel at intervals during the night and that he would have a better chance of making his recording at Heathrow! He looked at me in disgust: "I've come all the way from Stamford tonight especially to make this recording. I picked Saturday night because I thought it would be quiet" he exclaimed.

"Well, my friend, if I were you, I would go home to bed." I left the poor man packing up his equipment.

I have often thought about this encounter and have since wondered whether he was in fact who he said he was. There is a Royal Air Force base at Luffenham and another at Cottesmore just a couple of miles away and it was in the days of the cold war. And further more, I didn't notice his means of transport. Was he concealing it? A bit of a mystery.

I found the points, secured and locked them. My watch said 2100. I was running to time. Actual work was to start at 2200. I made my way back to the car and drove to Harringworth, where a train was waiting to come into my possession, to the site of work. I instructed the crew, assured them that the catch points at Glaston were clipped and locked, sent them on their way to the site and then returned to Manton.

The first part of the job was 'set up' and the work started on time at 2200. I explained to the Tracklayer Driver that there was a train just inside the tunnel which would prevent him from running away and that he could start work. He was happy with the arrangement. It was time for coffee.

Whilst I had been away the platelayers had removed the fishplates and bolts from the track to be lifted. The tracklayer lifted the track in sections and loaded this onto the empty train standing on the Up. In came the bulldozers and diggers from Wing.

The ballast was loaded into the train which I had allowed in from Harringworth and had acted as a dead end for the tracklayer. This departed to the north fully loaded with the spent ballast at about 01.00 hrs. The tracklayer shunted into the sidings at Manton to allow its passage. Another empty train came in from the south and the loading of the ballast continued.

The train, which had been loaded with the old track, was propelled back to Manton. Standing at Manton on the Up was the train of new track from the north. The locomotive was uncoupled and attached to the rear end of the train of old track. This train of old track then departed north, leaving the original locomotive standing at Manton. The locomotive which had brought the old track was attached to the train of new and I conducted this back to the site of work.

I will not go into any more detail about the movements of ballast trains during engineering but the reader should now see that the guy in charge must have his wits about him. He must have a clear understanding of what is required in order to avoid delay, confusion and especially accidents. Hence the planning in my office on Saturday morning.

When an engineering job is set up and all the trains are in their correct position, the actual work is directed by the Permanent Way Supervisor. The Movements Inspector will have satisfied himself that all the safety rules have been applied, that all the trains are where they should be and that everyone understands exactly what is taking place – he can then relax a little.

The Permanent Way Supervisor and I had a little discussion. We were both happy with the position. I advised him that I was going to sit in my car and watch the proceedings whilst eating my sandwiches. The time was about 0300. I was dead tired and grabbed '40 winks.'

It was 0340 when the PW Supervisor knocked on my window. I was told that I had to ring the control at Nottingham. I couldn't for the life of me think of any reason for this as I made my way to Manton signalbox. The signalman put me through to Control. "Hello John, I am afraid I have some bad news for you." said the voice at the other end: "The Inspector who was to relieve you at 0600 hrs has gone sick and there is no replacement."

I knew that this man would have worked until 1400 when he would be further relieved by the Inspector who would finish the job at 2200 hrs Sunday night. I asked the Control to wait until about 0800 then ring the afternoon Inspector and ask him to come at 1000 for the final 12 hours work. The Control did as I had requested and I was pleased to see my relief walking along the track at 0950. I handed over to him, explaining the situation with the trains. I gave him my track plan of trains on site and signed off duty in the signalman's log. I don't know how I kept my eyes open on the drive back home.

I had worked on Saturday morning from 0800 to 1100 to plan the job, snatched four hours sleep in the afternoon, departed for work at 1800 on Saturday night and arrived home at 1130 on Sunday morning. A total of 20.5 hours at work in the previous 27.5. That was the end of the long weekend that I had been promising my wife. It's a miracle that I'm still married!

There were many occasions like this one and some were worse than others. I can remember being half frozen to death one night in a blizzard at Ambergate in the Peak District with no shelter at all, except a chipping bunker and a signal post to stand behind. My overcoat was frozen solid. At home I had been in the bath a good hour before I thawed through.

There was also the time at Avenue on the Erewash Valley line when the weather closed in and froze the ground so solidly that the Engineers could not complete the job. In that instance, the Main Line was kept closed until half way through the following week. Working as a PICOP (Person In Charge Of Possession) was and still is a hard way to make a living.

General Purpose Grade 'E'

On the June 19 1978, I was told that as a result of an independent enquiry I was to be upgraded to Grade E. This is the most senior supervisory grade possible on the BR network. If I was to be promoted further, the next stage would have to be into the management grades.

It's a strange arrangement on the railways because the first step into management means a tremendous drop in your earnings. It's promotion in name only. A supervisor would work overtime at the weekends and would be justly rewarded for the inconvenience. A manager on the other hand would have to work for the glory only. It's not surprising that many senior supervisors were reluctant to make the 'crossing' between grades from supervisor to management.

I have to say that I was one of those supervisors who dreaded the move. I was therefore a grade 'E' supervisor until 1993 when I was finally persuaded to make the change. During the period between 1978 and 1993 I had done pretty well. I was able to take a couple of foreign holidays each year, have a new car every two years and generally live a full and active life. Money was the last thing I was bothered about. I worked hard and lived hard.

Senior Managers, however, would constantly badger me to join them. Some were even envious of my life style. One in particular, on seeing my latest car openly commented: "You are earning too much!" I retaliated by telling him "No that's not true. It's the other way round - you are not earning enough. Anyway, where were you last Saturday night? I certainly remember where I was, and it wasn't out with my wife!" This particular manager would say: "Ah, but my pension will be greater than yours." I could honestly tell him: "I can afford to make my own arrangements, I will not need a bigger pension when my investments mature."

The reason why I mention all this is to indicate to the reader just how silly the management structure was, explain the reason for my reluctance to join the management grades, and why I was a top grade supervisor for 15 years. Would YOU commit financial suicide? This also meant of course that the railway was denied some potentially great managers because they would not entertain the pay cut required to make the jump.

As a senior General Purpose Supervisor, my duties were wide and varied. One week I would be working as a Movements Inspector, the next week I would be a Yard Supervisor or a Trip Supervisor. I may even be working as the Area Freight Assistant in charge of all of Toton yard. It was a very busy position indeed. It called for a vast and wide knowledge of the job. Other than those lovely days of steam, they were the best years of my working life.

Below: Standing in for a failed HST IC125, swallow-liveried Class 47/8 No. 47833 passes Hathern, north of Loughborough, with an up express for St Pancras on February 2 1992. John Woolley was called out to take charge here after the driver of an express reported hitting a person on the tracks. *Gavin Morrison.*

Fatality

It was an August Monday in the 1970s. I will not mention the exact date or the name of the young lad involved. I was on call and at home, enjoying my day off. The telephone rang.

"Trent Power Box here, can you get out to Hathern, John? The driver of the Master Cutler (express from London to Sheffield) has reported hitting someone at Loughborough."

I arrived at Hathern and the express stood at the signal on the Down Main. The driver was from Sheffield and I knew him by sight, from my footplate days. "Hello driver, are you all right? What's happened?" He told me that as he passed Loughborough at 90mph, he noticed a small boy standing in the track, with his back to him. He sounded his warning horn and applied the emergency brake at the same time. The young boy did not turn. The noise of the approaching train and the warning horn was drowned by another express passing the young lad on the Up Main at the same moment. The driver told me that the young fellow was struck in the back at a speed of about 75mph. He couldn't have felt a thing.

I asked the driver if his locomotive had been damaged and he was able to tell me that he had looked at the front and apart from the obvious marks the locomotive was untouched. I knew that the driver must have been in shock and I doubted whether he could continue on his journey. Although he insisted that he felt fine, I walked through the train to see if there were any off duty drivers on board who could take the train forward. I obviously had to consider the delay to the hundreds of passengers on this prestigious service.

I was unable to find a driver but I did find a Senior Conductor who volunteered to ride to Derby. After arranging for the train to be taken out of service at Derby, and I knew that the driver would be met and accompanied home, I allowed the train to continue.

That walk from Hathern to Loughborough is one which I will never forget. I will leave you to work out why.

I arrived at the site of impact to find police and ambulance men wandering all over the track. I was furious! I found the most senior officer in charge and told him to clear the lines of all personnel until I could stop all trains. I had visions of an even worse disaster.

When I had received assurances from the Power Signal Box at Trent that the line was clear, the Doctor, Ambulancemen, Police and I examined - and cleared - the track. It was not a pleasant task.

The inquest was at Loughborough and I attended with the driver. The Coroner questioned me in detail and recorded an accidental death verdict. The driver and I left the court. We had finished work for the day so I asked him to join me for a quick pint. Passing him a pint of Bass, I said: " Well John, it's all over now, try to forget it".

He replied: "I must be the unluckiest driver on BR. The very next week after killing that poor boy, I caught a platelayer off guard coming out of Sheffield station. The inquest for that is next week."

Mick

It was in 1983 that I first met Mick. He had left the armed forces in 1977 and had started shunting at Toton. Although I had seen Mick carrying out his duties, he pretty well kept his nose clean and I had no need to really get to know him. Mick had applied for a position of goods guard. I was to be the Inspector who would re-examine him on his rules and regulations. My boss had told me that another Inspector had failed Mick. The boss asked me to take him under my wing and try to coach him and bring him up to scratch. The other Inspector told me of his shortcomings and, to be honest, there were plenty.

I met Mick on the Monday morning and took him into Toton Yard. I started by going through the procedure of examining the train and working out the brake force and total tonnage for a particular route. In railway terminology it is called 'train preparation.' I must admit that the other Inspector was right. Mick was pretty hopeless. I decided that the place to spend the rest of the week would be in the classroom. On reflection, Mick was fortunate that the boss had decided on one-to-one coaching.

The week went well and Mick seemed to be getting the message. I couldn't help but like the man, even when he frequently went off at a tangent and required bringing back 'on line.' He had heard that I kept ferrets and used them for catching rabbits. He too kept ferrets and asked if I would allow him to accompany me on my outings. I replied that he ought to forget rabbits, at least until he had secured his job.

Out in the sidings again, I found Mick much improved but still lacking in some respects. I decided that I would take him out on a colliery trip and ask the guard in charge to stand down and allow Mick to perform all of the necessary duties. The train we chose was one to Bennerley's open cast mine.

Mick had assessed the train, coupled up, and carried out the rest of the procedures correctly. He completed the necessary paper work for the driver and informed the yard foreman that we were ready to depart. We were away. The job went smoothly to Bennerley and

I was quite impressed with his performance. We had delivered the 'empties' and were now on the loaded train for Toton. When an empty train is exchanged at a colliery for a loaded train this is called 'slip working'. 'Merry-go-round' working is where an empty train is loaded and unloaded without detaching from the locomotive. It was getting dark and I asked Mick to light his tail lamps.

Mick brought the lamps inside the brake van, removed the paraffin holders and lit a match. The lamps refused to light. He removed the wick holder and peered into the vessel. It was empty. No paraffin. The rest of the lamps were also dry. He could not look me in the face. He had forgotten to fill them at Toton. He was horrified at what I might say. My reaction must have taken him by surprise. I calmly asked him to place his electric hand lamp on the brakevan bracket so as to display a red light in the rear. Although this class of train required three lamps I knew that there were no signal boxes between us and Toton who could spot the shortcoming.

Mick asked me what he should say to the signalman at the Trent Power Signalbox should anyone advise him that a train was running without the regulation lights in the rear. I told him to say that the lamps were full of black oil (a lubricant used for steam engine pistons). Of course Mick had never heard of the stuff. This was an excuse often used by the old steam men when they had either run their lamps dry or had forgotten to fill them and black oil fitted the absence of a light to a tee! In the days of steam a fresh supply of paraffin could always be obtained from the nearest signalbox but alas, these are now very rare outposts.

The journey back to Toton was uneventful and I decided to overlook this small (but serious) error on Mick's part. After a few more days in the classroom, Mick was just about good enough to take charge on his own. I warned him that I would be responsible for his performance for the next few months and that should he let me down I would be down on him like a ton of bricks. I duly signed his pass certificate and let him loose.

I spoke to my boss about him and assured him that although Mick did not appear to respond quickly to tuition, he was nobody's fool and, with some practical experience under his belt, would soon become a good man. I watched Mick's progress through the years and I was right - he never put a foot wrong. Furthermore, he was always immaculately turned out at work and eventually he was spotted by a new boss. Mick was promoted to Safety Officer, took numerous national examinations and passed them all. He became a very competent lecturer in all aspects of safety. He was further promoted to Traincrews Supervisor in charge of Toton and Leicester. We became the very best of friends and yes, we have caught hundreds of rabbits together, with our ferrets.

Speedlink

It was in the early 1970s that Toton went through radical changes. British Rail had decided to abandon single wagon load traffic to concentrate on 'block trains' (traffic for one destination, from supplier to customer – steel, oil or aggregates, for example). Single wagon load customers had, in any case, been declining for a number of years. This was mainly brought about by changes in industry, the building of motorways, the growth of reliable road haulage, the exploitation of natural gas and the Clean Air Act.

Gone were the days when trains loaded with house coal formed a continuous stream from Toton to London just to keep domestic fires burning in the Home Counties. The great London smogs of the 1950s were caused partly by the millions of open fires burning coal mined in the north and transported to the south east on the Midland Main line - all from the huge yards at Toton.

Legislation led to smokeless zones. Houses were modernised. Central heating powered by gas became the norm. Open fires disappeared by the thousand. Coal merchants along the Midland went out of business. The use of coal as a fuel was now confined mainly to the coal gas plants, smokeless fuel plants and electricity generating stations.

The discovery of North Sea gas had a dramatic effect on reducing demand for coal. Almost weekly, it seemed, as outdated coal gas plants closed, Toton would lose a flow of coal traffic which in my early days would have been unthinkable. Most of the few remaining coal merchants found that the new motorways provided a quicker and cheaper means of transport for the little coal that they required. Rail traffic declined. The largest of our customers was now the electricity power stations.

It was time for us to change the way we did things. One of the great innovations was the Merry Go Round (MGR) train. These are loaded 'on the move' at the coal mine, moved directly to the power stations where they are automatically discharged and returned to the mine for reloading without the locomotive either having to uncouple, or even to stop. They are both productive and cost effective.

It is also true to say that in the 1970s single wagon load customers

were turned away by a BR that did not want their business. We could no longer transport their requirements and hope to make a profit. Our machine was too big and costly to run for the small man. It needed radical thinking and change if the railways were to survive. At Toton, the still massive complex was beginning to overwhelm the dwindling traffic. It was time for another Beeching-style contraction.

The Down Hump at Toton was therefore closed and all remaining traffic that required shunting was diverted to the Up sidings. Although hump shunting had been declining steadily on both the Up side and the Down, the concentration of all of the traffic to the Up had the temporary effect of creating a reprieve for the activity of hump shunting at Toton. However, BR had decided that single wagon load traffic was no longer viable in any form. It was inevitable that hump shunting would eventually cease altogether.

In the interim Toton became a Speedlink distribution point. At night, fully fitted trains from many destinations would arrive at Toton Old Bank Sidings. They would exchange their traffic with other trains for forwarding. The principle of speed freight was based on sound thinking. There were depots all over the system dedicated to Speedlink. A vehicle might start in Scotland and change trains at these depots three or four times before finally reaching its destination. The TOPS system (which kept track of where each and every vehicle was) was now fully operational and the advanced traffic information provided by the computers allowed us to plan traffic movements with an efficiency undreamt of only a few years previously. We would study the incoming consists and decide well in advance how we would deal with the trains as they arrived.

Timekeeping was paramount. We were allowed perhaps 30 minutes to receive a train, remarshal it and send it on its way. If a train was late arriving it could have a disastrous effect on the others with which it connected. In an effort to try and recover the situation we would often send a train on its way without some of its intended connecting traffic. This was good for the train as a whole – but it was not good for the customer whose traffic was delayed 24 hours until it could join the following night's train! It was even worse for the operators who would have to explain in detail why a vehicle had missed its connection. They were a headache.

One problem was that Toton Old Bank sidings (where Speedlink shunting took place) were not designed for this type of work. Each shunting move required signalling onto the running line. The track occupation by other trains and the Power Box Signalman therefore dictated our performance to some degree and if he didn't let us out when we needed to do so, shunting was delayed. In many ways we were not totally in charge of our own destiny. This was frustrating.

For these reasons, I would leave my office at night when the trains started to arrive and take personal charge of the activities until all the Speedlink trains had departed. Even then, with both hands firmly on the job, things could still go wrong. I had many a sleepless

Above: This was the most modern railway John Woolley had key responsibilities for in his four-decade career at Toton, which spanned four decades, from 1954 to 1994. An unidentified Class 37 passes Toton, heading north up the Erewash Valley with a down empty wagon train as English Electric Type 1 (Class 20) No. 20054 shunts in the background on October 6 1984. Close examination of the photograph reveals, immediately above the '37', a single Type 1 Bo-Bo of the even then obsolete British Thomson Houston variety. The up yard is on the left while on the horizon, the cooling towers and flue chimney at Ratcliffe on Soar power station lurks in the mist. Although a busy scene, the indications of contraction are evident: note how the group of loops in the left middle distance have been disconnected at this end, leaving them as single ended sidings. *Brian Stephenson/Rail Archive Stehenson.*

morning going over the previous night's events. I was constantly searching for solutions to recurring problems. In all though, the system worked as well as could be expected with the resources available. However, the Speedlink operators did not agree that we had done all that we could. They consequently later moved their activities to Bescot yard and Toton became dedicated to moving coal once again. This time it was by bulk MGR service direct to the power station. There was no need for them to enter the yards and MGR trains did not need dividing and remaking into new trains and so hump shunting ceased altogether. The once-mighty Toton complex began to shrink as yards progressively closed. The little shunting still required was carried out conventionally on 'the flat.'

I remember one incident during the busiest period of Speedlink operations. It was about 2300 and a Class 25 had backed onto a reformed train for Severn Tunnel - I believe the reporting number was 6V80. The guard was having difficulty releasing the ratchet brake of a continental van, coded VDA. I took charge and asked the driver to apply the air brake. This would have the effect of taking the pressure off the hand brake mechanism as the brake was applied even more firmly by air.

I was just about to show the guard how easy the brake handle could now be moved when in his haste to leave on time, he picked up the handle and threw it into its release cradle. The result of this was that he trapped my finger between the handle and the vehicle framing. Blood spurted everywhere.

He was most apologetic and I quietly asked him to rejoin his train and get away to time. The local hospital placed four stitches into the wound and I returned to work. The next night the guard came early and made his way to my office to see how I was. He remarked that he had never seen a man more calm and still dedicated to the job despite the circumstances. I told him that the pain from my finger was mild in comparison to the agony I would suffer from the boss should his train have been delayed!

Chapter 7
BACK TO THE TRACTION DEPOT

Above: Until the 'Peak' Class 44s (followed by 45s/46s) arrived from 1962, Toton had been an MPD which provided only freight locomotives. The 'Peaks' changed all that and thereafter expresses roaring past the MPD and yards were hauled by Toton engines. No. 45121 runs through Toton South at the head of the up 'Master Cutler' (Sheffield-St. Pancras), on May 17 1979. The down yard control tower is above the third carriage. *John Chalcraft/©www.railphotoprints.co.uk Collection.*

By April 1981, I had enjoyed seven years in the Operating Department. There was now to be major changes amongst the traincrew supervisory staff. The once pre-eminent Class 45 'Peaks' had been replaced by the new HSTs on the backbone of the Midland Mainline expresses. These new trains were to be serviced at Derby and as a consequence the number of locomotives requiring service at Toton declined. Toton had turned full circle and became a freight only depot once again.

It had been decided that because of the decline in the numbers of locomotives handled at Toton, one supervisor could handle both the operating of the traincrews and the traction arranging. The old TCIs would be allowed to retire and the younger men would run both jobs.

I was approached by the management and asked if I thought that the scheme would work. I had to admit that the new post would be a busy one – but that yes, it could be done. For my trouble, I was asked to apply for one of the new posts. I took charge on April 19 1981. The boss asked me to form a team and make recommendations for the appointments of my colleagues.

One of these was a fellow traction arranger from my earlier years by the name of Ron who had moved to Stoke on promotion to Grade D. I rang Ron and told him of the new arrangements at Toton and asked him if he would consider moving back to Toton on further promotion in the new organisation. Ron jumped at the chance.

There was another young traction arranger still at Toton by the

name of Jim, who was also appointed. All we needed then was a general purpose relief man and the team would be complete. There was a supervisor working at Westhouses (which was about to close) by the name of Brian. He fitted the bill perfectly. He signed up and the new job was 'on the road'.

All but one of the older supervisors retired. He was a wise old owl called Albert. He would be the rest day relief man. Albert elected for this post so that he would not have to work nights. The rosters were such that all rest days were either on days or afternoons.

The team was excellent and every one of us worked tirelessly together. We had an unwritten rule that we would plan as far as was possible into the next man's shift. This ensured that there were no surprises or problems for at least two hours at the beginning of the shift. The depot ran like clockwork. I was very proud indeed of this new team and the team effort.

There is more to running a busy depot than organising

locomotives and men. There was the depot links (traincrew's booked rosters) to formulate and agree with the drivers' and guards' staff representatives. These men were known as the LDCs (Local Departmental Committees). Jim was given this task and he became an expert on traincrew rostering and agreements.

I was given the task of formulating, rostering and the record keeping of Bank Holiday working. It was important that all records were accurate. Obviously it would be unfair if any man worked more or fewer Bank Holidays than his colleagues. It could be a daunting task particularly at Christmas and New Year when no one really wanted to be at work. Records became particularly important at these times to prove to a man that it really was his turn.

I loved the work and enjoyed working with the LDCs. We shared mutual respect and pulled together to ensure that the depot ran smoothly at Bank Holiday times. At Christmas we ran the depot with the minimum staff possible. I remember reading in one of the rail enthusiasts magazines that they had noticed that the Ratcliffe Power Station-Fletton (waste ash) train always ran double-headed at Christmas. They asked in the magazine if anyone had any reason for this. At that time, I was not at liberty to say, but it was my idea and for the record, I will now explain my thinking.

During the Christmas break most locomotives would be stabled for long periods. Sometimes when we tried to restart them after the festive break, we would find numerous locomotives with flat batteries. That created traction shortages and excessive shunting to sort them out and get them running again. I made the decision (and this was sanctioned by Power Control) to couple several pairs of 56s and 58s and use these alternately on the Ratcliffe-Fletton services to keep them in good operating order.

Another advantage of this was that should one of the locomotives fail en route, the train could still carry out the diagram without the necessity of Toton having to provide an assisting crew and locomotive. These arrangements worked well and without a hitch over the years and allowed me to minimise the number of men I needed to roster. It was a 'belt and braces' approach which worked well.

Albert & Ron

Although Albert was an excellent operator, he could not get used to extra demands of arranging the traction. He had never operated the fuel line and the locomotives. In addition, Albert had heart trouble and he really needed a less stressful job. I remember relieving him one Saturday afternoon when there were locomotives queuing on the fuel line awaiting disposal instructions. Albert

apologised. I told him not to worry and go home. I added that the job would quieten down as the day progressed and as there was little to do later, I had all the time in the world to 'square it up'.

Sometime later, I had sorted it out and all was in order. The telephone rang and I answered it immediately. It was Albert's wife. The shock of what she had to tell me struck a hammer blow. She told me that Albert had arrived home in a cold sweat and told her to call an ambulance. He collapsed and died within a few minutes. It was a very sad loss.

Ron was allocated the task of organising and monitoring of drivers' and guards' route learning. This was no mean feat. Ron had to work out and agree with the LDCs how long it would take a driver to learn a new route. He had to ensure that the depot could cope with the constant changes to the traffic flow. This was because Toton men were now going over routes which had traditionally been allocated to other depots.

Further Changes

Changes were now coming fast and furious! Westhouses closed as a depot and all their remaining work was transferred to Toton, together with the staff. Coalville was to follow some time later. Toton therefore became a hybrid depot and the men who were transferred to the depot from Westhouses and Coalville (who historically had been adversaries) were now part of the same team. Both management and the staff 'reps' bent over backwards to ensure that these men were welcomed and assisted in settling down in their new environment.

Because of the changing workload and ongoing loss of traffic, there were changes taking place in the Control organisation. The Nottingham Control Centre was moved from Furlong House and centralised at Crewe with a loss of many positions.

The Nottingham Divisional Offices were closed and more and more responsibility was placed on the Traincrews and Operating Supervisors. Toton Yard lost its Shift Manager (known as the Area Freight Assistant) and his work was handed down to the Yard Supervisors. Management was confined to Depot level and

Below: A down Midland Main Line HST IC125 passes Hasland, where on May 14 1997, the Avenue coking plant dominated the skyline. Much to the delight of its neighbours, this has since been completely demolished. The arrival of the HSTs (which were maintained elsewhere) followed the demise of Toton's 'Peak' diesel electrics in the 1980s and thereafter the depot reverted to its traditional freight-only role. *Gavin Morrison*.

Divisional Management at Nottingham was disbanded.

Never a week went by without change and loss of someone's position. What was once a massive machine changed to a slimmer, more effective and competitive organisation. The changes were well justified when one considers the amount of traffic we had lost as industries changed and closed during the recession. I was never averse to change and progress, but sometimes I must admit to having some reservations (and fears) about the constant changes and lack of stability. In retrospect, I must state here that my concerns were mainly based on the old traditions. Perhaps I was not in tune with the new thinking? This thought crossed my mind

Above: Class 37/7s are receiving attention in Toton MPD on February 27 1996, including Mainline No 37798 (left). *Brian Morrison.*

constantly and helped me to come to terms with the changes.

As for privatisation, some railway managers favoured the forming of separate businesses by commodity – this meant separate businesses for coal, steel, oil, aggregates, passengers and so on. Certainly, one brilliant manager for whom I worked set up his own organisation with its own resources and staff and called it Trainload Coal. His business encompassed the coal moving depots

The Class 58s were maintained at Toton for virtually their entire career. In this line-up on the depot front are (from left): 58010, 58014, 58007, 58003 and 58013. Friday October 12 1984. *Gavin Morrison.*

in the area. Namely Worksop, Toton and Barrow Hill.

I was seconded to work out his locomotive power requirements for the new business and reopen his own power control office at Nottingham. The business was effective, economic and soundly based financially. The man was a genius but the organisation fell short of government thinking! The organisation was further expanded to take in the aggregate business in Leicester and renamed East Midlands Freight.

The government favoured an even more competitive market place. It decided that the best way forward would be to divide up the country in regions, each with its own resources. These would compete with each other for the available traffic.

In addition to Toton, Worksop and Leicester, Nottingham now took over Peterborough, March and Parkeston Quay. The area covered was renamed yet again and called Trainload Freight

South East. The new company dealt with all of the freight traffic generated in that area. That is how the organisation remained right up until the sell off.

The Trainload Freight South East business (and others) was bought by the Americans (Ed Burkhardt's Wisconsin Central) and renamed EW&S. What do the initials stand for - East, West and South? Not a bit of it. The initials mean ENGLISH, WELSH & SCOTTISH. They bought the lot! So much for the government's idea of a competitive market. Wisconsin had the railfreight monopoly.

The railway, before privatisation, was not the dinosaur that the public was led to believe. Managers were always looking at ways to improve service and reduce costs. To justify my statement, you only have to look in detail at the changes that I have already described. Certainly, the railways prior to privatisation gave the customer a service. At the time of writing, a passenger franchise called South West Trains has been highly criticised for not providing a service. They are in danger of losing their franchise. They made a large number of drivers redundant and cannot now cover their commitments. It's a shambles.

This week there was criticism of the massive profits made by the train leasing companies. A report in the 'Financial Mail On Sunday' dated February 23 1997 says: "A public outcry greeted last weeks sale of Eversholt for £788 million, netting £57 million for its five man management team." They were among investors in a group that shared a £192 million increase over the price paid when the company was privatised 13 months ago.

"Porterbrook was sold by its investors in August for £825 million seven months after they paid £527 million."

For an investment of a few thousand pounds, millionaires have been made at the taxpayer's expense. The government has got it appallingly wrong and had vastly undervalued the railway network and its assets.

Michael Benniman Sams.

It was the spring of 1993. I was on the day turn in the traincrew office at Toton. The Traincrew Manager at that time was a guy called Ian. I must admit that he was one of the best managers I had ever worked for. He was a super guy. It would be about 1200 when Ian came into my office.

"John," he said. "Can I introduce you to Detective Inspector Calter from the West Yorkshire Police." I shook the detective's hand and wondered what on earth I could do for him? Ian spoke again: "Detective Calter would like your assistance".

I looked questioningly at the detective. Ian said: "I will leave you both to talk" and left the office to continue his daily routine. The detective was tall, dark and imposing. He carried an aura which suggested to me that he knew what he was about. He struck me as a man who was very easy to get along with. His manner was pleasant and he smiled easily. The detective spoke: "I suppose that you have heard of the kidnap of the estate agent Stephanie Slater?"

I was familiar with the case and answered in the affirmative. The detective went on to explain that although Sams was under arrest for the kidnap of Stephanie, there were other unsolved crimes which he could have committed. One of these was the murder of Julie Dart. He went on to say that Sams had been questioned about this but had stated that he was at Toton train spotting on the day that Julie had gone missing.

To verify his claim Sams had produced his photo album which showed locomotives in Toton yard. The date that these were supposedly taken was written below each picture. Sams had cross referenced these with entries on his computer. The entries seemed to cover him for the time when poor Julie disappeared.

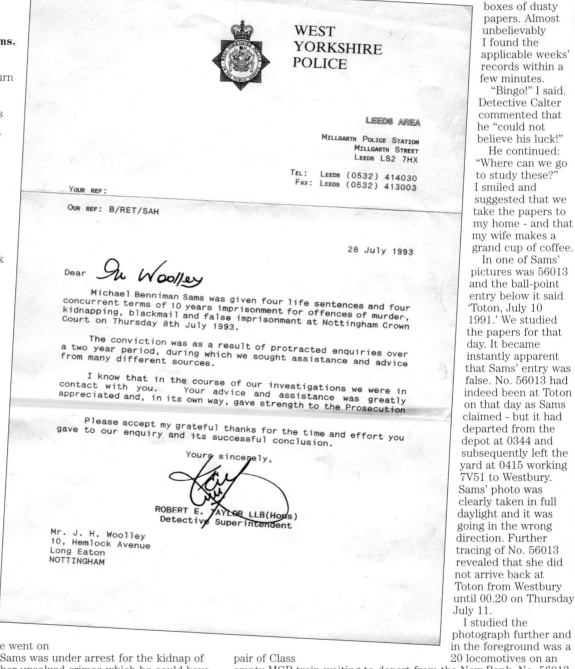

WEST YORKSHIRE POLICE

LEEDS AREA

MILLGARTH POLICE STATION
MILLGARTH STREET
LEEDS LS2 7HX

TEL: LEEDS (0532) 414030
FAX: LEEDS (0532) 413003

YOUR REF:

OUR REF: B/RET/SAH

28 July 1993

Dear Jn Woolley

Michael Benniman Sams was given four life sentences and four concurrent terms of 10 years imprisonment for offences of murder, kidnapping, blackmail and false imprisonment at Nottingham Crown Court on Thursday 8th July 1993.

The conviction was as a result of protracted enquiries over a two year period, during which we sought assistance and advice from many different sources.

I know that in the course of our investigations we were in contact with you. Your advice and assistance was greatly appreciated and, in its own way, gave strength to the Prosecution

Please accept my grateful thanks for the time and effort you gave to our enquiry and its successful conclusion.

Yours sincerely,

ROBERT E. TAYLOR LLB(Hons)
Detective Superintendent

Mr. J. H. Woolley
10, Hemlock Avenue
Long Eaton
NOTTINGHAM

Inspector Calter asked me if there was any way that the photos could be verified as being taken when Sams said that they were. He produced the album and I instantly recognised the locations. The trouble was however, that the photographs had supposedly been taken two years previously. My colleagues and I had always been meticulous about keeping accurate records, and were obliged to keep all records for at least a year. The old documents were kept in a redundant signalbox at Toton Centre. I remembered that the very week previously we had organised a bonfire to burn some of the old papers. My heart missed a beat.

I rang the gang who had been allocated to destroy the old papers. They told me that they had started with the oldest and that they had left untouched the papers for the previous four years. I told them not to burn anything else until I gave them the 'all clear'.

At 1400 I was relieved by the next shift. Inspector Calter and myself made our way to the old signalbox. There we found boxes upon boxes of dusty papers. Almost unbelievably I found the applicable weeks' records within a few minutes.

"Bingo!" I said. Detective Calter commented that he "could not believe his luck!" He continued: "Where can we go to study these?" I smiled and suggested that we take the papers to my home - and that my wife makes a grand cup of coffee.

In one of Sams' pictures was 56013 and the ball-point entry below it said 'Toton, July 10 1991.' We studied the papers for that day. It became instantly apparent that Sams' entry was false. No. 56013 had indeed been at Toton on that day as Sams claimed - but it had departed from the depot at 0344 and subsequently left the yard at 0415 working 7V51 to Westbury. Sams' photo was clearly taken in full daylight and it was going in the wrong direction. Further tracing of No. 56013 revealed that she did not arrive back at Toton from Westbury until 00.20 on Thursday July 11.

I studied the photograph further and in the foreground was a pair of Class 20 locomotives on an empty MGR train waiting to depart from the New Bank. No. 56013 was in the background heading north from the North Yard. It was obvious to me (by studying the shadows) that the photograph had been taken in the early afternoon. Further, that specific combination of trains at that time of day could only apply to the 1400 to Oxcroft and the 1420 to Denby.

We studied the rest of the records and we also found the same locomotives in that same combination some weeks earlier. Sams was clearly lying! Inspector Calter asked me to check some other photographs of Class 58 locomotives allegedly also taken on that

day. None of these appeared in our records either. I knew that there was only two places they could have been. Either in the Maintenance Depot undergoing repairs or at Worksop working coal trains in the north.

The first possibility was ruled out because they did not appear on the maintenance computer printout. I rang my colleague at Worksop and after a short delay he was able to prove that both locomotives had indeed been working in his area all of that week. We had exposed Sams' lies.

Inspector Calter took a long statement from me and took away the records as evidence. I had been promoted further before I was called to Nottingham Crown Court to give evidence in the murder trial. Sams was found guilty. He finally confessed to Julie's murder after being imprisoned.

On July 28 1993, I received the letter shown on this page, from the West Yorkshire Police. It seems to me unbelievable, even now, that our everyday operations and records proved so valuable in a successful murder investigation.

Above: No. 56013 was used by suspect Michael Sams as his alibi in the investigation into the kidnap of estate agent Stephanie Slater (for which he was under arrest) and the murder of Julie Dart. Sams claim - backed up by a dated photograph of 56013 - was that he was trainspotting at Toton on Wednesday July 10 1991, when Julie went missing. John Woolley proved that 56013 left Toton for Westbury with 7V51 at 0415 that day and did not return until 0020 on Thursday July 11. John gave a formal statement, plus evidence in court and on July 8 1993 Sams was given four life sentences and four concurrent terms of 10 years imprisonment for murder, kidnapping, blackmail and false imprisonment. 56013 was withdrawn on December 17 1993 and is dumped at Toton on July 28 1997. It was scrapped in September 2001

Below: Class 08 No. 08703 pulls away from the depot at Toton with a loaded ballast train heading north, seen from the A52 dual carriageway bridge on September 1 2004. Compare this with the broadly similar view, on page 14. *Both: Gavin Morrison.*

CHAPTER 8
MANAGER

It was the week before the Easter Holiday in 1993. I was putting the final touches to the Bank Holiday rosters. The telephone rang and it was for me. "Hello John, Phil here, how are you?". Phil was the resources manager at the head offices in Furlong House, Nottingham. I instantly assumed that the call was about extra traffic for the Bank Holiday. It was not unusual for a customer to order a train with little or no notice. "Hello Phil, nice to hear from you, what can I do for you?" I replied.

"Well John, there is a vacancy for a Shift Manager in my control organisation - can I interest you?" I asked him what the pay would be and he answered.

"Phil," I replied after some thought. "You might interest me rather more if you sharpen your pencil!" He replied that he would get back to me after he had spoken to the Personnel Officer.

Some while later Phil rang me again with an improved offer. He also pointed out that the position that I was holding would be 'good for the millennium' and that should I have any thoughts on early retirement I would be better placed at Nottingham. I had set my sights on finishing with 40 years service and it seemed that Phil had 'got wind of it.' I accepted his offer, turned up for the interview and took charge of the Area Operations Control on June 21 1993.

The railways were now really gearing up and preparing for privatisation. The job was fragmented and as a consequence my area of responsibility became vast. I was in charge of all freight operations at Toton, Worksop, Leicester, Peterborough, March and Parkeston Quay. Anything to do with day to day freight operations in these areas was my responsibility. Any problems with running, 'the buck stopped on my desk'.

Of course, as well as having competent supervisory and clerical staff in my office, I now had hundreds of staff under my command at all those outstations. As big as it was, the organisation was very effective and ran with few problems which could not be quickly remedied. Items such as signalmen going sick, shunting staff and traincrew shortages were generally no problem to solve. There were exceptions however. When things went really wrong, the job was hectic.

I remember one early morning in 1994. The railway had been running without a hitch all night. Then the telephone rang.

Above: An intriguing picture because of its fascinating mixture of traditional infrastructure and then-modern train. The modest Midland Railway brick-built station at Melton Mowbray, with its ornate cast-iron and glass canopies, had barely changed from the steam era and even in 2013 retains its curious cantilevered signalbox and mechanical semaphore signalling. It looked virtually identical - if grubbier back then - when John Woolley fired Beyer Garratts and 'Super Ds' through here. On June 28 1986, problems on the MML meant that this unidentified HST IC125 had been diverted via Melton Mowbray, Oakham, Harringworth Viaduct and Corby before rejoining the Midland Main Line at Glendon South Junction. *Gavin Morrison.*

"Leicester Power Box here, there has been a serious derailment at Knighton. One of your trains loaded with stone from the Bardon Hill quarries has become derailed on the crossover. The track is so seriously damaged that it will close the Midland Main Line out of Leicester to London. Passenger trains will have to be diverted via Melton, Manton and Corby". The news was very serious indeed.

In these circumstances there are defined laid down instructions. The first priority had to be the safety of my staff and protection of the wreckage. The second had to be to define whether we needed the emergency services - ambulances and fire brigade. Only when the safety and the welfare of the men and the public had been defined could we concentrate on emergency working and planning a full recovery.

At that time, the new company Railtrack was forming and although they had not yet fully taken over the infrastructure they would also call out their own inspectors to investigate. I called out my 'on call' traffic inspector and asked him to attend for a joint site enquiry. At the same time, I rang the Traincrew Supervisor at Toton and asked him to crew a locomotive and couple it to the 75 tonne crane and breakdown train (these were kept at Toton) and stand by for further instructions. Whilst I was waiting for more information from the site, I arranged for the signalbox at Corby to open. This box (which has since been burned down by vandals) was normally closed on nights.

The next task was to inform the Permanent Way Supervisor so that he could call out his men and instigate track repairs. I checked

my check list of things to do - and found I was spot on.

Because of the anticipated serious disruption to the passenger services I rang the 'on call' manager and informed him. This was primarily so that he could inform whoever he decided would need to know. He had no other contribution unless I specifically asked him to attend the site and I would only do this if there was a dispute between the parties involved. This was not the case.

My inspector was soon at the site and more information was coming in. The train had been derailed all the way across the main lines and although there were no injuries or further danger, the track was very seriously damaged. I gave specific instructions to the breakdown train crew at Toton and sent them on their way. The diversions were organised and I had processed the job as far as I could when my relief came at 0600. My daily computer log was updated and contained all the details of my actions. This log was transmitted at 0600 to all of the managers in the organisation.

I was surprised when the Regional Manager approached me the

Above: The diesel railway from Toton operated and managed by the team of which John Woolley was a part, was the rationalised steam railway he had grown up with, using modern power. On June 28 1986, the MR signalbox, its semaphore signals, jointed track and 1950s vintage BR Mk 1 carriages are all steam age hardware. Even the 'Peak' dated from the diesel 'pilot' scheme of 1955. Class 45/1 No. 45122 is passing Corby North with the diverted 1410 St Pancras-Sheffield.

Below: John Woolley's last 'drive' was aboard an HST IC125 and as he roared up the MML he glanced at the lineside fixtures which had changed or disappeared since his cleaning days. This is Glendon South Junction, north of Kettering, where the Corby line peels away to the east. This HST IC125, led by 43106, was rejoining the MML after having been diverted via Melton Mowbray, Oakham, Manton Junction, Harringworth Viaduct and Corby on its route south. Since then, this line has been singled although Corby's station, closed on April 18 1966 and demolished, was rebuilt and reopened in 2009. *Both: Gavin Morrison.*

Top: Leicester London Road in transition. Brush Type 2 (Class 31) No. 31305 is in charge of the 10.15am Birmingham-Norwich on April 24 1979. *John Chalcraft/©www.railphotoprints.co.uk Collection*

Above: Leicester London Road in steam days. Stanier 'Black Five' 4-6-0 No. 45273 rolls in with a St Pancras-Manchester train on July 9 1957. *©www.railphotoprints.co.uk Collection*

following week. He spoke: "John, that derailment last week, why did you not inform me? I was in an embarrassing situation when I came to work that morning. I had the Passenger Manager at Derby down my neck on something I knew nothing about!" He spoke these words for everyone in my office and under my charge to hear.

I sprang to my defence. "I informed the 'on call' manager, surely it was his duty to advise you." I explained that the mishap procedure manual had been followed to the letter. He retaliated "In such a serious incident as this, I would expect you to advise me personally!" I was inwardly furious and replied: "Look here boss, I had enough to do organising diversions, signalbox openings, rerailing gangs, inspectors, traincrews and platelayers. I was at the sharp end and my

main task was to get the job moving. If your 'on call' manager should decide to go back to sleep after hearing of the mishap from me first hand, so be it on his head. I suggest you ask him why you were not informed?"

I added: "The next time there is a derailment on my shift, I will ring the Chairman. Perhaps he will pass it down!"

The boss looked at me and could see that I was upset and correct. He realised then that he had got the wrong man. It was a shame that he could not have approached me in private. He walked out of my office and the matter was forgotten. My senior Traffic Supervisor looked across the office and said "Good for you John, they live on a different planet don't they?"

Above: This was the MML on which John Woolley drove his last HST to St Pancras. On January 23 1995, the 1324 IC125 from Sheffield to St Pancras approaches Leicester, with power car 43069 at its head. On the right, the modest English Welsh & Scottish locomotive depot looks neat and tidy and has a handful of engines at home. Although still used by a private operator today, the shed is all-but invisible from the HST's position because of a mature row of trees near where the wagons are standing! *Gavin Morrison.*

Left: When John started work in the 1950s, this is how that same EWS depot site looked in terms of infrastructure - but it was probably much tidier than see here. This is Leicester's MPD in 1961 - it was descending rapidly into filth and neglect. Just as John talks about at Toton, interest in steam fell off quickly when the diesels arrived. The locomotive is Stanier '8F' No. 48518. Other engines lurk in the murk in the right distance. ©www.railphotoprints.co.uk Collection

My last drive!

In the spring of 1993, I had occasion to travel to London. I was to meet an Operations Inspector who would show me around the Kew area. I had never worked as far as this and now that I was in charge it was imperative that I could look at the locations and meet the men.

I arrived on the platform at Nottingham to catch the Robin Hood HST express. Also on the platform was a Toton driver by the name of Alan. We had been cleaners together all those years ago and were good friends. Alan asked me where I was bound for? I told him, and I was happy to hear that he was making his way to Cricklewood to pick up a train bound for Toton. I would have his company all the way to St. Pancras.

The HST stood in the platform and Alan knew the driver. After speaking to the driver, Alan asked me if I would like to 'ride up front' and of course I was delighted to do so.

The Robin Hood stops only at Loughborough and Leicester and then is non-stop to London. I sat in the second man's seat and Alan stood behind the driver. Alan told the driver who I was and a little about our history and relationship.

"This is John Woolley," he began. "He is a Shift Operations Manager for Trainload Freight South East in Furlong House, Nottingham. He is an ex-footplateman and we were cleaning steam engines together in the 1950s".

The driver looked at me and said: "I remember you when you were a Running Foreman at Toton. We used to bring express '45s' to Toton from Nottingham for repairs and change them for 'good uns'. Welcome aboard!"

The train started from Nottingham and I watched the driver's every expert move. I was thrilled by the power of the machine. She leapt away like a race horse. We were soon at Leicester and spot on time. The driver turned to me and smiled broadly as he asked:

"How would you like to take her from here to St. Pancras John? You've only got one stop at St. Pancras to think about."

I was sitting at the driving desk as quick as a flash.

Alan took the vacant seat and the express driver stood behind me. I said, "You'll have to keep a close watch on me, I ain't seen the road through the front window for years! Have you got a list of the temporary slacks?" I asked. He pointed to his schedule in the clip on the desk in front of me. The guard gave us the tip and we were away.

I was thrilled to bits as I applied the power. The twin Paxman 12 cylinder 2,250 h.p. engines gently took the strain. With 4,500 horses working in unison the train glided smoothly out of the station. I spoke to the driver: "Do you know, there are many people who would pay thousands of pounds for this experience!" He replied "Yes, and I reckon that the company realises this. That's why they expect us to do it for nothing!" I laughed.

He added "Do you know, the first 200 trips on these are superb. After that, it's just like mowing the lawn - boring, but a chore that has to be done…" I chuckled again.

Since my driving days the main line to London had been upgraded. The line speed was now 100mph for most of the way. Where it was allowed, I was soon running at the maximum. The feeling of power was exhilarating. I had the impression that there were no bounds to the power available on this wonderful machine and that the only controlling influence stopping us from going into orbit was the speed of the track.

The driver advised me to try the brakes. "Give her a shot of brake John and get the feel of them in readiness for when you will need them." I did so and was just as impressed by her powerful braking effort as I had been with her boundless power. The HSTs are beautiful tools.

As I ran along the route I reflected on my youth and memories flooded back of all those trips in the 1950s with steam. Passing Market Harborough, I glanced at the site of the old steam shed, now an industrial estate. I remembered the many times that I had visited the depot in the steam days. I looked at the site of the old track bed to Northampton and thought about the gauge glass, Frank and Clipstone Tunnel. All now long gone.

In front of me lay the Crimean Bank. I could almost hear the sharp bark of the Riddles Class 9Fs, the clanking and banging of the 'Austerities' and the eight beat muffled roar of the Beyer Peacock Garratts of the past. The 4,500 horses of the HST glided the train up the bank as if it wasn't there. I wondered what the grumpy old steam men of years ago, who I first worked with, would have made of that. It all seemed so very long ago, but cherished memories all the same.

As we cleared the summit at Desborough I eased back on the power and enjoyed the sound of the Turbo Chargers as they ran back from a scream to a gentle hum. Approaching Glendon I noticed the cows drinking in the field at the bottom of the embankment on the down side. I recalled the hot summer's day in the 60s on the footplate of a Riddles 9F when I was envious of the cattle drinking there.

I was given plenty of warnings about the speed restrictions along

the route. The driver was watching me like a 'cat watching a mouse.' He was a fine instructor and he made sure that I didn't put a foot wrong. I enjoyed running alongside the M1 motorway and leaving the south bound road traffic for dead. I could see the faces of the drivers as we overtook them. Some would look out of the window as we passed and then glance down at their speedometer. They probably thought that they had stopped!

The permanent speed restriction is reduced in 10mph steps as London is approached and all too soon I was entering St. Pancras at a crawl. We stopped smoothly and exactly on time. The driver spoke: "Well John, you ain't lost your touch". I was incredibly happy at that moment.

I said my goodbyes to Alan and thanked the Nottingham driver and came back to reality and the task in hand. If that Nottingham driver ever reads this I should like to express my thanks once again to him for allowing me the very great honour and privilege of that last, great footplate experience.

March Depot

It was whilst I was working in the AOC (Area Operations Centre) that it had been decided that the Peterborough and March area needed to be rationalised.

I was given the task of looking at the area and making recommendations. March depot had not changed since the railways had come out of single wagon load freight, when Speedlink ended. The depot was set in the middle of a vast tract of land surrounded by redundant track.

Phil (my boss) released me from my duties for six weeks in the glorious summer of 1993. My first sight of March depot and

Above: Even the freight of the far flatlands of the Fens was under John Woolley's management in the last few years of his four decades of service at Toton. On March 26 1985, Class 37 No. 37173 approaches March station from the east, with a freight for Whitemoor yard. *Gavin Morrison.*

marshalling yards since my footplate days came as quite a shock. Gone were the hundreds of wagons and shunting staff that went with them. There were weeds all over the sidings. It looked derelict. The train crew accommodation was run down and when I spoke to the men, their low morale came through instantly.

I was met at the depot by the local traffic supervisor. He had been advised of my impending arrival and instructed to assist me in any way that was necessary. He introduced me to the drivers' LDC secretary. The driver eyed me suspiciously. "Come to close the place then, have you?" he asked.

I smiled and replied: "I really have no pre-conceived ideas at all. Certainly, the depot has some work and you are the depot furthest east in our company." I asked him to answer the same question: "Do you think the depot could be closed?" I could see that he was taken aback. "Well, no." he said. "I think the depot still has a role to play."

"Yes, I agree," I replied. "But perhaps some changes are necessary if only to make the depot more viable. We will see. I might need your help and co-operation."

The point of the conversation was to put his mind at rest. Whilst ever there was work, there were jobs. Providing, of course, that the work was on a commercial footing.

After spending a couple of weeks looking around the area, examining the depot's work load and looking over Peterborough, it was time to list the options. They were as follows, it seemed to me:

Transition era March. 'Whistler' English Electric Type 4 (Class 40) No. 40124 is heading coal empties at March East Junction on March 10 1979. Brush Type 2 (Class 31) 31169 is visible in the distance. *Gordon Edgar/©www.railphotoprints.co.uk Collection*

- Close the depot and move all of the work and men to Peterborough.
- Close the depot and reopen another at Ely.
- Relocate the men and the work to March station.

My report was written giving the 'for and against' points for each option. I had to prove that the first option was viable. This necessitated re-writing all the train crew diagrams and theoretically reprogramming the trains to Peterborough. The end result had to reflect the same performance (or better) for customers.

I also had to prove that the extra activities in the Peterborough area - sidings occupation, trains stopping for relief on running lines, depot locomotive stabling accommodation and the accommodation

Above: As at Toton, Whitemoor Yard at March suffered rapidly declining trafic and heavy rationalisation from the mid-1960s. On January 1 1995 the vastly-reduced yards are in the background as Class 37 No. 37376 comes off the Wisbech line with Hertfordshire Railtours' 'The Brown Cow' excursion, with Class 47/8 No. 47820 on the rear. Next port of call was the Nene Valley Railway. The new Whitemoor prison was eventually built on the northern part of the former March marshalling yard. *Gavin Morrison.*

for the extra staff - were all viable operationally.

My conclusion was that it could be done – this therefore was a 'for'. The 'against' was that by moving the depot further west we

Above: Parkeston Quay also came under John Woolley's command, from Toton, as Area Operations Control Manager in his last years with British Rail. This was an amazing achievement for a 15-year old engine cleaner who joined the railway expressly against his father's wishes, and after a poor start at school, on October October 25 1954. He retired 40 years later to the day, on October 25 1994. With an ancient tank wagon for company, Brush Type 2 (Class 31/1) No. 31278 is at the head of a car train at Parkeston Quay on April 16 1984. *Gavin Morrison.*

Above: Plenty of interest in this pre-electrification scene at Peterborough on September 12 1981. Class 56 No. 56057 is heading north with a down rake of flyash wagons. This traffic dumped power station ash on the merry-go-round principle from a continuous loop at Fletton. A London-bound HST IC125 is braking for Platform 2, on the left. The large rectangular Royal Mail sorting office linked to the covered bridge over the station is long gone. *Gavin Morrison.*

would lose our influence at the east extremity. This could have dire consequences for infrastructure servicing (weekend engineering operations).The second option was a non-starter from the beginning. Although Ely is on a major junction and many senior managers had favoured the option, there was no spare space which could be turned into a traincrew depot. Furthermore, I could not make the work fit the location economically.

The third option became the obvious choice. With little effort the men could be moved to a building on the station. The work diagrams would need only slight modification. Locomotives could be accommodated in a siding nearby and great areas of land could be given up and sold off if necessary.

It was the cheapest option giving the greatest savings and 'ye can't' git berrer en that!' I had retired when I heard that option had been implemented.

Time to go home!

The business was now at the very brink of the privatisation sell-off and I was coming up to my 40th year of railway service. Phil called me into his office in the summer of 1994. "Hello John, how are you? Grab a seat." What he was to tell me then came as a welcome relief. "John, I reckon that it could be made possible for you to retire."

Above: **The everyday railway of the later years of John Woolley's railway career. In lovely sunny weather, Class 45 'Peak' 45123** *The Lancashire Fusilier* **leaves Toton light engine as it heads for Nottingham on May 17 1979. Immediately above the rear cab is the hump room on the down side, while on the right hand edge of the picture is the down side control tower. The high level line leading to the flyover is marked by the two signals above the 'Peak's front cab. Disused after closure of the down yards, this is now covered by mature trees as seen from this viewpoint today on Long Tom's bridge.**
John Chalcraft/©www.railphotoprints.co.uk Collection.

Phil went on to say that yet another reorganisation was on the cards and that he had plans to make one of the AOC managers redundant. He had drawn up a new roster which altered the relief arrangements for the posts.

I was the most senior man in the organisation but was not the most senior man in the post. In fact, I was the most junior. The railways regard seniority as the longest term in a position. Except for one, the other managers were too young to retire. Phil asked me to have words and obtain a written note from the others stating that they would stand down for me to go.

It was about a week later when I was able to advise Phil that I was in possession of the 'stand down' letter. Arrangements for me to leave the service were made. The date would be October 25 1994. That was exactly 40 years to the day since I had started as a boy, as a cleaner, in those lovely days of steam.

On October 25, I came to the office at 0900. My duties on the last day were to return keys, books and empty my desk and locker. I remember that I had mixed feelings. In a way, I was pleased to be finished with a lifetime of shifts and total commitment and I asked myself 'was it worth it?' I was at the same time, however, feeling very sad indeed.

I shook hands with all of my staff and turned to leave. Phil was blocking the door with all of the managers and administration staff.

"You don't think we would let you go just like that do you?" he asked. I was given some beautiful gifts, including a rare bottle of malt whisky. They knew how much I loved a good drop of malt! As much as I love the bottle, however, I know that I will never open it, because to me it is far too valuable as a keepsake. A speech was wcalled for and although I tried very hard to give a brief history of my career and to thank them for the lovely gifts, I was just too upset to make the best of it They understood and I was not the only person present that day with damp eyes. The finance manager was a lovely young lady. She asked me how long I had worked for the railways. I answered her "About 60 years love!" She looked amazed and asked: "How do you make that out John, you are only 55 years old?" I looked at her, smiled, and said "Based on a 38-hour week, it's probably longer You have to take into account Sundays, Bank Holidays and overtime, normal jobs do not call for that degree of

commitment" I left the building for the last time as a railwayman and drove home to Long Eaton. Because of the thoughts going through my mind, I reckon a taxi would have been more appropriate. But it was over and it had been worth it!

Postscript.

In the following January, I received a telephone call from the Area Manager at Toton. He asked me to drop in and see him. I walked into his office. "John," he said "How are you? Would you like to come out of retirement for a couple of months?"

It is strange but although I had been pleased to finish with the railways, I was nevertheless missing them terribly. "OK, Roland, what can I do for you?"

He outlined his thoughts on yet another reorganisation of Toton yard, where I had spent my working life.

I worked on the project for six weeks and produced a report showing massive savings. The few months away from the job had been refreshing and I could see the job in a different light. Thoughts and ideas came easily, I found. I am not at liberty to say what my findings were at this time because they are still ongoing. The project however, had eased me into retirement. I would like to thank Roland for that.

Nowadays, it's trout fishing, gardening, my 'local' and last - but most certainly not least - my wife Caryl.

Above: Just as the articulated Beyer-Garratt 2-6-0+0-6-2s symbolised Toton from the 1930s to the 1950s, so the BR diesel pilot scheme Class 44 'Peaks' did the same job from the late 1950s to their withdrawal by the 1980s. John Woolley was lucky - and proud - to have worked closely with both in his 40-year Toton career. No. 44001 (the erstwhile D1 *Sca Fell Pike*, see also page 61) keeps company on the shed front with Brush Type 2 (Class 31) No. 31147 and a pair of nose-to-nose English Electric Type 1s (Class 20s) on June 7 1976. By this time, the nameplates had gone from a locomotive built in 1959. When new, it worked West Coast Main Line trains until April 1960 when it was transferred to Toton with rest of the class, where it worked freight services until withdrawal in October 1976, four months after this picture. *Gavin Morrison.*

Above: A moody and evocative reminder of the everyday railway of the early years of John Woolley's footplate career, from 1954. A lone cyclist - passenger or railwayman? - pauses on the damp platform at Syston to watch Stanier 'Black 5' Class 5MT 4-6-0 No. 45269 hammering through the deserted station on December 12 1961. Syston closed on March 4 1968. *Tony Cooke/Colour Rail*

TOTON AND LONG EATON

A brief history by

NIGEL HARRIS

Above: Long Eaton station, August 27 1932. Midland Railway Class 2P 4-4-0 No 482 passes Long Eaton with an up express. A single clerestory-roofed carriage is behind the tender. This station, on the Erewash Valley main line immediately south of the yards, closed on January 2 1967 and the former Sawley Junction station (see map, page 127) was renamed Long Eaton. *T.G. Hepburn/Rail Archive Stephenson*

In 2013, Toton Traction Maintenance Depot still plays a major role in today's freight railway as the heavy engineering centre and biggest UK depot for DB Schenker, Britain's biggest railfreight operator. I defy anyone interested in railways who drives west along the A52, which straddles the depot throat mid-way between Nottingham and Derby, not to slow down slightly as they pass, in order to steal a fleeting glimpse down into the depot yard and sidings, which is usually filled with the crimson-liveried diesel locomotives of the DB Schenker fleet. Sadly, many locomotives are often stored out-of-use these days, but as times improve DBS does repair and refurbish from the stored fleet to ensure there is sufficient traction to meet business needs. And this makes sure that in 2013, after 143 years of continuous work, the locomotive depot not only remains busy – but also continues to be at the heart of the neighbouring communities of Toton, Sandiacre and Long Eaton.

It is significant that it is Toton's *locomotive depot* which is well known today and is seen as the railway operation of scale at this location. It was a very different story in the past, for although the Motive Power Depot (MPD) was certainly always large and important (it was a triple roundhouse in steam days) it was the once-massive surrounding marshalling yards which were the real headline and attention grabbers. The MPD was servant to this sprawling complex, which at its peak stretched for two miles along the Erewash Valley line from Long Eaton to Sandiacre.

At its peak in the early 1950s, this massive complex was handling one million wagons a year. It was an endlessly busy, round-the-clock

hump shunting, remarshalling and train receipt/despatch operation, which sustained those surrounding communities of Sandiacre and especially Long Eaton. These are small towns, which are actually much bigger, relatively, than the small village of Toton, which gave its name to this enormous railway complex. Even though the marshalling yards are long gone, the name 'Toton Sidings' is still very commonly used in the region. Even in their glory days, however, the name 'Toton Sidings' sounded more like a modest country goods yard to those unfamiliar with this once-massive facility.

As this book advanced towards publication, in 2013, 'Toton Sidings' was actually headline news in Britain's national media as the favoured location for the East Midlands station planned for the proposed High Speed 2 rail link, destined to connect northern England with London and thence Europe, via High Speed 1 and Eurotunnel, at 300kph (186mph). The Toton railway story which many had sadly come to believe was perhaps largely now already told, looks like having yet another exciting chapter. Maybe there's even a whole new story to write.

That new tale would be a passenger story of course and the massive HS2 station would sit precisely half-way between Derby in the west and Nottingham in the east, where the city's light rail metro (tramway) would be extended to connect the new complex with one of its biggest catchments. This would not be without cost locally, of course, for whilst the massive site will easily accommodate the very large station required (the trains are a quarter of a mile long) the high speed approach from the south implies some residential demolition, including some historic Midland Railway cottages in Long Eaton. Progress always has a price, just as it did in the mid-19th century, when the yards themselves were built on open farmland.

The arrival of HS2 would not only represent a dramatic reversal of long-term decline in the yards, it would also represent a complete about-turn for Toton in terms of traffic type, because its railway history has been built since the 1850s on freight – especially coal. Millions of tons of coal. It is hard to imagine today, when Britain's deep mining industry is all but dead, but for three quarters of the 20th century, this country mined coal on a truly epic scale. This applied in coalfields nationally and in the East Midlands specifically, from where just about every ton was handled by Toton. There was a massive network of collieries whose coal was staged through Toton in those million wagons a year.

19th century roots

In the early days of coal mining, canals took over from horses and carts on rutted muddy tracks, carrying coal where it needed to go. A single horse could move many cart-loads in a single working boat and although it was only 2-3mph this was very efficient compared with unmade roads. Then, pioneering engineering work first by Cornishman Richard Trevithick, who came up with the first effective steam locomotive for the Penydarren coal tramway in 1804, and subsequently by father and son north eastern engineers George and Robert Stephenson, changed everything. First, in 1825, the Stephensons' *Locomotion* was the icon of the Stockton & Darlington Railway (the world's first public railway) and then *Rocket* made 30mph history in 1830 on the Liverpool & Manchester Railway, the world's first inter-city passenger line.

The railway revolution thereafter exploded across the country and it did not take long for mine owners in Derbyshire and Nottinghamshire to see and seize the opportunities. In August 1832, the mine owners of the Erewash Valley set their minds to linking Pinxton and Leicester by rail, with a branch from Derby to Nottingham, to carry their coal south. This was the Midland Counties Railway (MCR).

Not surprisingly, local canal owners faced with destruction of their business made maximum mischief whenever possible and successfully sought to frustrate the MCR plan, which as a result proceeded at a snail's pace. Also, a rival company, the North Midland Railway (NMR), wanted to link Derby to Leeds and it had its eye on a line from Derby to Birmingham. Scarce capital to pay for construction was being fought over and this meant that the MCR plan did not move forward quickly – if at all.

After a few years of struggles and setbacks all round, plans were cut back to linking Derby and Nottingham only, with a further line south from Long Eaton to Rugby, which would thereafter reach London via the London & Birmingham Railway. This amended scheme was complete by 1840 and the ground was thereby laid for Toton's future development as a railway centre of considerable significance.

1856 – Toton's first yards

Within four years, the famous Midland Railway (MR) - which made Derby its spiritual, business and engineering home - was born when the MCR, the Birmingham & Derby and the NMR merged and chose the town as its headquarters. Its first job was to strike north and actually build the Erewash valley line, through Toton, to serve its fast-growing and very extensive coal mining industry. The first section (to Codnor Park) opened in 1847 and by 1856 the first yards at Toton had been laid, named after the tiny village of the same name lying just to the east. The yards were laid on what had previously been undeveloped farmland north of Long Eaton and bordered by Sandiacre and Stapleford in the north. The strip of land ultimately used was wide enough for nearly 100 tracks and no less than a mile and half in length – and it eventually reached nearly two miles. This was a major railway facility (see aerial picture, page 128)

In the mid-19th century, industrialized Britain lay at the heart of a fast-growing and powerful global empire and was known as

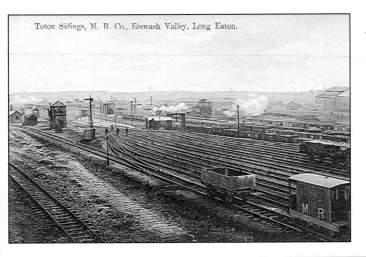

Toton Sidings, M. R. Co., Erewash Valley, Long Eaton.

Left: A postcard of the up yard at Toton before 1923, looking from east to west, with the MPD on the extreme right of the picture.

Below: A similar but much busier apparently pre-Grouping view of the north end of the up yard, looking across the Erewash Valley main line to the locomotive depot beyond. Although there is other freight present, coal predominates. *Keith Reedman Collection*

TOTON SIDINGS, NEAR LONG EATON

'the workshop of the world.' The British Empire would eventually encompass one-fifth of the globe. The Royal Navy was the most powerful fighting force on the planet, enabling this relatively tiny island country to project military prowess on any coast, just about anywhere. Right across Britain industrialization had pushed the agrarian economy firmly to one side. Towns and cities were growing exponentially around their factories, mines and other industries – and all of it was fuelled by coal. The Nottinghamshire and Derbyshire coalfield thrived.

Output in the East Midlands soared and 'Toton Sidings' expanded rapidly to not only concentrate the output for distribution nationally, but also collect empty wagons for recycling back to the pitheads for refilling. In 1883, the noted railway historian Frederick Williams published the third edition of 'Our Iron Roads' in which he says: *"The amount of business done at Toton day and night is enormous, but it varies with the season. In a summer month 18,000 wagons will be received and dispatched, in a winter month as many as 26,000."* At this time, shunting in the Toton marshaling yards was carried out by up to 40 horses.

By the turn of the century, sidings flanked the Erewash Valley line on both sides and to enhance capacity both in and out, a high level route into the yards from the south was opened in 1901. This direct access into the south end of the yards was built over a number of years. The new Red Hill tunnel, for instance, is dated 1893. The high level lines through Long Eaton to Toton sidings were part of a scheme to provide a separate set of lines to London. The line did not have a connection which would have allowed traffic to Derby and the west. This grade-separated route eliminated conflicting moves on the flat junctions and ran from Trent Junction on bridges and embankments between Long Eaton and the existing railway - it delivered traffic directly into the down side (northbound) yards on the western side of the Erewash valley main line.

Although other goods passed through, Toton has always had a single principal commodity: coal. Until Dr Beeching came along in the mid-1960s and introduced merry-go-round block trains of coal running directly from colliery to power station, this multi-million ton traffic

Above: An aerial view from the west across Long Eaton showing Granville Avenue in the foreground and Britannia Mill, fronted by Bennett Street, to the left of Britannia Road, which runs up the side of the mill to the Erewash Canal. The area sandwiched between the canal and the winding River Erewash, occupied by allotments and a variety of buildings, is now open parkland known locally as Dockholme Fields - or 'Dockie.' The down (nearest) and up yards with the Carriage & Wagon Works in the right distance, are vast. A rough count reveals around 1,500 vehicles in the sidings. *Keith Reedman Collection.*

ran in largely unbraked, four-wheel wagons of around 10-16 tons capacity. What is more, until a degree of standardization came along after nationalization, many of the wagons were privately owned, with primitive grease axle boxes, and with bodies and frames made largely of wood. Many were dubiously maintained and in poor condition. After filling at the pithead, they would be 'tripped' (transferred, empty) in groups from the pitheads to Toton, where they would be concentrated and made up into trains for despatch around the country. And remember that there were many grades of coal too, including best steam coal and house coal. Further complexity arose from the fact that users nationwide often ordered specific coals from specific pits and frequently in small quantities.

Coal wagons were typically marshalled and re-marshalled maybe twice on their journeys and at Toton these conflicting demands and thousands of wagons all came together and had to be made sense of. It is hard even to comprehend in today's digital high-tech age, let alone imagine it being done in the days of ledgers, inkwells and handwritten wagon labels.

Coal was needed to power just about everything, in all parts of the country: from ships to power stations, steam engines, iron making foundries, gas works and domestic houses. There was a massive demand for coal in London and Toton was the perfect place to concentrate East Midlands coalfields' production before running it up the Midland Main Line to the capital. As demand and output soared, Toton continued to grow in size, activity and importance.

Toton's first MPD

Above: This picture accompanied John Woolley's original manuscript with the caption: 'Toton MPD as I knew it.' The view is from the top of the coaling plant, so it's a 1930s view. No. 1 shed is nearest, with 2/3 sheds beyond. Garratts are parked alongside No. 1 Shed and alongside the ash plant in the foreground. Wagons of locomotive coal are right of centre, with wagons already unloaded alongside. On the left, a new pit is under construction alongside the Garratt. It's immediately clear why MPDs were very dangerous places to work. *Courtesy Caryl Woolley.*

This massive coal traffic was the reason why in those days the yards were the master and the Motive Power Depot was its servant. The MPD dates from the same period as the sidings were first laid – the shed is first mentioned in formal MR minutes of 1855-57. The minute reads: *"Sandiacre: resolved that the tender of G. Thompson be accepted for the construction of a small engine shed and cottage at the new sidings there."*

Plans for Toton's first roundhouse date from March 2 1869 and it cost £16,100 to construct. The first shed, completed in 1870, was a standard 24-road depot with a covered 42ft turntable. A subsequent 'No. 2 shed' was built alongside in 1873. As the coal business soared, yet more engines were needed and the MPD expanded yet further – in 1899 plans were drawn up for a further two roundhouses. There was resistance within the MR's financial management teams about such a large expansion and in the event only a single new roundhouse was built. 'No. 3 shed' was constructed by J. Walker & Sons and it opened in 1901 at a cost of £17,256. It had a larger 55ft turntable given that locomotives were growing to meet the demands of weight and speed being placed upon them. The 42ft turntables in the older buildings were also replaced, by 55ft (No. 1 shed) and 60ft (No. 2 shed) in 1926/27 at a cost of £6,622.

Inevitably, there were incremental improvements and developments to the MPD infrastructure over the years. For example, in 1903, the MR invested £1,779 for what the minutes describe as 'unspecified improvements.' The 'cenotaph' mechanical coal and ash disposal

plants were provided later, in the early 1930s. Further major works followed in the late 1940s.

Locomotive water was originally piped some distance to the MPD's water tanks and cranes from the Top Lock of the Derby canal, until 1956, when a new supply was installed from the closer Erewash canal. Interestingly, a diesel depot was proposed as early as 1944, but the increasing numbers of diesels, usually shunters, were generally housed in No. 2 shed.

The Midland Railway introduced its shed codes in 1898, Toton becoming No. 17, with shedplates initially being fitted inside the cab. Fitting shedplates to the smokebox door began in 1908/09 and Toton's code was later changed to 18A. In *1963, a* new diesel depot on site was coded 16A. The shed officially closed to all steam locomotives on November 7 1966. The three roundhouses are long demolished although part of the old water softening workshop building survived as a plant and machinery workshop.

The Beyer-Garratts

Toton Motive Power Depot provided the locomotives needed to power the railway's very heavy and seemingly endless coal traffic to London. Even the old Midland Railway's Derby hierarchy, with its obsession with small engines (which demanded extensive double heading) realised after the Grouping of 1923 that bigger locomotives were needed. In 1927, the LMS came up with the mighty 2-6-0+0-6-2 articulated Beyer Garratt locomotives, designed and built by Beyer-Peacock of Gorton, Manchester, specifically for the 126-mile Toton-Cricklewood coal trains. They were controversial and not regarded as a success. Renowned LMS historians the late David Jenkinson and Bob Essery (a former LM fireman himself) described the 155.5-ton Garratts as an "aberration" of LMS locomotive policy in the 1920s.

The Garratts with their many axles, were partly an answer to the problem of lightly-built bridges on the Midland Main Line, giving rise to concerns about weight. The Garratt principle of dividing the total weight amongst numerous axles was therefore sound. But about the execution of Garratt design they are scathing. Management rivalries

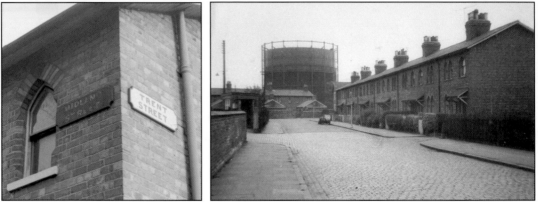

Top: A view of Long Eaton before the various post-war developments got under way. The Erewash Valley main line runs diagonally beyond the gasworks (with two gasometers) - a site now occupied by Tesco. Toton yards were off to the left. In the centre distance, to the left of the railway beyond the main right-left road lies two parallel rows of terraced houses. These were Trent Street and Midland Street. Both streets are still there today, but the houses are long gone because they now border the Asda car park, the supermarket occupying the site of the sidings beyond the terraced houses. The health centre and car park now occupy the open space to their left.

Above: The view east along Trent Street showing the lone gasometer at the top of the picture and the street signs on the corners of the brick cottages, built in the 19th century by the Midland Railway for its workers.

Left: Just one of the classic gas lamp posts put up in these streets by the MR. *All: Keith Reedman Collection.*

Articulated Beyer Garratt 2-6-0+0-6-2 No. 47967 clearly has fresh coal on the grate as it arrives in Toton yard with a down iron ore train in June 1957. *D.T. Greenwood/Rail Archive Stephenson*

within the LMS and interference from Derby during design combined to produce a 30-locomotive order which they describe as assuming the character "of a not very good French farce."

The first three locomotives were ready by 1927 and they went to Toton – much to the relief, it was said, of the enginemen at Wellingborough. But it was a temporary escape – they came to see Garratts before too long. Builder Beyer Peacock supported the LMS order for 30 engines with some brash (for the time) advertising, proclaiming to one and all that 1,500-ton coal trains formerly worked by two locomotives were now being handled by a single Garratt.

Well, maybe! As to whether this was economic is quite another question – certainly their massive appetite for coal comes across clearly in John Woolley's memoirs. You don't have to be a genius to work out that a single crew of two was also by definition doing the work of four men – with one fireman doing a job previously done by two.

The Garratts maybe looked the part and in theory they should have been masters of their work. Sadly, they were hobbled by the

Above: Toton not only played its part for king and country by doing its day job - it also helped the 'PR' battle on the Home Front through this 'somewhere in England' wartime propoganda photograph showing six new Stanier '8F' 2-8-0s built to defeat the enemy. The picture also pinpoints the MR hostel, beyond the flyover. *Keith Reedman Collection*

interference from Derby, whose small thinking and biased meddling torpedoed their potential advantages. A chief weakness was the small MR '4F' 0-6-0 axle boxes which Derby insisted they be fitted with – they simply weren't up to the job and 'ran hot' too often. The more generously-sized bearings, which Beyer Peacock had wanted to fit, would have been unlikely to have caused this trouble.

Even watering caused problems. The MR practice of double heading had led to water columns being placed in pairs on the Midland goods lines so that two engines could water simultaneously to save time. The Garratts could easily have been designed with water fillers carefully

Above: Another wartime picture at Toton, showing a 1943 visit from London to the Motive Power Depot by the South African High Commissioner, Colonel Denys Reitz. *Courtesy John Cornell.*

Right: A view of the down North Yard at Toton, with Meadow Yard to the left, looking north, with the Erewash Valley main line off to the right. Long Eaton is to the left and the MPD is in the distance, marked by the coaling tower. This shows the yard after the LMS upgrade of the late 1930s, completed in 1939 shortly before the outbreak of war. The points and their ballast look very new and unused compared with the sorting sidings themselves.
Keith Reedman Collection.

Above: A comparable viewpoint, following closure of the down North Yard and with track dismantling just getting under way. This picture accompanied John Woolley's original manuscript with his caption: 'Where have all the wagons gone?' Remaining shunting was transferred to the up yard. *John Woolley.*

spaced so as to likewise allow dual filling at the same time – but even this 'obvious' opportunity was missed. Watering had to be done via a single filler, with a small diameter balance pipe supplying the second tank. Given the maximum capacity of 4,500 gallons, this made watering a lengthier business than it could (and should) have been, leading to locomotives standing for far longer than was ideal at water columns before being moved up to allow rapid filling of the second tank. On busy goods lines this was disastrous and caused operational chaos.

The cabs were draughty, very dirty and unbearably hot in the summer. The bunkers (of seven tons capacity) on the first three engines were not self-trimming which made life very hard for the fireman, while leaky flexible steam pipes between the articulated units made life even more difficult for the crew. Even when coal pushers and rotary bunkers were fitted to solve the bunker problem; (nine tons on the later engines, and the modified first three) they didn't work that well and created problems of their own.

After a couple of years their steaming performance fell away sharply and attempts to solve this problem by sharpening the exhaust (making the engine 'chuff' with greater vigour, thereby 'drawing' the fire to burn faster, brighter and hotter) led to higher coal consumption of about one hundredweight per mile. This was about the same as the

two 0-6-0s which they had been designed to replace – but on the Garratts this had to be shovelled in the same period of time by a single fireman.

Although designed and built for the Toton-Cricklewood coal traffic, they also subsequently worked trains to York and other north eastern destinations. Noted and published Long Eaton historian Keith Reedman recalls them on the Castle Donington line, to the south west.

Builder Beyer Peacock had been building very successful (and some very large) Garratts for a host of overseas countries for many years and should have been allowed to design and build as their experience suggested. If this had happened, it might have been a different story for the Garratts on the LMS and BR. As it was, they were not popular locomotives and they were difficult to operate – as John Woolley makes clear.

Woolley started at Toton in October 1954 and although the Garratts

Above, left: Looking north from the summit of the up hump, to the east of the Erewash Valley main lines. The hump room would have been to the left rear of the photographer. The hump looks long out of use although the sorting sidings are full of rolling stock.

Above, right: Looking south up the down hump, showing the later retarders, fitted to to replace those shown on page 99. *Both: Andy Lymn.*

Above: On the left, Meadow Sidings on the down side have now been lifted, as have the points and track leading down from the hump to the North Yard sorting sidings, alongside the Erewash Valley main line on the right. The up West Yard, Old Bank Sidings and West Stowage sidings are beyond the main lines, to the left of the famous hill flanking the east side of the complex. The now dead end sidings of the North Yard, accessible only from the MPD end, are seemingly in use only for the stabling of withdrawn wagons and 'Peak' locomotives whose days are now over. It was very sad for John Woolley to witness this sad decline in size, status and activity. *Andy Lymn.*

were all gone by 1958 (sadly all scrapped) John had been a main line fireman on them as recalled in this book. Thereafter, Toton men kept the coal conveyor to London moving using conventional Stanier Class 8F 2-8-0s and then-new Riddles Class 9F 2-10-10s of both conventional and Franco-Crosti variants.

The endless stream of coal going through the yards was the reason Toton MPD existed and the shed and its men were kept busy round the clock. John Woolley was a part of this for the last decade of steam traction, through the overlap period when steam and diesel served side by side and into the diesel-only era of rapid decline.

At the time of the Grouping of 1923, and for some time afterwards, the London Midland & Scottish Railway was the biggest joint stock company of its kind in the world. It was a forward-thinking, modern company and introduced the first successful diesel shunters in the early 1930s. You can see their direct descendants today – they were the forerunner of the BR Class 08 shunters once common everywhere, and to which they were almost identical in appearance.

1930s modernization
The down sidings

It is hardly surprising that the LMS set out to modernize and mechanise Toton in the 1930s. It is also self-evident that the pits cold not send out loaded trains without a continuous supply of empty wagons to replace those being sent out full. To make sure the empty wagon supply chain ran smoothly, the down yards were done first, with the installation of fully-mechanised gravity hump-shunting, worked by operators in control towers and diesel shunting locomotives on the ground. The work was completed in the nick of time in May

1939, less than four months before the start of the Second World War.

Yard capacity was significantly enhanced as trains could be handled much more quickly. After the engine of an arriving train had detached and departed to the MPD the diesel shunter hooked onto the brake van at the rear and drew the train into a headshunt, from where the wagons could be propelled towards the hump.

On the ground, a shunter identified which groups of wagons needed to stay together and then uncoupled them into 'cuts' of several wagons each. On the leading wagon of each 'cut' he chalked the number of the siding the group was destined for. This was big enough for the tower operator to read.

When all was ready, the train would be propelled up the hump near to the optimum speed of 1.75mph. The hump operator in the tower set the first of the points to send the wagons in the correct direction and he also keyed-in the number of the final siding in the fan where they should stop. This information was sent to the control tower further down the yard, where a second operator set the remaining points leading to that final siding.

A controller in the control tower used retarders, which could retard any wagons which were running maybe too fast, to ensure they arrived in their final siding at a slow enough speed to buffer up gently to other wagons already there without a major collision. This was a highly skilled job – Toton's Meadow Yard had 18 roads while the North Yard had 17. On the downside of the hump, the track sloped down at 1 in 20, this then eased first to 1 in 80 and then 1 in 200 before levelling off. The sidings then sloped up at 1 in 330 to help stop moving wagons.

On weekdays, Toton was open round the clock on a three-shift basis with up to 70 trains arriving each day. Average wagon handling was

about 3,000 a day at this time, in 'cuts' of three vehicles, but at busy periods this would rise to 4,000 vehicles. Between 1939 and 1961 up to a million wagons were handled each year.

1950s Modernization
The up sidings

Plans by the LMS to upgrade Toton's up side were thwarted by the Second World War and given that the conflict left the railways exhausted and extremely run-down, the company couldn't afford to do the job after 1945 either. It wasn't until after Nationalization in 1948 that the new British Railways announced plans to carry out an even bigger job on the up side than the LMS had done in the 1930s on the down lands. Ten arrival lines were provided, capable of handling the longest trains. Where possible, all arrival lines and sidings were laid completely straight.

Major earth moving was required for the up side upgrade and the mound of earth created is still there on the eastern side of what remains of the up yards. The sidings and hump were mechanised with an enhanced version of the down yards system and the upgraded up side (for southbound traffic) reopened in September 1951. BR was very proud of the work and published a special leaflet, several copies of which turned up in local collections as part of the research by the Woolley family and *Steam World*, for this book. This leaflet mentions that electric lighting was provided in the yard for the first time, to replace gas. Four new signalboxes were provided on the main line, to control access in and out of the new yards.

In the down yard, the hump points only (known as the 'king, queen and jack points') were controlled from the hump room, after the wagons came over the hump, with the remainder controlled from the tower. The up side operator controlled access into all 37 of the sorting sidings available. As on the down side, retarders were operated by the control tower although the gradients were

gentler on the upside as the wagons were loaded and rolled easier and faster. Communication took a leap forward with the arrival of radios in the hump rooms, control towers and shunting locomotives.

In the early 1950s, the yards at Toton were at their zenith in terms of both size and modernization. When John Woolley started as an engine cleaner in October 1954 he witnessed this massive facility at its peak – even 20 of the 33 Garratts were still working, but with just two years to go before extinction. At this time the yards were handling one million wagons a year – a fantastic achievement for the railway staff there. The maximum number of wagons sorted in a single eight hour shift at this time was 1,549. That is an average of 26 vehicles every minute.

Although other similar marshalling yards at Carlisle Kingmoor, Tyne (Gateshead), Tees (Thornaby), Healey Mills (Wakefield) , Sheffield Tinsley, and Margam followed as part of the 1955 Modernization Plan, they were all very expensive white elephants. Rail freight had changed, freight was being lost to the railway at an alarming rate as road haulage became increasingly sophisticated, flexible and cheap. Within a decade these massive mechanized marshalling yards were redundant. Most had their humps abandoned and were stripped down to serve as much smaller flat yards of dead-end sidings. This is what happened at Toton and John Woolley's later career documents this decline, from the mid-1960s of a once mighty marshalling facility. Today, a handful of sidings chiefly on the up side serve to store unserviceable locomotives and wagons with very little active freight handling, other than a few through services which pause to change crews. It is mainly engineering trains that begin or end their journeys at Toton today, using a small yard to the west of the depot. Yes, coal – as ever - is still the most common freight to pass the depot although few trains stop (and then only for signals) and these days there are no booked locomotive changes. The massive facility which in 1950 saw 1m working wagons pass through the sidings today handles no working wagons at all – they simply pass the much-reduced sidings on the Erewash Valley main line.

The depot, however, continues to thrive. After privatization, which was just taking place when John Woolley retired in 1994, the facilities were expanded and upgraded by Wisconsin Central, which acquired the bulk of BR's freight business.

The new owners named the business English Welsh & Scottish Railway and made Toton its engineering headquarters. In the privatized era – and especially after the arrival of the Class 66s from August 1998 – the traditional practice of depots carrying out servicing and limited overhauls, with major rebuilds being done at a separate works facility, finally came to an end. It had been changing for some years. Nowadays, owned by DB Schenker, which bought

EWS in 2007, all engineering is done at Toton, so while the yards are undoubtedly a pale shadow of their former glory, the locomotive depot is more important than ever in terms of the scope of its work and its national role.

A recent project involves completely stripping and rebuilding the Brush Class 60s for their first major overhaul since they were delivered from nearby Loughborough in 1989-1993. There are even staff members working on that project at Toton who helped build the locomotives at Brush Traction's Falcon Works.

After over a century and a half and various changes of fortunes, there are plenty of railway families of Toton, Sandiacre and Long Eaton who still work at Toton Sidings and the potential arrival of High Speed 2 would mean that by 2026 it may be possible to buy a ticket at Toton International and travel direct to Paris, Brussels and maybe even Milan or Budapest. That is a prospect that the 15 year old John Woolley, cleaning engines on his first morning, on October 25 1954, would probably have dismissed as impossible.

The Toton railway story goes on with confidence into the 21st century. Long may it continue to do so.

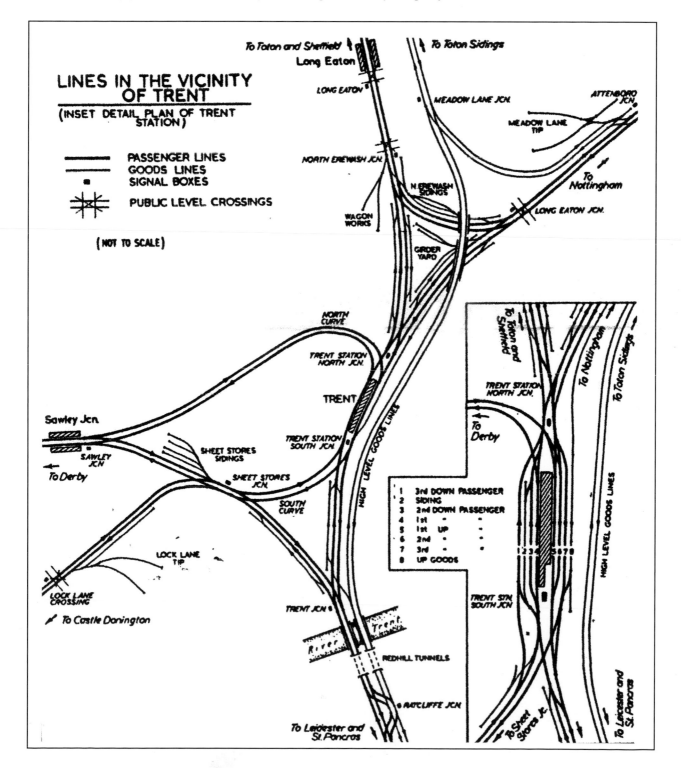

The very essence of the railways of Toton in the second half of the 1950s. When John Woolley was a steam footplateman, this was his working environment. LMS Stanier 'Jubilee' 4-6-0 No 45566 *Queensland* passes Stapleford & Sandiacre station (closed January 2 1967) with the up 'Thames-Clyde Express' for London St Pancras as a Stanier Class 8F 2-8-0 makes its way over the final approach to the reception sidings at Toton's up yard on June 1 1957. *T.G. Hepburn/Rail Archive Stephenson.*

Above: This is where it all started - the seeds of a career on the footplate were sown for John Woolley during many hours watching trains here, at Trent station - especially the three-cylinder LMS Stanier 'Jubilee' 4-6-0s. On May 18 1957 LMS Stanier 'Jubilee' Class 5XP 4-6-0 No 45560 *Prince Edward Island* passes Trent Station North Junction and enters the station with an up Class C fitted freight. John Woolley started work as a 15-year old engine cleaner at the important Toton Motive Power Depot on October 25

1954 and retired 40 years later to the day, on October 25 1994 after 40 years service. On his first day in 1954, he could never have imagined that not only would he achieve his boyhood dream of driving expresses on the MML, but that he would end his career in charge of freight operations over a vast area from Toton, taking in Worksop, Leicester, Peterborough, March and Parkeston Quay. *B.K.B Green/Initial Photographics.*

APPENDIX 2
JOHN HENRY WOOLLEY
AS RECALLED BY FORMER COLLEAGUES

Interviews & photography by
SARAH MIDDLETON-WOOLLEY

Whilst a well-written and absorbing autobiography tells us a great deal about a writer's view of life, it doesn't tell us anything at all about how that person was seen and experienced every day, by their workmates.

Families can't really help with this question either because it's surprising how often the person at work is very different to the one who comes home after their shift on the railway.

So, was John Woolley - my dad - easy-going or impatient? Was he approachable or aloof to those who worked for and with him? Was he kind and helpful or cool and distant with newcomers to the railway he loved so much and which he took so very seriously? And he did love the railway. As his brother Dennis told me, he was stunned when dad said he was going to retire early because it was "in his blood." Dennis just couldn't imagine dad not being a railwayman.

Was dad deadly serious at work or shot through with good humour? What was he *really like* as a railwayman and colleague?

I really wanted to know. So, in preparing this book, whilst Nigel grappled with the text, pictures and layouts, I toured Long Eaton, catching up with some of dad's former workmates, who were also his friends. I asked them to share their memories of him with me – and I absolutely insisted they didn't hold back. I wanted to know what John Woolley the railwayman was like to work with - I wanted the unvarnished truth 'warts and all.' And so I came to hear the nickname 'King John' for the first time - and as for the mug in which he offered visitors tea...I'll let you discover for yourself! I've given the interviewees their last job title, and their years of railway service.

I'd like to sincerely thank all the men whose candid opinions you'll read over the next three pages. They were open, funny, respectful and as honest as I asked them to be. Plainly, every one of them loved the railway as much as my dad did. I found out plenty I didn't know and had confirmed quite a lot of what I'd always suspected. But most of all, I was moved, amused - and really proud of my dad.

"I got closer to John when he was Trip Supervisor in the up hump. He was brilliant to work with - absolutely brilliant – but there was no escaping the fact that if he didn't like you, things could get difficult, pretty quickly. But it wasn't personal - if he had to be tough, it was always justified. He didn't suffer fools. Fortunately, I got on absolutely famously with him.

"The thing I always admired about John more than anything was his willingness to embrace almost anything. If there was something useful in whatever was under discussion, he would always take an interest – but if there was something that he could do himself, he'd almost take over and make it his own, which was in no way a bad thing.

"He was very, very humorous. When he was flying his model aircraft I had some of the funniest times of my life with him. It was just extraordinary. When you have someone who trains Boeing 737 pilots say "John can't fly a real aircraft, but he can fly the models better than me," that's quite something..

"He always had to be 'in there' – to be ahead of the game. If something needed doing then John had it half-done in no time. He turned the way ferret nets worked into an art form and he was consequently widely respected by the ferreting fraternity.

"He was very fair to work with and for. One of the most revealing tales I can tell about John is this. He was very self-assured on the surface. He was almost angular in his confidence. But there was a hint of doubt too

ROGER LYMN
Top Shift Supervisor, 1969-2005

and he would always just question things. He'd had a bust up with a Hither Green driver near Radlett. It was a stone train and it failed on the main line. There was a big argument with the driver and while John was seemingly self-assured about what he said, there was clearly a doubt. He told me this story over a pint; he was really upset. Then he went quiet took a big breath and said: "I was right, wasn't I?" And yes, he was right, but he just wanted to check that he'd done the right thing. He was direct, but always measured in what he did. Was he helpful to people? In excess. He would always help anyone who came to him. He liked being among confident people.

"Was he fun? I couldn't begin to tell you how much fun he was. He was very special was John – and I still think so. You'd fuel

him with a bit of energy and it would come straight back at you. He was a one-off. There was no-one quite like him. He'd lead you through things and get you involved in what he was doing. And he'd involve himself in our life too. I remember once when I was playing in a band - and what he did was really quite touching. We'd gone all the way up to the north side of Barnsley and the club was in the back of beyond - right at the back of God's arsehole. And the crowd was indifferent– they were there for the bingo. It was hard. Anyway, we did the first spot and then got into the second spot and it was really starting to drag, because the bingo was over and they had even less interest! Then the door opened and there was John and his wife Caryl. All the lads in the band loved him – he really became part of it. He'd taken the trouble to find the place and come and support us. He was a real 'diamond geezer'.

"Then, he went and got it into his head that he wanted to start making Indian curries - and, of course, they were absolutely brilliant. Then there was the exploding cigarette. John was Trip Supervisor at the time and this bloke made it known he had an exploding cigarette and was going to give it to John. We told him he wouldn't dare. Not to John. Anyway he did, and it duly exploded right under your dad's nose...John chased him at a speed none of us thought possible, round the office, four or five times, and he caught him, then smacked him on the back of the head. That was allowed then too!"

"He didn't suffer fools lightly and he was the sort of guy that you either liked him or you didn't. He was tough because he had high standards, he but he was really fair too. If you messed him around you'd have trouble, but if you did a good job and he was always on your side. He taught me a hell of a lot.

He was more like a father to me than a brother. He always had to have something on the go – he never stopped. How his

DENNIS HAWKSWORTH
Relief Driver, 1962-1981

wife put up with it I'll never know! She was devoted to him. He lived his life to his rules. I was amazed when he told me he was going to retire, because railways were in his blood. He absolutely loved his job. Loved it."

DES HARGREAVES
Train Crew Roster Clerk
1984-1994

"If you didn't know John, you'd think he was very blunt, but he had great enthusiasm. If people didn't think like he did, they could regard him as difficult. Personally, I always found him spot-on and we had great times.

"He was enthusiastic about everything – like when he discovered new hobbies, which was quite often. He never did things by halves. When he took up flying model aircraft - he quickly had a squadron of the bloody things! He'd go all out at whatever it was and once he'd sussed it, he'd move on and find a new challenge. The thing was, this rubbed off on you and almost without realizing it, you found yourself sharing his enthusiasm.

"John worked hard but he also made you realize that there's more to life than work. But he was a bit Marmite, frankly. You either loved or hated him! People would say: "Hell, he's blunt" - but I have to say he was usually right and when he was most direct he was usually just saying what the score was, making clear what he wanted doing. People sometimes took offence! He didn't suffer fools gladly. But he really knew what he was doing and I worked well with him. People used to say: 'If Des and King John can't sort it, it can't be sorted!" But he was a prankster. He'd make tea for a visitor and when they tipped it up they'd glimpse a false turd in the bottom. He thought it was hilarious.

"He was a very generous man – when he moved on from home brewing, he sold me his whole kit for a tenner. It was worth much more so we argued for a good ten minutes – it was all top of the range and in very good condition. I lost of course. A tenner it was.

"He loved a few pints with his wife and his mates - he was a great bar-room philospher – and crib player! I still miss him a lot. With new starters, he'd either help directly or he'd get someone to help. It was sometimes seemingly grumpy: "Go and see what his ruddy problem is!" – but behind the words was a kindly desire to help someone along.

"He was extremely knowledgable and I know that he was proud that he knew what he was talking about. He *never* talked rubbish. He always did his research with anything new. He never jumped into anything with both feet – he'd always do his homework first which gave him great confidence."

JOHN POTTER
Chief Inspector, 1956-1996

"I had some laughs with John when he was a Train Crew Supervisor – I did the same job. We got the job done but we had fun. He was very straight but there was a jovial side to him too. He took it very seriously but he knew how to have a laugh. You have to understand that he could be very serious and he meant what he said and you couldn't run rings round him – he was very strict. He was straight up-front and if he thought there was something wrong he wouldn't rest until he found out what was amiss. He was that kind of man. And then he'd sort it. We got on very well, John and I. He was incredibly helpful out of work too – I remember once I needed to copy some video off a camcorder and he just couldn't have done more to help, in his own time. At the time, I didn't know he'd died - I was on holiday and missed the funeral. I was very upset to miss it. He was a grand chap."

"John wanted to learn about signalling so he shadowed me at Oakham and Melton Mowbray. I liked him. I've got to speak as I find and he was fine with me, as a signalman. Maybe he was tougher on the drivers he worked with like the Signalling Inspectors were tough on us! John was a very fair man as I saw it. I remember seeing him going by my box on the footplate. I know he wasn't impressed with Railtrack,

PETE SALMON
Signalman, 1962-2012

which was coming in as he retired. He was passionate about the job but sad about privatization. I don't think he'd like it now if he came back - I just wish he could come back to see it and find out."

LEE 'EGGY' EDMONDS
Fireman/Second Man, 1964-2000

"John was good at his job, but you would also see him laughing and joking - and when he got going, it was like he couldn't stop. But then he would change in a second and he would suddenly be serious. I'm a bit happy-go-lucky and this totally threw me! I used to think: 'what the hell happened there?'

"He had a responsible job so he needed to know when to stop laughing. I clearly remember John working with the police and what he did just about clinched it in convicting Michael Sams for murder.

"Sams claimed he'd been trainspotting at Toton and seeing certain engines on a crucial day. He was able to prove that while they were Toton engines in the pictures, John's records proved that they weren't on-shed on the day Sams claimed they were - and this completely destroyed his alibi."

BILL BOTT
Driver, 1977-2010

"John was good to work with – they were brilliant in that office - and he was 100% trustworthy. He was a really good, old-fashioned railwayman and he was brilliant to work with. I remember him being angry one day. He was in one Christmas Day and his was the only car in the car park. Anyway, this other chap came in on his bike, the worse for drink – and he cycled straight into your dad's car! He told him in no uncertain terms to go and sleep it off. He

helped me a lot. We became good friends. We even went on holiday together. He worked very hard at his job and played hard when he wasn't working. He had a great sense of humour – at one of his Christmas Eve parties in the small hours your dad suddenly appeared with the milkman! I said why have you brought him in - and he said "Well he brought a bottle!"

MALCOLM PALING
Driver, 1962-2005

"He was very good. If you did your job he never bothered you. You'd sign-on, have a laugh with him and then clear-off and do your job. But if you didn't do your job properly, that's when he could get nasty with you. I never had any trouble. He was great fun. Especially on a Saturday night if it was quiet, the rest of us would sleep and he'd work with his rabbit nets. Most of the chaps at Toton liked him and got on well with him. You had to make sure that you let him know he was in charge. He was the foreman. There were one or two didn't like him at all - but that's inevitable at such a big place – it goes with being the foreman.

"He was a rum bugger when he wanted to be...."

STEVE PETERS
Relief Supervisor, 1970-1982

"I first met John in 1974. At the time they were creating supervisory posts at Toton as if they were going out of fashion and John and I were both beneficiaries of that policy. John had previously been a fireman and he was great company and I only ever fell out with him once – and that wasn't for long. I made the mistake of correcting his spelling! He would tell a rubbish joke then laugh at it so much himself that you couldn't help doing the same. He couldn't use the expression 'slope off' without falling about.

It's a shame that John sloped off…"

GEOFF CROWDER
Driver, 1966-1977

"I was having a pint with John one night. After a shift we used to go in the Midland Hotel at Sandiacre, by the railway bridge. There were one or two other drivers. John had just finished work, got his pint and sat down and the barmaid and barman were larking about throwing a dishcloth at each other. It flew towards us and this cloth knocked John's pint all over him. But the barman thought this was funny and was laughing his head off. He said 'I'll get you another one.' The barman pulled another pint alright, as he'd promised - but he was still leading the laughing around the pub. At least, he was until John took the newly filled pint and poured the lot right over his head."

JOHN SUMNER
Locomotive Inspector, 1957-2006

"I started at Toton on Janury 7 1957 and I knew your dad well. I used to watch John play in the Deltic Rhythm Band at Long Eaton Empire on a Sunday evening. They used to have a skiffle group play between the two films. We had been engine cleaners together. The last time I worked with your dad was as his second man on diesels. We had about 60 wagons and had left the Toton ballast sidings and we were approaching Stanton Gate and the signal was green.

I said to John – can you stop at the signal, I can't see a brake van at the back, I can only see wagons. We stopped and I phoned Trent power box and asked them to ring Sandiacre

box to see if he could see our brake van. We hadn't got a brake van and the guard was just walking up.

We had to set back with 60 wagons over all the crossings for the brake van. We were going to Westhouses."

PETE DUNN
Traction Maintenance Engineer, 1949-1994

"John and I met at school. We were always friends since then. We had a similar sense of humour – he was a very funny man. I started on the railway in 1949 and worked 45 years. worked all over Britain as a traction engineer but eventually got back to Toton. There was three of them ran the job as Train Crew Managers – the others were Harry Smith and Bill Jacques. Your dad was really good at his job – man mangement isn't easy but John really had it sorted. You can't coerce men to work for you – they had to want to work and John was good at making them want to. He was such good fun. He came in my office one night for a cup of tea and God knows where he got it, but he had this hand-held megaphone. The next thing, he's booming round the shed: "No. 9 come on in, your time's up…..I say again, No. 9 will you come in your time's up……I say, No. 6 – are you in trouble?" Or as we had our food he'd be showing me copies of Viz – we laughed till we nearly cried sometimes at his comments. We'd start on earlies after a bad night and I'd sometimes say: 'We're in the shit this morning John' and he'd just say "Don't worry! We'll sort it Dunny…" And he did, every time. John was a really hard worker. A grafter. He was very highly thought of and very highly skilled. I liked him a lot and personally I couldn't fault him. You can't say that about many people. The railways back then were more than a job – they were a way of life. It was a wonderful job."

PETE MEE
Driver, 1957-2000

"When we started work as engine cleaners, they sent us off for our first issue of bib and brace brace overalls - and, of course, the greasetop hat.

There was only two sizes of hat though. small, and big - and they were quite extreme. Small was too small for me and Bob Burnham so they gave us a big one – but every time we blinked the new cap just dropped over our eyes!

John, having started a couple of years before me and being an old hand, offered helpful advice.

As he walked by, called 'Those hats are too big – you know how to make them smaller?" He said "Put them on the locomotive safety valve." Being 'green' - we did. Anyway, when the engine blew off, Bob's went across the shed while mine went through a hole in the shed roof. When I got it back it wouldn't fit me – it was too small!

John said "I told you not to put it on the safety valve." That was John. I knew him well. He was alright. He burned his hair off one day. He had a teddy boy haircut and he had a blowback on a steam engine and it burned all his hair off. He could be a rogue. We would play cards in cold fireboxes – three-card brag, everything.

"John could be a right one."

VINCENT GORDON
Shunter, 1962-1965

"I started on the railway in 1962 - I was a shunter at Toton sidings - and left in 1983. John was a lovely man and he was my very good friend. He was a good man. Providing you did your job you had no trouble. He showed me respect and I miss him a lot. If the new lads were struggling he would be very helpful, very friendly. A lovely man."

APPENDIX 3

Trent's junctions evolved over the decades until reaching maximum complexity just after the turn of the 20th century. Toton's peak use came in the early 1950s and then declined quickly after 1965. The junctions facilitated the massive north-south goods traffic in/out of Toton, whilst allowing unhindered traffic on both the Midland Main Line and the east-west Derby-Nottingham axis.

Right: A 1998 snapshot highlighting Toton's key role with regard to the Nottinghamshire coalfield.

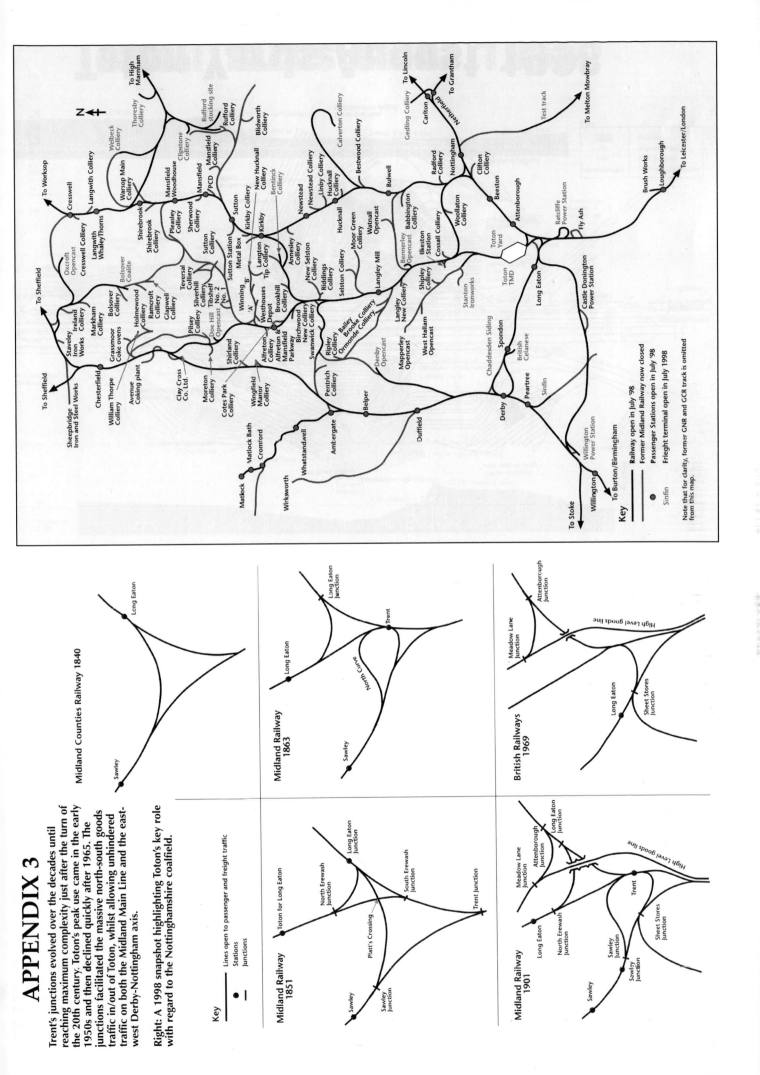

APPENDIX 4
TOTON YARDS TRACK LAYOUT 1951 & 1960

Facing page: This 1951 Aerofilms view of the yards and MPD at Toton emphasises the scale of a facility which was handling up to 2m wagons each year. More than 3,900 wagons can be counted here. The view is from the south. The approaches to Toton South are at the bottom of the view, with Stapleford & Sandiacre at the top. Long Eaton is to the left. The A52 now cuts across the top of the picture, just this side of Stapleford & Sandiacre signalbox.

1: To Nottingham, Leicester and the south.
2: Meadow storage sidings
3: Down yard, North Sidings
4: Carriage & Wagon Workshops
5: No. 2 Fan - sidings
6: West Yard
7: Toton Motive Power Depot
8: Site of current DB Schenker Diesel Depot
9: Coaling Tower
10: New Bank Sidings
11: Position of current A52 road
12: Stapleford & Sandiacre station
13: To Chesterfield & north
14: Down Yard Control Tower
15: Meadow Sidings
16: Erewash Canal
17: Up Hump Room.
18: Old Bank Sidings
19: Up Control Tower
20: Toton Centre signalbox

Key

	Buildings
	Signalboxes
	Rail Brakes
	Station platforms

Toton Engineman 141

APPENDIX 5
TOTON STEAM LOCOMOTIVE ALLOCATIONS, 1954-1965

COMPILED BY NIGEL HARRIS, DATA BY RICHARD STRANGE

This details Toton's (18A) steam allocation from John Woolley's first day as an engine cleaner, October 25 1954, through to steam's last full year, 1965 (closure to steam was on November 7 1966). In 1954, with the marshalling yards recently at their peak and handling one million wagons a year, the MPD had 138 locomotives. In October 1965, there were six.

Toton was emblematic for the massive, but ultimately disappointing articulated Beyer-Garratt 2-6-0+0-6-2s introduced in 1927 for the 1,500-ton coal trains to London. When John Woolley started work in 1954 there were 20 (of 33 built) still working at the depot. This declined by just two in 1955 to 18, but plummeted to four in 1956 - their last full year. None were listed in capital stock at Toton by October 1957, so John was lucky to have two years experience with them. All went for scrap. The new BR Riddles Class 9F 2-10-0s started arriving in 1955 (nine examples) to accompany around 60 Stanier Class 8F 2-8-0s typically allocated to the shed, to take the load previously carried by the Garratts. In 1956/1957 there were 22 '9Fs' in each year but by 1958 they had declined to 12 and they remained in the 10-14 range until 1962, to handle the declining freight traffic, with a smaller fleet of '8Fs'. 1961 was the last year of a large allocation of 'Big Eights' - in 1961 there were 54, 34 in 1962, 31 in 1963 and just 16 in 1964, their last full year, accompanied by just seven '9Fs' In their best year (1957, the first non-Garratt year) there had been 55 '8Fs' and 22 '9Fs' giving a combined fleet of 77 heavy freight engines. Just seven years later, there were 16 '8Fs' and 7 '9Fs' in 1964 - just 23 engines. No '9Fs' survived 1965.

The allocations are taken each year at the closest date to the anniversary of John's starting date of October 25 1954.

SATURDAY OCTOBER 23 1954
LTS/LMS Class 3P 4-4-2T (1): 41966

MR Class 3F 0-6-0 (17): 43251, 43292, 43309, 43405, 43453, 43499, 43631, 43650, 43751, 43793, 43795, 43810, 43823, 43825, 43826, 43828, 43832

MR Class 4F 0-6-0 (11): 43923, 43933, 43943, 43961, 43969, 43974 43988, 43990, 43994, 43995, 44012

LMS Class 4F 0-6-0 (17): 44047,44088, 44091 44106, 44133, 44136, 44145, 44154, 44157, 44161, 44190, 44200, 44233, 44250, 44289, 44362, 44376

MR Class 3F 0-6-0T (1): 47234

LMS Class 3F 0-6-0T (2): 47551, 47619

LMS Beyer-Garratt 2-6-0+0-6-2 (20): 47967, 47969, 47970, 48971, 47972, 47975, 47976, 47979, 47981, 47984, 47985, 47987, 47988, 47989, 47990, 47991, 47996, 47997, 47998, 47999.

LMS Class 8F 2-8-0 (64): 48007, 48037, 48075, 48112, 48117, 48128, 48145, 48152, 48168, 48176, 48178, 48182, 48183, 48184, 48185, 48186, 48187, 48194, 48195, 48196, 48197, 48200, 48201, 48203, 48204, 48205, 48221, 48271, 48273, 48284, 48303, 48304, 48319, 48324, 48332, 48350, 48361, 48362, 48367, 48370, 48384, 48400, 48412, 48419, 48461, 48463, 48490, 48507, 48538, 48543, 48606, 48607, 48615, 48618, 48636, 48637, 48638, 48655, 48662 48672, 48681, 48685, 48694, 48772

MR Class 2F 0-6-0 (5): 58146, 58159, 58171, 58173, 58197

TOTAL OCTOBER 1954 ALLOCATION: 138

SATURDAY OCTOBER 22 1955
LTS/LMS Class 3P 4-4-2T (1): 41966
MR Class 3F 0-6-0 (15): 43251, 43309, 43405, 43453, 43499, 43631, 43650, 43751, 43793, 43795, 43823, 43825, 43826, 43828, 43832.

MR Class 4F 0-6-0 (8): 43943, 43961, 43969, 43988, 43990, 43994, 43995, 44012,

LMS Class 4F 0-6-0 (16): 44047, 44088, 44091, 44106, 44133, 44145, 44154, 44157, 44161, 44200, 44217, 44233, 44289, 44362, 44376, 44427.

MR Class 3F 0-6-0T (2): 47234, 47247.

LMS Class 3F 0-6-0T (1): 47551.

LMS Beyer-Garratt 2-6-6-2 (18): 47967, 47969, 47971, 47972, 47974, 47976, 47979, 47981, 47984, 47987, 47988, 47989, 47991, 47994, 47995, 47996, 47998, 47999.

LMS Class 8F 2-8-0 (60): 48037, 48112, 48128, 48145, 48152, 48168, 48176, 48178, 48182, 48183, 48184, 48185, 48186, 48187, 48194, 48195, 48196, 48197, 48200, 48201, 48203, 48204, 48205, 48221, 48271, 48273, 48284, 48303, 48304, 48313, 48319, 48324, 48332, 48350, 48361, 48362, 48367, 48370, 48384, 48400, 48461, 48463, 48490, 48533, 48538, 48543, 48606, 48607, 48615, 48618, 48636, 48637, 48638, 48655, 48662, 48672, 48681, 48685, 48694, 48772.

MR Class 2F 0-6-0 (4): 58146, 58159, 58171, 58173.

BR Class 9F 2-10-0 (9): 92051, 92052, 92053, 92054, 92055, 92056, 92057, 92058, 92059.

TOTAL OCTOBER 1955 ALLOCATION: 134

SATURDAY OCTOBER 20 1956:
LTS/LMS Class 3P 4-4-2T (1): 41947

MR Class 3F 0-6-0 (13): 43251, 43309, 43405, 43453, 43499, 43650, 43751, 43793, 43795, 43823, 43826, 43828, 43832.

MR Class 4F 0-6-0 (9): 43845, 43865, 43941, 43946, 43961, 43988, 43990, 43994, 44012,

LMS Class 4F 0-6-0 (15): 44091, 44106, 44133, 44140, 44145, 44154, 44157, 44161, 44200, 44217, 44224, 44289, 44362, 44376, 44427.

MR Class 3F 0-6-0T (3): 47247.
LMS Class 3F 0-6-0T (1): 47551.

LMS Beyer-Garratt 2-6-6-2 (4): 47981, 47987, 47994, 47995,

LMS Class 8F 2-8-0 (56): 48128, 48145, 48178, 48182, 48183, 48184, 48185, 48186, 48187, 48194, 48195, 48196, 48197, 48200, 48201, 48203, 48204, 48205, 48221, 48271, 48273, 48284, 48303, 48304, 48314, 48319, 48324, 48332, 48350, 48361, 48362, 48367, 48370, 48384, 48395, 48400, 48463, 48490, 48530, 48538, 48543, 48606, 48607, 48615, 48618, 48636, 48637, 48638, 48655, 48662, 48672, 48681, 48685, 48694, 48772.

MR Class 2F 0-6-0 (6): 58146, 58153, 58165, 58166, 58171, 58173.

BR Class 9F 2-10-0 (22): 92048, 92049, 92050, 92051, 92052, 92053, 92054, 92055, 92056, 92057, 92058, 92059, 92077, 92078, 92080, 92081. 92100, 92101, 92102, 92103, 92104, 92109,

TOTAL OCTOBER 1956 ALLOCATION: 130

SATURDAY OCTOBER 26 1957
LTS/LMS Class 3P 4-4-2T (1): 41947

MR Class 3F 0-6-0 (12): 43251, 43309, 43405, 43453, 43499, 43650, 43751, 43793, 43823, 43826, 43828, 43832

MR Class 4F 0-6-0 (7): 43845, 43865, 43961, 43988, 43990, 43994, 44012

LMS Class 4F 0-6-0 (12): 44091 44106, 44140, 44145, 44154, 44161, 44200, 44224, 44289, 44362, 44376, 44427.

MR Class 3F 0-6-0T (3): 47223, 47234, 47247

LMS Class 3F 0-6-0T (1): 47551

LMS Class 8F 2-8-0 (55): 48128, 48145, 48178, 48182, 48183, 48184, 48185, 48186, 48187, 48194, 48195, 48196, 48197, 48200, 48201, 48204, 48219, 48221, 48271, 48273, 48284, 48303, 48304, 48314, 48319, 48324, 48332, 48350, 48361, 48362, 48363, 48367, 48370, 48384, 48395, 48490, 48530, 48538, 48543, 48606, 48607, 48613, 48615, 48618, 48636, 48637, 48638, 48655, 48662, 48672, 48673, 48681, 48685, 48694, 48772

MR Class 2F 0-60 (4): 58146, 58153, 58166, 58173

BR Class 9F 2-10-0 (22): 92050, 92052, 92054, 92055, 92056, 92057, 92058, 92059, 92077, 92078, 92080, 92081, 92100, 92101, 92102, 92103, 92104, 92128, 92129, 92130, 92131, 92153

TOTAL OCTOBER 1957 ALLOCATION: 117

SATURDAY OCTOBER 25 1958
LTS/LMS Class 3P 4-4-2T (1): 41947

MR Class 3F 0-6-0 (10): 43251, 43309, 43405, 43453, 43499, 43650, 43751, 43793, 43826, 43832

MR Class 4F 0-6-0 (6): 43845, 43865, 43921, 43990, 43994, 44012

LMS Class 4F 0-6-0 (11): 44091, 44106, 44140, 44145, 44161, 44178, 44200, 44224, 44284, 44376, 44427

MR Class 3F 0-6-0T (2): 47223, 47247
LMS Class 3F 0-6-0T (1): 47551

LMS Class 8F 2-8-0 (58): 48099, 48105, 48118, 48128, 48145, 48167, 48182, 48183, 48184, 48185, 48186, 48187, 48194, 48195, 48196, 48197, 48201, 48219. 48221, 48271, 48284, 48303, 48304, 48306, 48314, 48319, 48324, 48332, 48338, 48350, 48361, 48362, 48363, 48367, 48370, 48384, 48490, 48507, 48517, 48530, 48538, 48545, 48604, 48606, 48607, 48615, 48616, 48620, 48636, 48637, 48640, 48662, 48672, 48681, 48685, 48694, 48698, 48728

MR Class 2F 0-6-0 (3) : 58153, 58166, 58173

BR Class 9F 2-10-0 (12): 92050, 92057, 92077, 92078, 92081, 92129, 92130, 92131, 92153, 92156, 92157, 92158

TOTAL OCTOBER 1958 ALLOCATION: 104

SATURDAY OCTOBER 24 1959
LTS/LMS CLASS 3P 4-4-2T (1): 41947

MR Class 3F 0-6-0 (9): 43235, 43251, 43309, 43453, 43499, 43650, 43793, 43826, 43832

MR Class 4F 0-6-0 (6): 43845, 43865, 43921, 43990, 43994, 44012

LMS Class 4F 0-6-0 (9): 44106, 44140, 44161, 44178, 44200, 44224, 44284, 44376, 44427

LMS Class 3F 0-6-0T (1): 47551

LMS Class 8F 2-8-0 (56): 48033, 48060, 48062, 48099, 48109, 48118, 48127, 48132, 48145, 48163, 48167, 48183, 48184, 48185, 48186, 48187, 48194, 48195, 48196, 48197, 48201, 48221, 48271, 48284, 48303, 48314, 48319, 48332, 48333, 48338, 48350, 48361, 48362, 48363, 48370, 48384, 48401, 48414, 48490, 48507, 48530, 48545, 48604, 48606, 48607, 48615, 48620, 48636, 48637, 48638, 48640, 48650, 48672, 48681, 48685, 48698, 48750

MR Class 2F 0-6-0 (3): 58153, 58166, 58173,

BR Class 9F 2-10-0 (10): 92050, 92057, 92077, 92078, 92081, 92130, 92131 92153, 92156, 92158

TOTAL OCTOBER 1959 ALLOCATION: 95

SATURDAY OCTOBER 22 1960
LMS Stanier Class 3P 2-6-2T (1): 40149

MR Class 2P 4-4-0 (3): 40439, 40443, 40511

LTS/LMS Class 3P 4-4-2T (1): 41947

LMS Class 4P 2-6-4T (1): 42383

MR Class 4F 0-6-0 (6): 43845, 43865, 43921, 43971, 43994, 44012

LMS Class 4F 0-6-0 (12): 44043, 44106, 44133, 44162, 44178, 44200, 44224, 44270, 44295, 44376, 44388, 44409

MR Class 3F 0-6-0T (1): 47231

LMS Class 3F 0-6-0T (1): 47551

LMS Class 8F 2-8-0 (59): 48057, 48060, 48062, 48099, 48109, 48118, 48127, 48128, 48132, 48145, 48163, 48167, 48184, 48185, 48186. 48194, 48195,

48196, 48197, 48201, 48204, 48221, 48271, 48303, 48314, 48319, 48332, 48333, 48338, 48350, 48361, 48362, 48363, 48370, 48384, 48401, 48414, 48490, 48507, 48530, 48538, 48545, 48604, 48606, 48607, 48615, 48620, 48636, 48637, 48638, 48640, 48650, 48661, 48672, 48681, 48685, 48698, 48750, 48770

MR Class 2F 0-6-0 (4): 58166, 58175, 58214, 58228

BR Class 9F 2-10-0 (14): 92014, 92055, 92056, 92058, 92059, 92070, 92077, 92078, 92113, 92114, 92130, 92153, 92156, 92158

TOTAL OCTOBER 1960 ALLOCATION: 103

SATURDAY OCTOBER 28 1961
MR Class 4F 0-6-0 (5): 43845, 43865, 43971, 43994, 44012

LMS Class 4F 0-6-0 (12): 44043, 44106, 44133, 44162, 44178, 44200, 44224, 44270, 44295, 44376, 44388, 44409

MR Class 3F 0-6-0T (1): 47231

LMS Class 3F 0-6-0T (2): 47367, 47551

LMS Class 8F 2-8-0 (54): 48002, 48007, 48057, 48060, 48109, 48118, 48127, 48128, 48132, 48145, 48149, 48163, 48167, 48184, 48185, 48186, 48194, 48195, 48196, 48197, 48201, 48204, 48221, 48271, 48303, 48314, 48319, 48332, 48333, 48350, 48361, 48362, 48363, 48370, 48384, 48414, 48507, 48523, 48530, 48538, 48545, 48606, 48615, 48620, 48635, 48636, 48637, 48647, 48650, 48661, 48672, 48681, 48685, 48698

MR Class 2F 0-6-0 (2): 58175, 58228

BR Class 9F 2-10-0 (13): 92055, 92056, 92058, 92059, 92070, 92077, 92078, 92113, 92114, 92130, 92153, 92156, 92158

TOTAL OCTOBER 1961 ALLOCATION: 89

SATURDAY OCTOBER 27 1962
MR Class 4F 0-6-0 (7): 43845, 43861; 43865; 43971; 43994, 44012, 44026

LMS Class 4F 0-6-0 (11): 44043, 44106, 44133, 44162, 44178, 44200, 44213, 44270, 44295, 44376, 44388

MR Class 3F 0-6-0T (1): 47231
LMS Class 3F 0-6-0T(6): 47283, 47367, 47442, 47449, 47551, 47645

LMS Class 8F 2-8-0 (34): 48056, 48082, 48095, 48145, 48149, 48167, 48186, 48201, 48204, 48212, 48221, 48271, 48284, 48313, 48314, 48319, 48350, 48361, 48362, 48363, 48384, 48414, 48494, 48545, 48606, 48635, 48637, 48647, 48650, 48661, 48672, 48681, 48685, 48698

BR Class 9F 2-10-0 (10): 92052, 92053, 92055, 92059, 92077, 92078, 92130, 92153, 92156, 92158

TOTAL OCTOBER 1962 ALLOCATION: 69

SATURDAY OCTOBER 26 1963
MR Class 4F 0-6-0 (7): 43865, 43947, 43964, 43971, 43991, 43994, 44012

LMS Class 4F 0-6-0 (21): 44038, 44043, 44051, 44106, 44133, 44162, 44200, 44210, 44213, 44235, 44270, 44278. 44294, 44295, 44376, 44441, 44529, 44531, 44541, 44572, 44575

MR Class 3F 0-6-0T (1): 47223

LMS Class 3F 0-6-0T: (2) 47367, 47645
LMS Class 8F 2-8-0 (31): 48056, 48082, 48125, 48145, 48149, 48167, 48170, 48186, 48193, 48201, 48212, 48221, 48279, 48306, 48313, 48314, 48350, 48361, 48362, 48363, 48384, 48414, 48494, 48606, 48635, 48637, 48661, 48672, 48681, 48685, 48698

BR Class 9F 2-10-0 (6): 92053, 92055, 92059, 92078, 92130, 92156

TOTAL OCTOBER 1963 ALLOCATION 68

SATURDAY OCTOBER 24 1964
LMS Class 3F 0-6 0T (1): 47645

LMS Class 8F 2-8-0 (16): 48056, 48116, 48125, 48167, 48193, 48201, 48212, 48279, 48314, 48361, 48363, 48414, 48661, 48681, 48685, 48698

BR Class 9F 2-10-0 (7): 92048, 92049, 92053, 92055, 92059, 92078, 92156

TOTAL OCTOBER 1964 ALLOCATION 24

SATURDAY OCTOBER 23 1965
LMS Class 8F 2-8-0 (4): 48037, 48142, 48167, 48193
BR Class 2MT 2-6-0 (2): 78044, 78055

TOTAL OCTOBER 1965 ALLOCATION 6

With very many thanks to Richard Strange for assistance with this appendix.

Left: Toton was a freight shed and whilst it had plenty of heavy locomotives (2-8-0s, 2-10-0s and the articulated Beyer Garratt 2-6-0+0-6-2s) it also had allocations of 'Derby 4' 0-6-0 freight engines, including examples from both Midland and LMS-built batches. At the turn of the 19th century, the 0-6-0 tender engine was Britain's most common goods type. The 0-6-0 was the Midland's biggest freight engine, which is why double heading was so common. On March 18 1961, LMS '4F' 0-6-0 No 44447 steams through Stapleford & Sandiacre station with an up goods heading into the up yards. Note the BR Riddles '9F' 2-10-0 on the Erewash Valley up main line, coming through the road bridge beneath the station building on the left. *M.J. Fox/Rail Archive Stephenson.*

APPENDIX 6
ACKNOWLEDGEMENTS & BIBLIOGRAPHY

This is always one of the most daunting sections of a book – offering heartfelt thanks to the many people without whose help, assistance, kindness and friendship it most surely could not have happened. As editor, the task falls to me and I approach it with trepidation and respect for those involved.

Starting at the centre, warmest thanks to John Woolley's widow Caryl, and their two daughters, Helen Lakin and Sarah Middleton-Woolley. You can meet them all on page 5. They have each, in their unique ways, worked on this project and have quite rightly left their individual marks on the book. This makes it very much a family affair. All three read the main proofs to make sure that in the trickiest (and biggest) sub-editing job I've ever tackled I did not inadvertently substitute my own vocabulary for John's. They did a wonderful job – especially Caryl, who could do very well as a freelance proof reader. She has the sharpest of eyes and a fierce and uncompromising eye for detail. Helen also spent a good deal of time reading the manuscript and this has helped ensure that the only voice you hear in the main text is John Woolley.

Sarah worked very hard as an especially effective editorial assistant and tackled a wide variety of tasks which saved a great deal of time as well as ensuring the job was done to a high standard. As well as sharing proof reading duties with her mum and sister she spent countless hours and drove many miles around Long Eaton seeking out photographs from former railwaymen, researching historical information for captions, interviewing her dad's former colleagues for the testimonials in Appendix 2 and taking their photographs. Finally, she promoted the book to not only book shops in and around Derby and Long Eaton but to newspapers and radio stations. Her dad would be proud.

Stephen Middleton also deserves a mention for supporting all this activity – not to mention painstakingly counting the wagons in the aerial photographs in the Appendices!

In and around Long Eaton thanks are due for the loan of photographs to: Lee Edmonds, Roger Lymn, Andy Lymn, Pete Salmon, John Cornell, Melvyn Rowthorne, Chuck Nurse, David Jones, John Fulwood, Judith Squires, Raye Richmond and Mick Boyd.

Thanks also to Keith Reedman, Long Eaton's long established and much respected local history expert for advice, guidance and some important photographs. Keith's invisible hand and expertise have enhanced many areas of the text and captions. For assistance locally, thanks also to Reg Sergeant, David Thompson, Tony Fountain, also Robert Hardy, for the cartoons.

Sarah also asked to express her thanks particularly for those who sat and talked about her dad for the testimonials section, so that the reader could know a bit more about the man who wrote the book. They were she said, a delight to talk to. They are: Roger Lymn, Des Hargreaves, Pete Dunn, Steve Peters, Dennis Hawksworth, Vincent Gordon, John Potter, John Sumner, Geoff Crowder, Peter Mee, Bill Bott, Pete Salmon, Malcolm Paling and Lee Edmonds.

To bring an autobiography like this to life, you need a good selection of appropriate photographs – and in this regard we have been humbled by the willingness of specialist railway photographers of national repute to 'go that extra mile' to make sure we had the right pictures to illustrate John's words.

So, sincere thanks to: Brian Stephenson (of Rail Archive Stephenson), Gavin Morrison, Brian Morrison, Paul Chancellor (of Colour Rail), Peter J. Robinson and the Armstrong Trust and William Wright.

Richard Strange (of Steam Archive Services) and renowned LMS historian R.J 'Bob' Essery both played important parts in taking this book from concept to production: their patient assistance and friendship are always appeciated. Thanks also to *RAIL* magazine for permission to use the maps and trackplans on pages 127 and 129.

My thanks to my old friend Mark Guest, who is second-to-none amongst the dozens of designers I've worked with over the years, for his expert tuition in the use of Adobe's Indesign page make-up software, which I used to put the book together. *Steam World* publisher Clive Nicholls also deserves credit for backing this idea.

Finally, my own very personal word of thanks to someone I sadly never knew personally but who I can't help feeling I've come to know at least a little, having worked so intimately with his words and talked to so many friends and family members who have told me so much about him: the late John Woolley. It's been a privilege to lead the shaping of his words into this book. I have very much enjoyed putting it together with the help of those listed above, who only added to the pleasure of producing it. My only hope is that John would have approved of the finished product, which I am assured he would have loved to see finally in print.

My apologies to anyone who I have missed from the list above and as is customary, I must conclude with the comment that any errors of fact or interpretation are mine and mine alone. If you spot any, please contact me via the publisher (see page 2) and let me know.

Nigel Harris
Tallington, Lincolnshire,

September 2013.

BIBLIOGRAPHY & FURTHER READING*

Locomotives of British Railways, H.C. Casserley & L.L. Asher, (Spring Books, 1963)

Passengers No More, Gerald Daniels & Les Dench, (Ian Allan, 1980)

British Railways Pre Grouping Atlas & Gazetteer, Fifth Edition, (Ian Allan, 1997)

Rail Atlas of Great Britain & Northern Ireland, S.K. Baker (OPC/Ian Allan, 2013)

British Railways Locomotives & Other Motive Power (Combined Volume), Various volumes.

The Complete UK Modern Traction Locomotive Directory, Colin J. Marsden, (therailwaycentre.com, 2011)

Toton Yards and the Erewash Valley: A brief railway history,
David M. Copeland (pub RAIL magazine/English Welsh & Scottish Railway, 1998)

LMS Engine Sheds Volume Two: The Midland Railway, Chris Hawkins & George Reeve (Wild Swan Publications, 1981)

An Illustrated History of LMS Locomotives Volume 5:The Post-Grouping Standard Designs,
Bob Essery & David Jenkinson (Silver Link Publishing, 1989.

British Locomotive Classes: Principal 'Big Four' classes as at 1945
A Steam Days Special (First published 1945, republished Ian Allan, 1991)

Toton Marshalling Yards (leaflet published by British Railways London Midland Region.

The Book of Long Eaton, Keith Reedman, (Barracuda Books, 1989)

Long Eaton Then & Now, Keith Reedman, (The History Press, 2011)

* Publication dates are of the editions used for reference in research for this book.

PERIODICALS
Trains Illustrated, Various issues.
The Railway Magazine, Various issues. Various issues.